THE
INNOVATOR'S
METHOD

THE INNOVATOR'S METHOD

BRINGING THE
LEAN START-UP
INTO YOUR
ORGANIZATION

NATHAN FURR
JEFF DYER

Harvard Business Review Press
Boston, Massachusetts

Copyright 2014 Nathan Furr and Jeff Dyer
All rights reserved
Printed in the United States of America

10 9 8 7

No part of this publication may be reproduced, stored in or introduced into a retrieval system, or transmitted, in any form, or by any means (electronic, mechanical, photocopying, recording, or otherwise), without the prior permission of the publisher. Requests for permission should be directed to permissions@hbsp.harvard.edu, or mailed to Permissions, Harvard Business School Publishing, 60 Harvard Way, Boston, Massachusetts 02163.

The web addresses referenced in this book were live and correct at the time of the book's publication but may be subject to change.

Library of Congress Cataloging-in-Publication Data

Furr, Nathan R.
  The innovator's method : bringing the lean startup into your organization / Nathan Furr, Jeff Dyer.
    pages cm
  ISBN 978-1-62527-146-4 (hardback)
1. Organizational effectiveness. 2. Management—Technological innovations.
3. Consumers' preferences. I. Dyer, Jeff. II. Title.
  HD58.9.F864 2014
  658.4'063—dc23

                                                          2014005467

ISBN: 978-1-62527-146-4
eISBN: 978-1-62527-147-1

The paper used in this publication meets the requirements of the American National Standard for Permanence of Paper for Publications and Documents in Libraries and Archives Z39.48-1992.

Contents

Foreword

At some point soon, please take a trip physically or virtually to New York City, Hong Kong, Singapore, and Dubai. In New York, go to the intersection of 6th Avenue and 57th Street and start walking south, away from Central Park. On the left side you will see Rockefeller Center—a set of skyscrapers that were built in the 1930s. Then look to your right, where you will see a set of even bigger skyscrapers designed and built in the 1960s. These are masses of rectangles and right angles reaching into the sky, differentiated only by the type of siding that was used and whether they had sixty or seventy stories.

Then go to Hong Kong, Singapore, and Dubai and contrast their skylines with those on the Avenue of the Americas in New York. Most skyscrapers in these cities that have been built in the last fifteen years are unique to the world. Most are *very* attractive—and some are truly stunning. The curves, angles, accents, and statements are unique to each building. What has changed? Have the architects simply become more daring and creative? Are the architects in those cities simply better at design than American architects?

The answer: No. Rather, the software that architects have been using in Hong Kong, Singapore, and Dubai—and around the world—has become so sophisticated that if an architect changes an angle, adjusts the weight-bearing or a new curve in an H-beam, or adds a new type of weld to be used in an ornament jutting out on the 23rd floor, the software automatically recalculates the design of every other piece, showing what each one needs to do and where it must be placed to account for interdependencies mandated by the unusual element of each piece. The software's power to calculate all the interdependencies among the elements of these massive skyscrapers has yielded a set of rules that say "If this, then that." These rules are not of the sort that say "Don't do this, because we have no idea what will happen." The rules of causality actually emancipate artistry in design.

The reason why skyscrapers designed in 1960s had so little differentiation is that there was little latitude for creativity: anything that was not a standard straight beam or a 90-degree angle was risky and very, very costly. Even the best architects struggled to come up with all the adjustments they needed to implement elsewhere in the structure to account for anything that was unusual.

So how does this relate to management? Historically, management is about "straight lines" and "right angles." The tools of traditional business planning—the "software"—that managers use today have helped them perfect the art of analyzing, planning, and executing when the problem is standard and the interdependencies are known. But innovation is about uncertainty and nonstandard processes—"curves" and "weird angles"—and the management literature and the tools we use have not yet caught up with the new kinds of problems that managers and innovators face. New "software" is needed—a new set of guidelines and rules—that managers can use for facing high uncertainty problems.

Furthermore, although most companies are laced throughout with interdependencies, most executives actually know little of what they are or how they interact. Some interactions in a company are static, occurring at a given point in time. Others are dynamic, doing their work over time. The reason why many executives and employees adhere to standard processes is that changes in interdependent processes are time-consuming, risky, and costly. Standard processes mitigate innovation, but many managers instinctively opt for less innovation nonetheless in their quest for order.

Executives face these paradoxes in part because so few researchers of business have achieved the comparable exquisite understanding of business interdependencies that software has brought to architecture. Many more of us must follow the lead of these few, because the impact these researchers have had on understanding systemic interdependencies of processes and organizational structure has been profound. For example, Steven Spear and Kent Bowen conducted a remarkable study of the Toyota Production System, examining the complete process of production in industries from health care to aluminum. From this deep understanding they were able to distill four rules for managing (summarized in the *HBR* article "Decoding the DNA of the Toyota Production System") that went beyond what prior researchers had tried to describe in simplistic terms. Similarly, in *The Anatomy of Peace*, Terry Warner and his colleagues at the Arbinger Institute chronicled the interdependent process by which conflict is created and resolved. Edgar Schein studied from beginning to end the process through which culture is created and resists change, summarized in his book *Organizational Culture and Leadership*. And finally, Chet Huber wrote *Detour: My Unexpected, Amazing, Life Changing Journey with OnStar*. As the innovator who built this very successful company within General Motors, Huber explains the static and dynamic interdependencies within the company. Huber did what nobody thought was possible, because he in fact distilled from his own experience and the research of a few others a set of rules: "If this, then that."

I owe much to these and a few other researchers and writers who have taught me to relish rather than retreat from the study and use of interdependencies in business and academia, in church, and in my family.

And for this reason I thank Professors Dyer and Furr. With *The Innovator's Method*, they are the first researchers I am aware of who have attempted to chronicle the process of innovation from beginning to end—laying out the static and dynamic interdependencies that historically have made innovation so hard. If one faces a high uncertainty problem, then the tools of lean start-up and design thinking they describe are valuable innovation tools. They, along with many others, are helping to build the management equivalent of the software architects use today to create amazing new structures.

With my gratitude,

Clayton M. Christensen
Professor, Harvard Business School

THE
INNOVATOR'S
METHOD

Introduction

As a successful scaled company, you cannot run the ship the way you used to. You'll get run over by a swarm of start-ups.

—Scott Cook, Founder and Chairman of
the Executive Committee, Intuit

HAVE YOU EVER come up with an idea for a new product or service that you thought would be very cool, but didn't take any action because you thought it would be too risky? Or maybe you just didn't know how to take the next step? Or at work, have you had what you thought could be a big idea for your company—perhaps changing the way you develop or distribute a product, provide customer service, or hire or train your employees? The fact is, most of us have these kinds of ideas at one time or another. But neither we, nor our companies, are very good at taking advantage of them. Why? Because typically there is significant uncertainty around whether these ideas will work. They are risky. And most individuals—and especially companies—are programmed to avoid risk. But what if you could take much of the risk out of it? What if you knew a process to quickly test and validate whether the idea had merit?

The key message in this book is that new tools and perspectives for validating big ideas characterized by high uncertainty are emerging in many disparate fields. Whether you call it lean start-up, design thinking, or agile software development, these new methods are revolutionizing the way managers successfully create, refine, and bring new ideas to market. These and other tools help entrepreneurs, designers, and software developers lower uncertainty and risk through cheap and rapid experimentation.

To help managers apply these new practices inside established companies, we offer a new method for managing innovation that we call *the innovator's method:* an end-to-end process for creating, refining, and bringing ideas to market. Drawing on our research of hundreds of established companies and start-ups, we show you when and how to apply the innovator's method, taking you step-by-step through these new practices. We answer such questions as: How do we know whether this idea is worth pursuing? Have we found the right solution? What is the best business model for this new offering? We focus on the "how"— how to test, validate, and commercialize ideas using the best tools from lean start-up, design thinking, and similar techniques used by a few corporations and most successful start-ups. We acknowledge that the innovation process is messy and unpredictable—and no process can fully remove the uncertainty. But these tools can be applied to create new innovations for customers or solve internal problems that have an element of uncertainty, whether in HR, finance, or another area.

Let's start with a story.

Rent the Runway

In 2008, Jenn Hyman, a second-year MBA student at Harvard Business School, spent Thanksgiving at her home in New York. During her visit, Hyman noticed her sister, Becky—an accessories buyer at Bloomingdale's—struggling to decide what to wear to an upcoming wedding. "Becky desperately wanted to buy a $1,500 Marchesa dress," said Hyman. "She felt compelled to buy a new dress—because she knew photos would soon appear on Facebook and she didn't want to be seen twice in the same outfit."[1] As she watched her sister wrestle with the cost of the dress, her sister's emotion was a clue to an important job-to-be-done for young women: helping them feel special and confident. Hyman realized that other fashion-oriented young women might have a similar challenge, an observation backed up by her years spent building a wedding event business at Starwood hotels and working in marketing and sales at Wedding.com. Hyman's insight led her to hypothesize a potential solution: instead of purchasing designer dresses, women might prefer the option of renting designer dresses online for special occasions.

Like many gifted young individuals—budding entrepreneurs and talented young managers—Hyman had used her powers of observation to generate a potentially valuable business idea. But what should she do next?

Pop quiz: imagine she came to you. What would you advise? For most business professors and executives, the answer would be, "Write a business plan." The plan would identify the customer need, describe the product or service, estimate the size of the market, and estimate the revenues and profits based on projections of pricing, costs, and unit volume growth. After all, without this type of analysis, how can we know whether an idea is worthy of investment? Indeed, Hyman received just this type of advice. *She didn't do it.*

Instead, Hyman recruited classmate Jenny Fleiss to help her test their proposed solution. Hyman and Fleiss set up an experiment to answer two key questions:

1. Will middle- to upper-class young women rent a designer dress if it is available at one-tenth the retail price?

2. Will women who rent dresses return them in good condition?

Then Hyman and Fleiss borrowed or bought 130 dresses from designers like Diane von Furstenberg, Calvin Klein, and Halston and set up an experiment to rent dresses to Harvard undergrads. They advertised around campus, rented a location, and invited young women. The experiment answered both questions. Of the 140 women who came in to view the dresses, 35 percent ended up renting one, and 51 of 53 mailed them back in good condition (the other two had stains that were easily removed). This experiment resolved some of the uncertainty reflected in the two questions it was designed to answer.

But would women rent dresses they couldn't try on? To answer that question, Hyman and Fleiss set up another experiment, this time on the Yale campus, allowing women to see the dresses before renting but not allowing them to try them on. In the second trial they had more dress options, because the first pilot revealed that many women didn't rent because they couldn't find an option they liked. The Yale pilot showed two things: women would rent dresses when they couldn't try them on, and the percentage of women who rented increased to more than 55 percent because they had more options.

Now Hyman and Fleiss were ready to test the big idea: Would women rent dresses they could not physically see? The entrepreneurs took photos of each dress and ran a test in New York, where one thousand women in the target audience were given the option to rent a dress from PDF photos. The final experiment showed that roughly 5 percent of women looking for special occasion dresses were willing to try the service—enough to demonstrate the viability of renting high fashion over the web.

So Hyman and Fleiss gathered data on whether designers would go for their idea and whether they could use designers' websites as their rental channel. Less than two weeks after conceiving the idea, the two women cold-called Diane von Furstenberg, an influential fashion designer and president of the Council of Fashion Designers of America. The initial idea Hyman proposed to von Furstenberg was to set up a rental option on the websites of existing designers. Hyman's start-up would take care of fulfillment—taking the order, shipping the dress, and dry-cleaning the returns. Von Furstenberg was intrigued by the idea and helped Hyman and Fleiss set up meetings with more than twenty designers.

The initial response from most designers was extremely negative. "We were going to designers asking to buy their inventory so we could rent it at the same time it's available at Saks Fifth Avenue and Niemen Marcus for 10 percent of the retail price," said Hyman. "In the first meetings their response was basically, 'over my dead body.'"[2] Designers were worried about cannibalization. Renting dresses instead of selling them seemed like a bad idea.

Hyman and Fleiss realized that to make their idea work, they would need to have their own website and inventory. So the idea of Rent the Runway—using the Netflix model to rent a wide variety of high-fashion dresses from multiple designers—was born.

Now that Hyman and Fleiss had resolved concerns about whether there would be demand for their product—and what their initial solution might look like—they were ready to launch. But the change in business model meant they needed capital to purchase inventory. The typical advice when you're going for capital is to make sure you have a top-notch business plan and get capital as cheaply as possible. *They didn't do it.*

Instead, as they took the idea to potential investors (including Bain Capital, which ended up financing their first round), they still had no formal written business plan. When asked why, Hyman replied, "We're anti-business plan people. We think that so many people just sit around all day and strategize but they don't act." Fleiss concurred, saying, "We had a bias for action, not business planning." In fact, one reason Hyman and Fleiss chose Bain Capital, even though it wasn't necessarily the cheapest capital, was the attitude of partner Scott Friend. "He shared our commitment to learning by doing," said Fleiss.[3]

With capital in hand, the two women were ready to build the team. The typical advice is to hire experts to head each functional area, perhaps someone who can leverage significant corporate experience to take the team to the next level. *They didn't do it.*

Instead, Hyman took on marketing, and Fleiss took on finance. They then looked for individuals having broad skills who could wear different hats. "Having Jenn serve as CMO and me as CFO is typical of our fluid approach to allocating responsibilities," said Fleiss. "We need managers who can wear different hats. We learned about the value of all-around athletes when Lara joined on an unpaid trial basis to help with our college market tests. Although she had years of experience at Coach, she wasn't afraid to move dress racks. Brooke, our director of customer insight, has had several different roles but she's never worried about the title . . . We make heavy use of unpaid internships to test whether employees have the same hungry jack-of-all-trades attitude."[4]

With a small team in place, the typical advice would be to carefully develop a flawless website and service with broad appeal, adding features that might attract a wider set of customers. *They didn't do it.*

Instead, Rent the Runway quickly launched a beta version of its service for five thousand invited members on November 2, 2009. RTR started with eight hundred dresses from thirty designers—a relatively small inventory. "We followed the minimum viable product approach," said Fleiss. "At the outset we just wanted to provide the capability to rent dresses. Nothing fancy." But with the help of a *New York Times* article titled "A Netflix Model for Haute Couture," initial demand for the small inventory proved almost overwhelming.[5]

Now with proven demand and increasing customer feedback on how to improve the service, RTR was prepared to invest in a complete solution. Over the ensuing months, as demand continued to increase, it expanded its inventory to more than thirty thousand dresses with help from a $30 million round of financing. "Our revenue growth is amazing," Hyman told us at the end of RTR's first year. "This is a dream come true." But a more visible sign of success, perhaps, is that "its inventory dressed 85 percent of the ladies who attended President Obama's second inauguration."[6]

Lessons for Managers: How to Turn Uncertainty into Opportunity

Rent the Runway's story provides a window into the innovator's method. In a nutshell, it's a process by which successful innovators manage the uncertainty of innovation—a process to test and validate a creative insight before wasting resources building and launching a product customers don't actually want. We've found that this method is widely used by the most successful innovators in start-ups as well as established companies.

The method doesn't include writing a business plan. Hyman and Fleiss refused to write one even though virtually every business school holds "business plan" competitions for "start-up" ideas like Rent the Runway. Why do management experts call for writing a business plan? The recommendation comes from traditional management theory that was developed to solve a certain type of problem: established firms attempting to optimize under conditions of relative certainty. Indeed a closer look at many of our management practices—such as strategic planning, the precursor to business planning—reveals that many of our familiar management practices were originally designed to capture value under conditions of relative certainty. However, most new business ideas (inside or outside the corporation) are characterized by a completely different set of conditions: uncertainty. For example, how could Hyman possibly know what the demand for rented designer dresses would be?

Increasingly evidence suggests that our familiar management techniques work poorly when applied to the context of uncertainty. For example, research shows that under conditions of uncertainty, planning simply does not work.[7] Most of the time it wastes time and resources as you conjure evidence that your hypothesis—that is, your guess—is right; it does not resolve the uncertainty. In our example, instead of writing a plan, Hyman designed a set of experiments to test the leap-of-faith assumptions behind her big idea. Each experiment was designed to test specific assumptions, answering specific questions to resolve the uncertainties surrounding her idea.

These experiments helped Hyman and Fleiss "nail it"—our term for deeply understanding the uncertainty and resolving it well. For example, the first RTR experiments were focused on resolving demand uncertainty: Were Hyman and Fleiss really undertaking a problem worth solving? The initial experiments showed that there was definitely a demand for renting designer dresses. The right designer dress for a big social event nailed the job-to-be-done: making a woman feel special, confident, and desirable.

But these experiments didn't show whether renting over the internet was a viable solution. To test this assumption, Hyman didn't waste time and resources building a website. Instead, she created a simple substitute, or *minimum viable prototype:* PDF pictures that she sent to potential customers in New York. This experiment provided crucial data on what customers wanted, and from there she iterated from the minimum viable solution to become an *awesome solution,* where RTR fashion advisers talk to customers "like a woman might talk to her girlfriend," suggesting shoes, accessories, and, when needed, shipping two dress sizes instead of one to make sure the dress fit.

Only after RTR nailed the problem and solution was it time to figure out the business model to ensure that the go-to-market strategy would work. Validating the business model involves experimenting to figure out how to communicate with your customers and capture value from them—developing the right pricing model to generate revenue streams that will cover the operational activities (cost structure) and the key resources and capabilities the firm will need to deliver the solution to customers. Hyman's initial hypothesis about the channel to the customer—designer websites—turned out to be wrong. A *pivot*—which we define as changing a key element of the problem, solution, or business model—was necessary. RTR pivoted from a business model as a fulfillment partner for existing designers to a Netflix-like business model.

Although this pivot turned out to be critical, the Netflix business model didn't exactly work either. It needed to be adapted to fit RTR clients' needs. Netflix customers don't need advisers to help clients choose a product, but RTR realized that its success depended on the effectiveness of fashion advisers to coach clients. Moreover, Netflix doesn't rent a movie for a specific night—and if the movie doesn't arrive as expected, the service isn't a failure for customers. So RTR searched for another

FIGURE I-1
___

The innovator's method

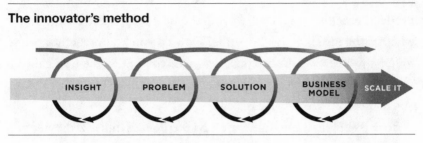

approach, finding an analogy in the airlines' model of selling a product (reserving a seat) for a particular time and place; RTR adapted its business model accordingly.

The RTR experience illustrates the "how-to" of the innovator's method: a series of experimentation cycles that resolve the uncertainties around the problem you're trying to solve, the solution you propose, and the business model to take your solution to market. We describe this method in a few steps—insight, problem, solution, and business model—during which your core tasks are to savor surprises (insight), discover jobs-to-be-done (problem), prototype the minimum awesome product (solution), and validate your go-to-market strategy (business model) (see figure I-1). Naturally, in a world of uncertainty, few things are linear. But we describe the innovator's method as a linear process to simplify a complex process and at other points in the book try to describe how the "steps" may overlap or be recursive.

Sources of the Innovator's Method

We conducted several overlapping research projects to understand how innovators successfully bring their ideas to market. This research starts with *The Innovator's Dilemma,* which first called for a different way of managing innovation, and then *The Innovator's DNA,* which identified the five discovery skills of disruptive innovators that help them generate insights.[8] Although *The Innovator's DNA* provides advice on how to generate innovative ideas, after you've generated an idea for a new product, process, or service, what is the next step? How do you know whether the idea is worth pursuing? How do you know whether you've found a problem worth solving? How will you know if you've nailed a solution to that problem? In short, what are the tools to test, validate, and commercialize new ideas?

To answer these questions, we reviewed and synthesized emerging perspectives from other disciplines about managing uncertainty. We're not the first to identify the need for a new way to manage the uncertainty of innovation. Each major discipline, upon encountering uncertainty, has developed its own answer, including engineering (design thinking), computer science (agile software), entrepreneurship (lean start-up), physics (active learning), the military (adaptive army), and so on. Each perspective offers valuable insights and valuable contributions that we have synthesized here. You may recognize elements of the innovator's method in other books, such as books on design thinking (Tim Brown's *Change by Design,* Roger Martin's *The Design of Business*), start-ups (such as Eric Ries's *Lean Startup,* Steve Blank's *Startup Owners Manual,* and Alex Osterwalder's *Business Model Generation*), innovation (such as Christensen's *Innovator's Dilemma,* Shona L. Brown and Kathleen M. Eisenhardt's *Competing on the Edge,* Bob Sutton's *Weird Ideas that Work,* or Rita Gunther McGrath and Ian C. MacMillan's *Discovery-Driven Planning*) or agile software (such as Jeff Sutherland and Ken Schwaber's *The Scrum Guide* or Kenneth S. Rubin's *Essential Scrum*). We respect and recommend these authors to you for their thoughtful contributions.

Even with valuable insights from their disciplines, these books often cover only a part of the innovation process. In this book, we pull the pieces together to provide a holistic model—starting with generating an insight, then moving to deeply understanding the customer problem, rapidly prototyping your way to an awesome solution, and finally aligning the business model with the solution before scaling it. As shown in figure I-2, design thinking is exceptional in helping people understand

FIGURE I-2

The method in detail

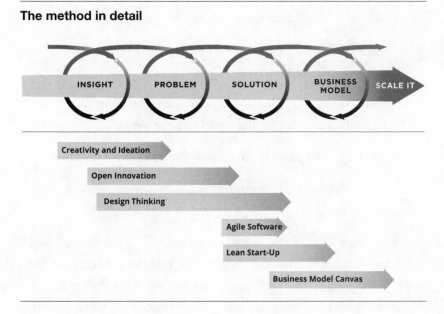

a customer problem, but it doesn't address the need to find the right business model. Lean start-up excels at prototyping the solution to a problem but often provides little guidance on generating ideas or determining whether you've found a problem worth solving. Books on business models provide excellent tools for figuring out other elements of the business model but do not address generating big ideas or how to deeply understand a customer problem. Our holistic model helps take you through the steps required to nail a business model before scaling it. And because most books focus on entrepreneurial start-ups, they don't take you through the crucial step of how to adapt these principles for a large company setting.

To understand how managers applied and adapted these principles in established companies, we conducted extensive research—both qualitative and quantitative—with hundreds of companies to understand what managers do to bring their ideas to market. We studied successful as well as unsuccessful companies to discover the differences between success and failure. These companies fall into four categories:

- Established companies that maintained their innovation capabilities after founding

- Established companies that had lost (or were losing) their innovation capabilities but then reignited them

- Successful and failed innovation initiatives in new ventures

- Successful and failed innovation initiatives in established companies

Although we do not describe all the companies in this book, table I-1 provides a sample of those that fall into the first three categories. These companies represent most of the case studies we use in the book.

Some companies, such as Amazon, Google, and Valve Software, have done a remarkable job of institutionalizing the entrepreneurial

TABLE I-1

Sample companies

Established companies that maintain innovation	Established companies that have reignited innovation	Start-up innovators
Amazon	Intuit	Rent the Runway
Salesforce.com	Hindustan Unilever	Qualtrics
Google	Procter & Gamble	Motive Communications
Valve Software	Mondelez	GitHub
Regeneron	Banco Davivienda	Asana
Starbucks	Godrej & Boyce Manufacturing	Chegg
W.L. Gore	AT&T	Ultimate Arena/Xfire
IDEO	Cemex	Big Idea Group

management principles on which they were founded. For example, under the leadership of Jeff Bezos, Amazon has sustained an extraordinary innovation track record since its founding in 1996. Indeed, the company has maintained an *innovation premium* (IP) that has averaged 73 percent.[9] (We introduced this metric in *The Innovator's DNA* and use it to rank the *Forbes* list of most innovative companies.) Amazon's IP means that investors are willing to pay a premium for its stock that is 73 percent higher than the net present value of cash flows from its existing businesses. Amazon's IP has been the highest of any company in the world during the past fifteen years.[10]

Other companies, such as Intuit, Procter & Gamble, and Hindustan Unilever, represent innovation turnaround stories. After years of stable but uninspiring innovation performance, these firms applied tactics we describe to dramatically boost innovation. Other companies are start-ups, such as Rent the Runway, Qualtrics, and Motive Communications, that provide rich insight into the process. Finally, some companies tried to bring techniques like lean start-up inside their companies but failed. Their efforts teach us about the challenges of such attempts.

Does the Innovator's Method Make a Difference?

We started this research by asking, "What processes do successful innovators use to validate their ideas and bring them to market?" Despite our claims of success, you may ask yourself, Does the innovator's method make a difference? Perhaps the most telling evidence comes from the established companies we studied that boosted their innovation performance after adopting elements of the method. Among the publicly traded companies we describe in this book, we observed that three to five years after adopting key elements, their IPs increased by an average of 57 percent (see table I-2).

Although it always takes time for innovations to bear fruit, these numbers are accompanied by growth in revenue, profit, and general excitement at the companies involved. For example, Hindustan Unilever increased its revenue by 40 percent in a single year; Intuit multiplied its

TABLE I-2

Growth in IP after use of the innovator's method

Company	Innovation premium before[a]	Innovation premium after[b]	Percentage increase	Additional value to market cap[c]
Intuit	20%	29%	45%	$1.8 billion
Hindustan Unilever	51%	61%	17%	$2.0 billion
Mondelez	17%	31%	78%	$8.3 billion
Procter & Gamble	18%	36%	95%	$40.5 billion
Godrej	40%	60%	50%	$0.9 billion
AT&T	−13%	6%	n/a	$35.8 billion

a. All "before" IP percentages are taken between 2006 and 2008 before the company initiated programs that included important elements of the innovator's method (except Procter & Gamble's, which is from 2000, the year A. G. Lafley became CEO).

b. All "after" IPs are from 2013.

c. Calculated as the difference in IP multiplied by the company's 2013 market cap.

revenue from successful new products tenfold over three years; Mondelez China was failing but turned itself into a successful $1 billion business; Godrej created a new category of consumer products sold through an entirely new distribution channel; Procter & Gamble created several multibillion-dollar businesses; and AT&T turned a negative IP into a positive one (investors in the mid-2000s were expecting AT&T's current businesses to shrink, but they now expect them to achieve growth).

Who Needs *The Innovator's Method*?

Anyone wanting to innovate or facing problems characterized by uncertainty needs to understand when and how to apply the innovator's method to increase their chances of success. We envision three primary audiences for this book:

- Managers from any function or division who want to innovate or solve problems characterized by uncertainty, but don't know the steps or feel frustrated by the impediments

- Leaders who face the challenges of declining growth, the need to sustain existing growth, or the difficulty of retaining talented managers who may leave for start-ups

- Entrepreneurs, many of whom may have been frustrated managers, who want to maximize their chances of success

Although the ideas in this book clearly apply to managers, leaders, and entrepreneurs, they are relevant to anyone trying to solve a complex problem—someone trying to reinvent education, improve political decision making, or even solve a challenging family problem. For example, we think US government officials would be more effective if they would design experiments and run them in parallel to see what they could learn before rolling out a policy to the entire country. (In fact, China has been successfully setting policy through experiments and is currently running, in parallel, seven experiments to determine the best way to control air pollution.) Ultimately, our goal is to teach you about the principles that you can use to solve any challenging problem.

The big idea that differentiates this book is that uncertainty requires a new set of management principles. While traditional management works well for problems of relative certainty, it works poorly for problems characterized by uncertainty. By using the tools described here, you will learn how to creatively solve high-uncertainty problems. You will learn how to transform an idea into a reality. This knowledge is valuable for leaders and managers in large organizations as well as budding entrepreneurs. For anyone who has thought, "I wonder whether this idea could work?" but hasn't known how to take the next step, *The Innovator's Method* is your operating manual.

1

The Innovator's Method

How do we turn Intuit into an eight-thousand-person
start-up? That's what we are trying to do.

—Brad Smith, CEO, Intuit

I N 2008, INTUIT celebrated its twenty-fifth anniversary and named Brad
Smith as CEO. Founded by Scott Cook, Intuit—maker of successful
financial software packages like Quicken, QuickBooks, and TurboTax—
had achieved remarkable success, growing revenues to more than $3 bil-
lion and creating a market value of $10.2 billion. But Cook and Smith
were worried. Intuit had seemingly reached a performance plateau,
and its market value had begun to fall. Annual revenue growth had
dropped in half, from 15 percent (1998–2003) to 8 percent (2004–2008),
and annual income growth had slowed even more dramatically, from
31 percent to 6 percent. Not surprisingly, Intuit's annual market value
growth had taken a hit as well, dropping from 14 percent to 5 percent.

Worse, after studying Intuit's new product launches over the prior
decade, Cook discovered that fewer than 10 percent could be called successful from a revenue and profit perspective. Meanwhile, Intuit's net
promoter score (NPS), a measure of whether customers like a product
enough to promote it to friends and colleagues, had flattened.[1] Finally,

the company's innovation premium (IP), a measure of stock price premium paid by investors because of expectations of future growth through innovation, had dropped from 57 percent in 2000 to 20 percent in 2008.[2] After twenty-five years, by every measure, it seemed as if the company had reached the telltale limit of the S-curve: Intuit was moving from growth to maturity, with the threat of failure not far behind.

Cook and Smith didn't want that to happen. But what could they do?

The Innovation Crisis: Unprecedented Uncertainty

Intuit was experiencing what happens to most successful start-ups as they grow into large, established corporations: execution becomes the highest priority as they scale the business to meet the demands of existing customers. Over time, the focus on execution crowds out innovation. Intuit was losing the ability to perform what Peter Drucker called management's fundamental task: "to create a customer."[3] Ironically, as companies focus on capturing value from customers, they often lose the ability to create customers.

And something more had changed. It's a cliché to say that the world is more uncertain than ever before, but few people realize the extent of the increase in uncertainty over the past thirty years. More important, they don't understand that greater uncertainty has created the need to change the way most organizations are managed. The challenge of creating a customer is more complex and uncertain than ever before. Here's why.

There are two types of uncertainty that influence a firm's ability to create a customer: *demand uncertainty* (will customers buy it?) and *technological uncertainty* (can we make a desirable solution?).* Uncertainty arises from the unknowns associated with solving any problem, which

---

*There is a third type of uncertainty called *environmental uncertainty*, which refers to the uncertainty of the macroeconomic environment and government policy; but demand and technological uncertainty are more directly relevant to creating a customer.

are sometimes called "unknown unknowns," such as hidden customer preferences or undiscovered elements of a technical solution.

The more unknowns there are about customer preferences and behavior, the greater the demand uncertainty. For example, when Jenn Hyman of Rent the Runway came up with the idea to rent designer dresses over the internet, demand uncertainty was high because no one else was offering this service.[4] In contrast, when Samsung and Sony were deciding whether to launch LED TVs, which offered better picture quality at roughly the same price as plasma TVs, there was lower uncertainty about demand because customers were already buying TVs.

Technological uncertainty results from uncertainty regarding the technologies that might emerge or need to be created for a new solution to emerge. For example, a wide variety of clean technologies (including wind, solar, and hydrogen) are vying to power vehicles and cities at the same time that a wide variety of medical technologies (chemical, biotechnological, genomic, and robotic) are being developed to treat diseases. As the overall rate of invention across industries increases, so does technological uncertainty.

To better understand the uncertainty facing firms like Intuit, we studied the depth and degree of the shift in demand and technological uncertainty. First, we looked at multiple measures of the rate of technological change. One measure is the rate of invention patenting (see figure 1-1).

This is an imperfect measure, but clearly it reflects a striking increase in the rate of invention in the past twenty years.[5] Not surprisingly, there has been a similarly dramatic increase in total R&D spending.

As new technologies emerge, companies are rising, and falling, at a much faster pace than ever before. This phenomenon is amplified by increasingly faster changes in customers' demands for a new mix of products and services. For example, consider how quickly entertainment preferences have changed. For more than three decades—between 1950 and 1980—we accessed TV shows and movies primarily through three networks (ABC, NBC, CBS) or at movie theaters. Then with the advent of the VCR, we've progressed to watching movies on our home TV screens

FIGURE 1-1

Total US patent applications

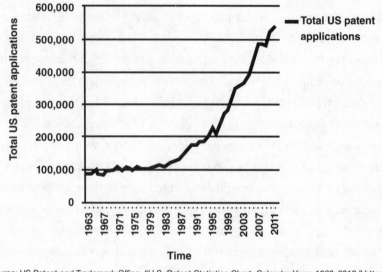

Source: US Patent and Trademark Office, "U.S. Patent Statistics Chart, Calendar Years 1963–2012," http://www.uspto.gov/web/offices/ac/ido/oeip/taf/us_stat.htm.

via videocassettes and then DVDs, to watching them on our computers, then on our laptops, then on tablets, and now on our phones, mostly via internet streaming. When the DVD emerged, it was adopted more quickly than any previous consumer electronic device selling just over three hundred thousand units in the first year—until the iPad, which sold three million units in its first eighty days.[6] In short, customer preferences are not only changing but also changing at an accelerating pace.

A closer look at demand uncertainty among the *Fortune* 500 underscores this pattern. The churn among this highest-echelon group increased significantly between 1964 and 2014 (see figure 1-2): a firm on the list in 1964 would, on average, have been on the list for sixty-one years before being replaced by another firm. By 2014, a firm that made it into the *Fortune* 500 would, on average, only be on the list for eighteen years. The churn on the *Fortune* 500 has increased five times over the past fifty years. Other academic studies confirm that competitive advantage has become harder to sustain over a broad range of high- and low-tech industries.[7]

FIGURE 1-2

Life expectancy of a firm in the *Fortune* 500

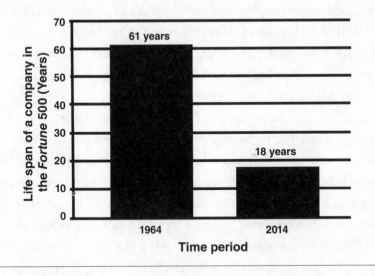

It's not an exaggeration to say that a second Industrial Revolution has occurred, a revolution fueled by new technologies and customers and accompanied by radical uncertainty. Companies don't hold on to customers as long as they used to, and new technologies and competitors are emerging faster than ever before. In fact, almost *one hundred million* new businesses are started globally each year—estimated to be almost ten times the rate from fifty years ago.

What drives these dramatic increases in uncertainty? There are many reasons, but two disruptive technologies have played a crucial role: personal computing and the internet. Another key is the emergence of capitalism in countries such as China, India, Russia, and Brazil.

Personal computing has placed powerful analytical tools into the hands of everyone having the motivation to master them. It has democratized and decentralized complex problem solving. Similarly, the internet has had a profound effect as a low-cost marketing and distribution channel for anyone wanting to sell a product. This means that more new products can be launched to a larger audience, and faster, than ever before.

Finally, as China, India, Russia, and Brazil have joined the global economy, they have expanded the pool of potential entrepreneurs by 2.5 billion people. These new entrepreneurs enjoy lower technical barriers to entry (with open source software, programming platforms, and cloud technologies), lower capital barriers (with the growth of venture capital, angel funding, and crowd-funding), lower production barriers (with the adoption of 3-D printers and global suppliers), and lower distribution and marketing barriers (with the internet and the emergence of direct shipping and social media). As a result, there are simply more competitors than ever before.

These changes have increased uncertainty to a tipping point—a threshold where the traditional ways we organized and managed corporations will no longer work to sustain growth in the future. This is especially true of companies in the industries having the highest uncertainty, such as computer software and medical equipment (see "How Much Uncertainty Do You Face?"). In fact, the computer software industry—where Intuit competes—is at the high end of the uncertainty spectrum, with volatile revenues, heavy R&D spending, and new entrants emerging at an unprecedented rate. Intuit's Scott Cook was aware of the difficulty of predicting and meeting customer demand. That's why many of the company's new products had flopped. He had also seen new competitors come along to attack Intuit in new ways, with different technologies and business models. He realized that he needed to figure out a new way to manage in the highly volatile computer software industry if he hoped to compete with the start-ups. Here's where the Intuit story gets interesting.

How Much Uncertainty Do You Face?

Not everyone faces the same levels of uncertainty. Some industries have greater inherent demand or technological uncertainty. Consider the 2×2 matrix shown in figure 1-3. The horizontal axis plots each industry based on technological uncertainty, measured as the average R&D expenditures as a percentage of sales in the industry over the past ten years. The vertical axis plots each industry's demand uncertainty, measured as an equal weighting of

FIGURE 1-3

Demand and technological uncertainty by industry (2002–2011)

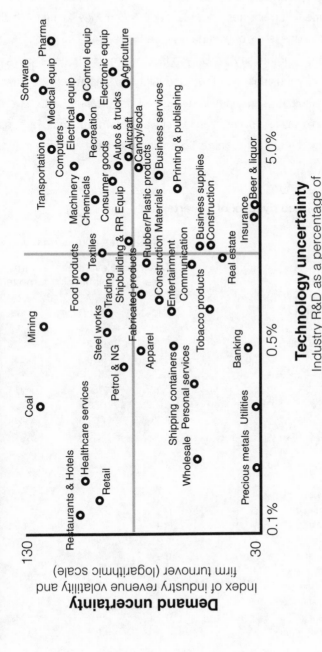

Source: Compustat, 2013.
Note: Quadrants drawn at median values: (1.4, 67.5).
Note: Beer & liquor, insurance, utilities, precious metals displayed at demand uncertainty = 30 for visual purposes. True demand uncertainty values are 28.9, 14.4, 21.6, respectively.

industry revenue volatility, or change, over the past ten years and percentage of firms in the industry that entered or exited over the past ten years. Although these are imperfect measures, they identify the industries facing the highest, and lowest baseline levels of uncertainty (see figure 1-4).

Where does your industry sit? Do you face high or low uncertainty? As you can see, some industries face low uncertainty; examples include providers of personal services, such as hair styling and dry cleaning, who have used similar technologies to provide solutions for well-known demands. By contrast, in the lower-right quadrant in figure 1-3 are industries that face lower demand

FIGURE 1-4

Industries ranked by level of uncertainty

	Measures of uncertainty		
Industry	**R&D % of sales**	**Revenue volatility**	**Firm turnover***
1. Medical equipment	8.2%	90.7%	13.1%
2. Computers	5.8%	98.8%	12.0%
3. Computer software	9.8%	69.9%	14.4%
4. Pharmaceutical products	17.4%	63.3%	12.7%
5. Measuring & control equipment	9.3%	97.0%	8.8%
6. Machinery	3.2%	100.5%	9.3%
7. Agriculture	10.8%	123.3%	4.9%
8. Electronic equipment	5.2%	61.5%	10.5%
9. Chemicals	3.0%	71.2%	9.2%
10. Electrical equipment	9.8%	35.0%	9.2%
24. Business services	3.2%	46.2%	6.5%
40. Business supplies	1.4%	34.8%	5.0%
41. Shipping containers	0.5%	65.1%	4.9%
42. Real estate	1.3%	57.6%	3.0%
43. Beer & liquor	2.3%	12.8%	3.7%
44. Personal services	0.3%	59.7%	4.4%
45. Tobacco products	1.0%	20.3%	5.2%
46. Insurance	2.2%	30.4%	0.9%
47. Wholesale	0.1%	14.1%	6.3%
48. Utilities	0.2%	45.6%	0.2%
49. Precious metals	0.1%	40.7%	1.5%

*Percentage of (entrance + exits) / total firms in the industry per year

uncertainty but high technological uncertainty. For example, aircraft makers can generally predict the demand for aircraft production. The challenge they face is technological uncertainty; Boeing and Airbus spend large sums developing advanced new aircraft like the Boeing 787 and the Airbus A350.

In the upper-left quadrant are industries that face high demand uncertainty but low technological uncertainty. For example, restaurants and hotels often have difficulty predicting demand for their services, because many factors influence whether, when, and where people eat out or travel. However, the technologies of offering food or lodging have not changed much over the years.

Finally, industries in the upper-right quadrant—such as software, pharmaceuticals, and medical equipment—face high uncertainty in both demand and technology. For example, who would have predicted that medical robots would perform surgeries? When Intuitive Surgical launched the Da Vinci System medical robot—which allows surgeons to operate using 3-D visualization and four robotic arms—the company faced significant technical as well as demand uncertainty.

Our analysis suggests that, on average, the top ten most uncertain industries require greater innovation management skills than the bottom ten. However, even if your industry provides clues about average uncertainty, every problem is characterized by its own level of uncertainty. For example, although Webvan was a food retailer in an industry with relatively low uncertainty, its online platform of home delivery faced both high demand uncertainty (will customers buy groceries online?) and high technological uncertainty (can we fulfill orders in a cost-effective way?). Demand uncertainty was high, because the company had few facts about demand and many assumptions. The same was true of technological uncertainty; it had many assumptions about which fulfillment technologies would work best.

The ratio of assumptions to facts equals your *uncertainty ratio*. If your problem is characterized by a low uncertainty ratio, you can probably apply traditional management. If you have a high uncertainty ratio, then *The Innovator's Method* should guide you. Unfortunately for Webvan's investors, the company was not successful in experimenting to resolve its high-uncertainty problems before a full-scale launch—$500 million—that proved disastrous.

A New Way to Manage: Intuit's Transformation

The story of Intuit's journey gives managers an archetype for a new way of managing in a high-uncertainty industry. Intuit's transformation arguably began in 2004 with its adoption of the net promoter score. NPS is based on a single question posed to customers: How likely are you, on a scale of 0 (not at all likely) to 10 (extremely likely), to recommend this product or service to a colleague or friend? A product's NPS is the percentage of promoters (those who score themselves 9 or 10) minus the percentage of detractors (scores 0–6).[8]

Net promoter score = % promoters minus % detractors

Historically, Intuit products had dominated their markets by being significantly easier to use than competitors'. But soon competitors were catching up, so Intuit launched an effort to improve ease of use and NPS. It spent even more time with customers, observed detractors, and redesigned products. "We put a big focus on making our products easier to use," says Kaaren Hanson, design vice-president. "And when this company decides to go after something, we do it. So we pulled the lever." But these traditional management moves failed to move the meter. "Our net promoter scores didn't budge," Hanson says. "And it didn't result in a big jump in sales, which is what we expected. We pulled the damn lever, and nothing happened."[9]

In other areas of the company, customer response to new products was especially disappointing. "We were humbled when we looked back at ten years of innovation," says CEO Brad Smith, who took over for Steve Bennett in 2008. "We'd launched fifty-four products, and fewer than five had achieved any commercial success, measured by revenue or profit. And we were bad at shutting down the failures. When we did, we got labeled as not being patient enough."[10]

Design for Delight

Intuit's leaders knew they needed to figure out what would move customers and discover how to improve the success rate of new products. So a team was pulled together. "We went out to understand what was beyond ease," says Hanson. "And we looked at a lot of the usual suspects. We looked at Nike, we looked at the W Hotels, we looked at Harley-Davidson, and we looked at Apple. You name it, we probably looked at them."[11] The Intuit team realized that the most successful companies didn't just offer products that were easier to use; they offered products that delighted customers.

Products that delight customers do the unexpected. They solve a problem customers didn't know they had, or they evoke a positive emotion. But how does a company create products that delight customers?

The team discovered that design thinking offered critical new tools not in their familiar management tool set. Cook had the benefit of sitting on the board of Procter & Gamble and saw up close how P&G incorporated techniques like design thinking into product development. Drawing on design thinking principles, Cook, Hanson, and her team created a training program called Design for Delight (D4D), a program intended to transform Intuit into a design-driven innovation machine. Intuit's D4D initiative was based on searching for a big unmet customer need and then applying three principles.

- *Gain deep customer empathy.* Understand customers better than they understand themselves.

- *Go broad to go narrow.* Generate lots of solutions before winnowing the list.

- *Experiment rapidly with customers.* Seek feedback early and often.

Hanson realized that to infuse D4D principles into the DNA of all eight thousand employees, she needed to get top management on board. To jump-start the process, Hanson and Cook helped plan a two-day offsite for Intuit's top three hundred managers. At first the group paid polite attention, but as the audience plowed through a five-hour PowerPoint presentation, Cook saw that the design thinking approach was falling flat. But then Alex Kazaks, a young associate professor at Stanford, led the team in a unique participatory exercise: Kazaks asked each person to design, and prototype, a wallet for the person next to him. As the managers worked through the design challenge, creating prototypes, getting feedback, and redesigning, the hands-on experience helped them see the value of design thinking as a tool to discover and deeply understand customer needs to create new value.

Hanson then organized a series of design forums, typically attended by roughly three thousand employees, to teach people the key principles and let them practice D4D. However, after several forums and a huge effort, Hanson discovered a disappointing fact: the company wasn't changing enough to produce different results. "We did this for about a year," says Hanson, "and what I was hearing in the hallways—that made me feel absolutely nauseous—was that 'design for delight' is this flavor of the month. This was very disheartening, because we actually had senior leaders involved and engaged. As it turns out, senior leaders are not enough."[12]

Innovation Catalysts and "Lean Start-In" Workshops

Structural changes were needed deep inside Intuit. Hanson and her team began thinking about how to create deeper expertise in D4D. If she could create D4D coaches—what Intuit now calls "innovation catalysts"—she thought they could coach teams applying D4D in their everyday work.[13] So she selected nine individuals from a variety of business units and fields—design, research, and product management—to become the new D4D experts.

The innovation catalysts were charged with assisting project teams to give them the confidence to use the D4D playbook. Hanson asked the catalysts to spend 25 percent of their time on "big-payoff projects." Why? Hanson knew that without a visible win, the program would fade quickly. As the first few successes trickled in, the demand for expert help grew. Over the next few years, Hanson's team recruited and trained an additional two hundred innovation catalysts, who spent roughly 10 percent of their time coaching teams.

As Intuit rolled out the D4D program, the catalysts found that design thinking provided highly useful tools for gaining deep customer empathy. But it didn't have great tools for testing potential solutions once customer pain points were discovered. Cook and his team became familiar with *lean experimentation,* ideas popularized by Eric Ries in *The Lean Startup* and by Steve Blank in *Four Steps to the Epiphany.* The tools of lean experimentation were well suited to test a *leap-of-faith assumption,* a term used at Intuit to refer to a hypothesis being tested through experiment.

So Intuit began running "lean start-in" workshops. Employee teams brought an idea to meet a big unmet customer need, and in two days the team went through the entire cycle of identifying a customer pain point, prototyping a solution, and testing with customers.[14] These workshops have become a useful vehicle for developing and prototyping new ideas. Indeed, the combination of forums, workshops, and catalysts has not only helped everyone at Intuit understand the new D4D playbook but also provided deep expertise to successfully execute the plays.

Implementing the Innovator's Method

What exactly was happening inside Intuit? As managers were adopting ideas from design thinking and lean start-up, they were learning how to systematically experiment their way to success. Moreover, they began to create start-up teams throughout the company that used a similar process to that used by start-ups to bring new products to market.

As we observed what was happening at Intuit—and what happened at other innovative corporations and start-ups—we realized that these companies were using a similar process for testing and validating ideas.

This process, what we call the innovator's method, consists of four steps to solve high-uncertainty problems and turn insight into a successful innovation (see figure 1-5).

> *Step 1. Insight: savor surprises.* Leverage the behaviors identified in our earlier book, *The Innovator's DNA*—questioning, observing, networking, and experimenting—to search broadly for insights about problems worth solving.

> *Step 2. Problem: discover the job-to-be-done.* Rather than starting with solutions, start by exploring the customers' need or problem—the functional, social, and emotional job-to-be-done—to be sure you're going after a problem worth solving.

> *Step 3. Solution: prototype the minimum awesome product.* Instead of developing full-scale products, leverage theoretical and virtual prototypes of multiple solution dimensions. Then iterate on each solution to develop a minimum viable prototype and eventually a minimum awesome product.

> *Step 4. Business model: validate the go-to-market strategy.* Once you've nailed the solution, you're ready to validate the other components of the business model, including the pricing strategy, the customer acquisition strategy, and the cost structure strategy.

FIGURE 1-5

The innovator's method

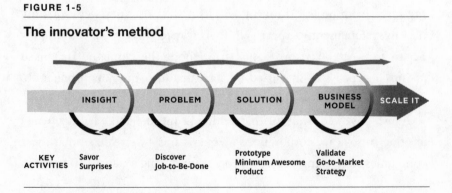

Each step in the method is critical and involves an experimentation loop to test leap-of-faith assumptions in a repeated "hypothesis, test, learn" loop.[15] Let's return to Intuit and see how it has applied the innovator's method.

Insight: Savor Surprises

The innovator's method starts with generating insights into potential customer problems by looking for surprises or other clues, such as symptoms of a problem. We use the word *problem* interchangeably to mean a need or problem that can exist for external customers or internal users. (For example, at Intuit, half the projects are targeted at solving an unmet customer need; the other half target internal needs, such as developing better technology tools to serve customers or creating a better working environment.) The insight can come from anyone, and that explains why Intuit gives 10 percent unstructured time to every employee to generate ideas and participate in a start-up team. In a convenience sample, we found that insights were developed most often through user or customer observations and through conversations with customers, Intuit employees, and various individuals outside Intuit.

Insights often start when you notice a symptom or a surprise, which provides the clues to an opportunity. For example, Intuit's Barath Kadaba and Deepa Bachu (an innovation catalyst) were looking for opportunities to create new businesses to improve the financial lives of the 1.2 billion residents of India. After initial observations and analysis, Bachu and a team of three other people decided to explore the needs of India's 150 million farmers, a large segment of potential customers with many challenges.

The team spent three weeks following farmers—in the fields, in their villages, and at the markets where they sold their produce. As they watched, they were surprised at the incredible challenges farmers had selling their produce at a good price. As they listened to farmers complain, worry, and often lose money, they had the clues of a potential problem to solve. Furthermore, the team was surprised by the powerful role played by middlemen in the market, who had no incentive to pro-vide farmers with accurate information on supply and demand. These symptoms and surprises pointed to a potential opportunity. If the prob-lem was as serious as Bachu thought it was, and if Intuit could come up with a solution that would translate into higher prices for farmers, Bachu knew it could be a big opportunity for Intuit.[16]

Problem: Discover the Job-to-Be-Done

Managers tend to start by building solutions, but we emphasize the need to first deeply understand the problem. Keep in mind that "prob-lem" may mean either a customer's pain or a customer's desire, such as a desire for connection, expression, fulfillment, and the like. At the core you are trying to discover the functional, social, and emotional elements of the job-to-be-done—the need for which customers might purchase your product. For example, although a BMW may do a similar functional job as another car (transport), a BMW can also accomplish important social jobs (prestige, status) or emotional jobs (feels "cool") that may be overlooked at first blush.

At Intuit, teams follow up on an insight into an unmet customer need by using a technique called *pain-storming*. According to Rachel Evans, one of the innovation catalysts who developed it, "The purpose of a pain-storm is to get crisp on what we think the problem is so we can test our hypotheses."

Pain-storming involves creating a customer's "journey line" to understand how customers now complete a task and identify their main pain points (and emotions) along the way. The team then conducts a root-cause analysis to understand the causes of the biggest pain points. Of course, it doesn't work if team members just sit in their offices and imagine what customers might want. Instead, Intuit's team members directly observe and talk to customers in their offices or homes. As CEO Smith told us, "To walk a mile in your customer's shoes, you have to take your own shoes off first."[17] In short, you must "be the customer."

As Bachu and her team spent weeks living with, observing, and talking to farmers and middlemen in seven agricultural markets, she learned firsthand about the pain farmers felt when faced with a decision to sell perishable crops, whose prices might fluctuate as much as 50 percent in a single day. The team validated their initial observation that the farmers had no information on supply or demand to guide them, resulting in spoilage or suboptimal prices. They also validated the fact that farmers were often exploited by the middlemen, who had an incentive to minimize market price transparency. As the team members gained confidence that they had identified an important problem worth solving, they translated the problem into a vision statement for the customer: "10 percent higher prices for farmers." Drawing on the insights into the causes of the farmers' problem—and using the vision statement as a guide—the team then was ready to focus its energies on developing a solution.

Solution: Prototype the Minimum Awesome Product

After identifying a customer problem worth solving, most managers unleash the product development team to build a full-featured, error-free product to attract as many customers as possible. Although this approach makes sense in familiar markets, it is the wrong thing to do when you face uncertainty. Instead, managers should search broadly for a variety of solutions and then use a series of four prototypes to converge on the solution that best solves the job-to-be-done (theoretical prototype, virtual prototype, minimum viable prototype, and minimum awesome product).

Although rapid prototypes may seem like old news, there is a subtle process to leveraging prototypes in the right way to rapidly validate your hypotheses. In the early days, although Intuit adopted the idea of rapid prototyping to test solutions, they found it led to premature development, as high-potential solutions were quickly thrown into Intuit's traditional software development process. This process often yielded long development cycles and disappointing results. Intuit's leaders soon realized that the better way to gain momentum was to fake the product in order to get something into users' hands more quickly. This *virtual prototype*, as we would call it, allowed the Intuit team to quickly test many, many solutions with customers to determine if they had any potential.

For example, the Mobile Bazaar team (Intuit's name for the team searching for a solution to the farmers' pricing problem) experimented with several simple prototypes to test potential solutions. One prototype was an eBay-like auction where the farmers could auction their products directly to buyers. However, initial tests of virtual prototypes, drawn in PowerPoint, suggested such a system would be complex for farmers to set up and use (most of them were not well educated, nor did they have experience with computers).

The team observed, however, that all the farmers had cell phones and knew how to send and receive text messages. So the team tested virtual prototypes, and then a minimum viable prototype, of a solution that involved gathering information on prices that buyers and middlemen were prepared to pay; this information was then sent to farmers in real time through text messages. Farmers then would use that information to decide when, and to whom, they would sell. The team "faked the back-end" by having three team members manually send text messages to farmers to see how they responded. Farmer response to this solution was extremely positive. Within one year, Mobile Bazaar had 180,000 farmer subscribers, and tests showed that farmers' prices had increased an average of 16 percent.

In addition to demonstrating the use of specific prototypes, the Mobile Bazaar example demonstrates a more general principle of the innovator's method: "go broad to go narrow." At Intuit, teams apply this principle by generating as many solutions as possible during what the company calls a "solution-jam" before reducing the concepts to a short list for prototyping. After selecting at least three solutions, the team initiates a "code jam," with the goal of creating a working software prototype of each solution that isn't perfect but is good enough to test with customers. In this way, Intuit progresses from pain-storming to a customer-tested prototype within four weeks, thereby enabling rapid experimentation with customers numerous times before the solution is put into software development.

However, as we will argue, truly delighting customers comes from the unexpected: it comes from understanding a problem in a way that others haven't and then going beyond customers' expectations in providing a solution. Therefore, the ultimate goal of this stage of the process is to create a *minimum awesome product*—one that remains "uncomfortably narrow" in feature set but is awesome at what it does.[18]

Business Model: Validate the Go-to-Market Strategy

At Intuit, Kaaren Hanson argues, "Until you've figured out how to delight a customer, don't even think about the business model."[19] But once you've discovered a solution customers want, you're ready to figure out the best way to get your solution into the hands of customers at a price that generates the revenues called for in your strategy. However, although most managers assume they understand how to get products to market, many companies have killed their new products by forcing them into existing business models. For example, managers often use the same distribution channels, a similar marketing strategy, a similar pricing strategy, and so on, as they use for existing products. But even when innovations appear similar, they often require their own unique business models. Properly aligning the business model involves discovering and validating your go-to-market strategy directly with your customers. This process requires validating how to acquire and influence customers, how to set price, and which resources will be required to deliver your solution to the market.

Intuit currently manages this process by dividing innovation into groups. Innovations related to its core financial software products (Quicken, QuickBooks, and TurboTax) are labeled "Horizon 1" (H1) products and generally borrow the existing business model. But products only partially related to the core are labeled "Horizon 2" (H2), and new or unrelated products are labeled "Horizon 3" (H3). The new H3 and H2 products, in particular, require rapid experimentation to test assumptions about the new business model. Furthermore, H3 products require a unique set of metrics to measure progress in nailing the new business model. Rather than measure financial performance, such as ROI or contribution to top-line revenue, Intuit starts by measuring what it calls the "love metrics" (see chapter 8). The point is that you can't assume that new solutions will work with your existing business model.

Mobile Bazaar typifies an H3 business, and the team is still in the process of experimenting with the business model. Unlike Quicken or TurboTax, the Mobile Bazaar distribution channel to customers will operate via cell phones (as will all digital marketing), and pricing must also be different (likely through subscription or a "free" advertising supported or freemium model). Intuit has not attempted to scale Mobile Bazaar at this point, because it has not yet validated a profitable business model.

A New Style of Leadership

Corporations are designed for execution, not innovation. But as uncertainty increases in the world around us, the way we manage has to change to meet these circumstances. To apply the innovator's method requires a new style of leadership. In the age of uncertainty, leaders are no longer chief decision makers. Instead, they're chief experimenters who formulate hypotheses with their team, conduct experiments, and let the data speak for themselves. "We want our leaders to be coaches and facilitators, not decision makers," says Cook. "The experiments that the team runs should provide the data to help the team make decisions so the leader doesn't have to."[20]

Thus the manager's role shifts to coach and facilitator of "fast and frugal" experiments. If the manager, or anyone else on the team, says, "I think we should do X" or "I believe X," that statement is translated into a leap-of-faith assumption, and the next question should always be, "What's the fastest way to run an experiment to help us know whether we should do X?"[21] "With our new focus on experimentation, our leaders should stop trying to be Jobs or Bezos and predict the future," says CEO Smith. "Our leaders should nurture innovation wherever it comes from. With lean experimentation, employees can come to leaders and have the boldness to say, 'I've got an idea, and here's the proof.'"[22]

So within each of the first few steps (problem, solution, and business model), Intuit teams follow this process: (1) writing down the most important leap-of-faith assumption, (2) designing an experiment to test it, (3) conducting the experiment to provide the answer, and then (4) looping back to figure out the next leap-of-faith assumption that the team needs to answer.

Leaders have to walk the talk. Key decisions they want to make should be tested as leap-of-faith assumptions. Remember, in high uncertainty, anything you believe to be true is only your best guess. What is your leap-of-faith assumption?

Intuit's Results

How has Intuit's application of the ideas we describe here affected innovation at the company? First, Intuit has become an experimentation machine. In 2006 the TurboTax unit ran only one customer experiment; in 2012 it ran more than six hundred, and by 2013 it had run almost 2,500 customer experiments in a single year. Not surprisingly, this increase in market experiments has produced a plethora of successful new products. Mobile apps have increased from zero in 2008 to fifty in 2013, including the very successful SnapTax app, which generated 350,000 downloads in its first three weeks.

But the proof is in the financial pudding. In 2010 Intuit generated $10 million in revenues from products launched in the prior three years. That number jumped tenfold—to $100 million—by 2012, and the company expects to earn much more as these nascent businesses mature.[23] Perhaps more important, Intuit's product launches and product improvements are being well received by the market, and profits are up considerably. Operating income has more than doubled, from 7 percent annual growth from 2004 to 2008 to 15 percent annual growth from 2008 to 2012.

And investors have rewarded Intuit. Its market cap jumped from $10 billion in 2008 to $17 billion in 2013—a 70 percent increase (for comparison Intuit's market cap increased only from $9 to $10 billion from 2003 to 2008). Moreover, Intuit's innovation premium has jumped from 20 percent in 2008 to 30 percent in 2012—a 33 percent increase. Intuit is once again acting, and performing, like an innovative company and, some might say, like a start-up (see "Is Your Company an Eight-Thousand-Person Start-Up?").

Is Your Company an Eight-Thousand-Person Start-Up?

If you're working in a larger organization, you may wonder, What does this start-up stuff have to do with me? Although we describe both start-ups and established companies, the issue isn't the size of the company. The issue is the type of problem you face and how you are solving it: uncertainty requires a different management approach that is critical for either entrepreneurial or corporate start-ups. However, because start-ups often spend their time solving high-uncertainty problems, you may incorrectly associate the innovator's method with start-ups rather than with the type of problem.

We define a start-up as does Eric Ries in *The Lean Startup:* as "a temporary organization designed to search for a business model under conditions of extreme uncertainty."[24] The definition includes three important dimensions. First, anyone (or team) who is creating a new product, service, process, or business—no matter the size of the company—is the founder of a start-up. The definition includes corporate and entrepreneurial start-ups.

Second, a start-up has a special purpose and structure; it's a temporary organization focused on searching for a problem, a solution, and a business model. Third, the founders are trying to launch something new under conditions of uncertainty. It isn't clear whether there will be demand for the new product (demand uncertainty) or whether the technological solutions will work as desired (technological uncertainty). If you're a start-up founder (manager or entrepreneur), you should apply this method to avoid the number 1 pitfall that kills start-ups: scaling the business before you've nailed it.

Similarly, we define "customer" as anyone with a problem or need, whether inside or outside the organization. You can apply the innovator's method to solve problems with some uncertainty *inside* your organization, whether in IT, HR, or finance. Wendy Castleman, an Intuit innovation catalyst, recalled such a process for an internal customer. An employee in IT observed that billing agents took fifteen minutes to answer customer questions. This spark of an insight and further observation identified the core problem: billing agents had to look across multiple systems to identify the various components of a customer bill. So she designed a series of experiments, testing different prototyped approaches to solutions for agents, ultimately finding a new tool that decreased call times from fifteen minutes to three!

Using a similar approach, Intuit's Full-Service Payroll team wanted to see whether they could improve the customer experience of calling in for support. One idea was to answer the phone in a more personal way. Instead of saying, "What is your EIN number?" they hypothesized that they would get higher customer satisfaction by beginning with, "How can I help you today?" They tried it with one agent, and the results were stunning. The agent's NPS scores jumped more than 20 points, well beyond the rest of the team (or her prior scores). They quickly rolled out the change to the rest of the team, and the experiment ultimately led to a 21-point increase in their NPS scores. The point? The innovator's method works for internal as well as external customers.

A Guide to This Book

In this chapter we've examined how an established organization can implement the key steps in the innovator's method, and we've introduced leadership principles that enable the method to flourish. Now you'll take a deep dive into the leadership principles that will help you apply the method as well as each step of the method. Rather than give you theory and let you figure out how to implement it, we focus on giving you both the big idea (why to) and the tools and tests we've seen successful innovators use (how to). (See appendix A for a summary of the model and the tools and tests discussed in each chapter. See www .theinnovatorsmethod.com for further tools and tips.) Here's an overview of the chapters to come.

In chapter 2, we explain why being a good manager can make you a bad innovator. We describe how your role changes when you're managing for innovation in a high-uncertainty environment. Chapter 3 discusses how managers generate insights—the seeds of innovation—by applying five key skills (questioning, observing, experimenting, networking, and associating) and by searching broadly to understand the job-to-be-done. Then in chapter 4 you'll learn how to determine whether your insight represents a problem worth solving. Discovering the job-to-be-done (functional, social, and emotional job) is the critical first step, and one that's often overlooked. This chapter has tests for determining whether you've discovered a worthwhile problem.

In chapter 5 you'll find tools to help you broaden and then narrow your solution ideas as you use progressively detailed prototypes to discover an awesome solution. Once you've generated a solution to a worthwhile customer problem, you're ready to figure out your go-to-market strategy. In chapter 6 we introduce the business model snapshot, which pinpoints six components of your business model that you need to identify before fully launching your product. These include value (your value proposition and pricing strategy), customer acquisition (customer relationships and channels), and cost structure (activities and resources).

The great benefit of the innovator's method is that it gives you the tools you need to resolve uncertainty; it teaches you how to experiment to answer your questions and then pivot when necessary. But because you face uncertainty, your chances of guessing right on the first try are nearly zero; this means that changes—pivots and iterations—are critical. In chapter 7 we reveal crucial principles for mastering the pivot.

Once you've turned many of your hypotheses into facts, you can scale your idea to reach a broader market. But the process that helped you nail the business model doesn't help you scale it. Now it's time to reapply traditional management while keeping your ability to test the remaining uncertainties. In chapter 8 we explain the often overlooked art and science of scaling.

Lastly, not everyone has support from the top management team, and at times you may find yourself the only believer in your idea. In chapter 9 we address how to adapt the method to work for you individually and for a team, or use it to ignite innovation in the organization more broadly. We also explain how to adapt the method based on whether you're pursuing disruptive or incremental innovations.

In the conclusion chapter, we tell the story of how Regeneron, an established corporation in a technically complex industry, used the ideas in this book to become one of the world's leading biotechnology companies. Using this example, we discuss the future of management and competitive advantage.

A tectonic shift has exponentially increased the level of technological and demand uncertainty faced by companies. Even established organizations need to be good at solving high-uncertainty problems—the kinds of problems they have tended to leave to start-ups. The need for managing uncertainty is a serious challenge, because established organizations must execute under an existing business model to meet the needs of existing customers. As a result, they typically adopt management practices that run counter to managing for innovation.

But Intuit, and dozens of other companies we studied, have shown that it's possible to reconceptualize the role of management and to create processes and infrastructure to radically decentralize the process of idea generation and assessment. When anyone in an organization is encouraged to be the founder of a start-up (a new product, a new service, a new process) and knows how to do it, it unleashes the kind of creative energy that can counter, or even embrace and exploit, uncertainty.

That doesn't mean that the innovation process is easy and clean. In practice innovation is always messy and recursive. There are often politics, contradictions, and setbacks. But with that caveat, we have tried to simplify the mess to clearly explain the most common steps and tools we observed successful innovators use. We describe the innovator's method in terms of four common elements (insight, problem, solution, and business model) to help you clearly grasp and understand them. Although we generally observed that successful innovations start with an insight into a big problem and then progress through the steps we describe, in practice, these steps often overlap each other, or sometimes occur in a slightly different order—that is the nature of dealing with an uncertain world. Ultimately each element of the innovator's method is more important than the order, as is understanding the key tools and tactics to turn your ideas into innovations. As you encounter these challenges and confusions, embrace them as part of uncertainty, remembering that although uncertainty can be frustrating, it is also the source creativity, innovation, and new growth. The innovator's method is your guide to help you recognize what to do when.

2

Leadership in the Age
of Uncertainty

*When MBAs come to us we have to fundamentally retrain them—
nothing they learned will help them succeed at innovation.*

—Scott Cook, Founder and Chairman of
the Executive Committee, Intuit

ABOVE, WE QUOTE Scott Cook criticizing traditional management training. Is he simply being inflammatory? Perhaps. But many other innovative leaders have also criticized traditional management training. For example, Elon Musk, founder of Tesla, SpaceX, and PayPal, argued that "As much as possible, avoid hiring MBAs. MBA programs don't teach people how to create companies . . . At my companies, our position is that we hire someone in spite of an MBA, not because of one."[1] While we all recognize that management training has immense value, why do some leaders of innovative companies offer such harsh criticisms? Here's our explanation of where we have made a wrong turn when it comes to innovation.

In 1911 Frederick Taylor wrote the landmark book *Principles of Scientific Management*. It had such a powerful impact on the emerging industrial corporations of the twentieth century that it earned Taylor the title "father of scientific management." Taylor's management principles were taught at the new, emerging business schools of the day and applied at rising industrial powers such as Ford Motor Company and General Electric. Indeed, Henry Ford, Alfred Sloan, and other corporate legends looked to scientific management as their management textbook, and Taylor's influence is still felt in business schools worldwide.

What were Taylor's principles of scientific management? First, he recommended that work be carefully planned and broken into separate tasks. The idea was that managers could analyze the tasks of production—for example, through time and motion studies—to determine the fastest and most cost-effective way to complete them. Then the manager's job was to make sure the task was standardized as much as possible and that workers followed the prescribed process. Taylor argued that task specialization was critical because it offered numerous benefits—for example, allowing for clear responsibility and accountability. It also enabled managers to match worker skills with the task, thereby facilitating a division of labor.[2]

These principles—task specialization, work standardization, accountability, and division of labor—quickly spread throughout US industry. Taylor's ideas greatly simplified the job of managing the complex tasks of the emerging industrial corporations. Moreover, his principles—when applied effectively—had a powerful positive impact on the performance of the large companies of his day. We see Taylor's handiwork everywhere. Every large company is broken into functions for task specialization— R&D, procurement, operations, marketing, HR, and finance. Every large organization seems to strive for division of labor, standardization of work, accountability, and the pursuit of best practices.

But even though Taylor's principles have done much good, there's one problem: they're exactly the wrong prescription for managing innovation. They're great principles for efficiently performing tasks to sustain a customer, but they work poorly for guiding work to *create* a customer (Peter Drucker's "central purpose" of business and the clear focus of start-ups).[3] They turn individuals into good managers (of execution) but bad innovators.

How does it happen? Consider task specialization and division of labor. Specialization makes sense when a problem is well defined and characterized by low uncertainty—the kinds of problems companies typically face as they move up the famous S-curve from growth to maturity (see figure 2-1). Let's say a company needs to produce a thousand widgets at the lowest possible cost, and to respond to five thousand daily service calls. The company knows roughly how many widgets to produce and how many calls to service; it needs to figure out the most efficient way to do it. Because these tasks are quite different, the company divides them into separate functions and hires experts in operations or service to perform the tasks. Managers are held accountable based on performance metrics—say, cost per unit produced or ratings of customer satisfaction with service calls. Managers quickly learn the value of hiring and developing specialists with deep expertise (as opposed to generalists with broad expertise), because the problems are

FIGURE 2-1

The S-curve and the right style of management

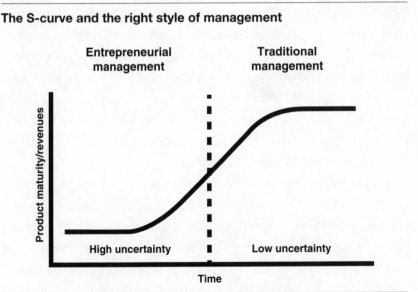

well enough defined that it's easy to match a specialist with the problem. These tactics are in fact the right ones for many problems that managers face, and applying them is simply good management.

Unfortunately, this is the wrong approach when you're trying to solve high-uncertainty problems, the kind a company or start-up faces at the introduction and growth stages of the S-curve (see "Sloan Versus Durant: A Contrast in Management Styles"). When you face high uncertainty about how to create a customer, you aren't sure what type of expertise will be most valuable. So you want people who have broad expertise, the kind of people who can see the problem, and possible solution, from various angles. That's why the practices that make someone a good manager can be roadblocks in efforts to ignite insights and bring new ideas to market.

Sloan versus Durant: A Contrast in Management Styles

Alfred Sloan is known as the father of the modern corporation, having transformed General Motors into the model corporation of his era by introducing principles such as specialized management roles, decentralized organization, and cost accounting. Sloan's ideas on dividing tasks into manageable chunks led him to break GM into divisions (Cadillac, Buick, Chevy, Pontiac), each focused on a different customer segment.[4] Sloan's management principles— along with those of contemporaries like Taylor as well as Henry Ford, who pioneered mass production techniques—contributed much to the early development of management theory and practice.

Sloan's influence is evident today in the number of institutions that bear his name and the number of business schools that teach his ideas. But Sloan's success and influence on management overlook an interesting question: Where did General Motors come from? Indeed, Sloan took the reins of GM only after it was generating nearly $4 billion in inflation-adjusted revenues.

In fact, GM was founded by Billy Durant, a creative entrepreneur who made millions in the horse-and-buggy industry before starting GM. Durant was an experimenter who pioneered products in both industries and grew GM until the board of directors, recognizing that he was a talented entrepreneur but a poor manager, replaced him. Durant then cofounded Chevrolet, eventually repurchased control of GM, and ran the firm until the board removed him a second time and replaced him with Sloan.[5] That Sloan is so well known, and Durant so little known, is intriguing. What were Durant's management theories? Why did they work in the early days but fail as GM became a large corporation?

The answer is simple: management theory was developed to solve the large-company management problem and not the innovation problem. The former emerged during the Industrial Revolution, when the economy was transformed from small workshops to large businesses of unprecedented scale, producing things like oil, textiles, autos, and railways. To make the trains run on time and increase the production of autos, these large corporations required a new profession: management. They needed managers to plan, coordinate, rationalize, and optimize the operations of large, complex organizations. Business schools emerged to train this new cadre of managers to be effective at resolving the problems faced by large corporations, such as "What new features should we add?" or "How can we lower costs by 5 percent?" These are low-uncertainty problems calling for incremental changes to existing products or processes.

In contrast, most start-up or corporate entrepreneurs are trying to launch new products that have disruptive potential. They face high-uncertainty problems such as "Will consumers want to use a personal computer (a demand problem faced by Apple), and can we make it easy enough for children to use (a technology problem)?" Or, "Will people buy products over the internet (a demand problem faced by Amazon.com), and can we provide fulfillment in a low-cost and reliable way (a technology problem faced by Amazon.com)?" "Will people make payments over the internet (a demand problem faced by PayPal), and can our technology provide them the ease of use and security they need?"

Although these firms successfully solved some high-uncertainty problems, business history is littered with failures—in many cases, because they applied the wrong theory: they followed business-school management theory (designed for low-uncertainty problems), and not innovation-school management theory (necessary for high-uncertainty problems).

Four Key Roles of the Leader

To apply the innovator's method, established companies must make a critical transition from their natural tendency to rely exclusively on traditional management to applying entrepreneurial management when facing the uncertainty of innovation. We've identified four key roles that leaders must fulfill if they hope to turn their organizations into successful innovators, composed of teams that innovate like a network of start-ups. These roles are critical to ensure that the innovator's method is incorporated into the company's processes and the day-to-day behaviors of employees.

First, and most important, the leader must become the chief experimenter and not the chief decision maker. As shown in figure 2-2, the other three roles support, and enable, the chief experimenter role. The second role is to set the grand challenge—not only to inspire others to

FIGURE 2-2

Be the chief experimenter

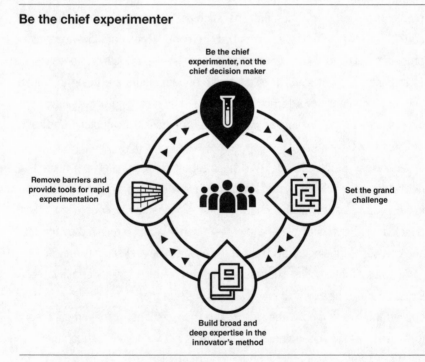

pursue an opportunity but also to challenge the organization to break free of Taylor's principles of scientific management.

Third, the leader must build broad and deep expertise in the innovator's method, which is needed to ensure that the organization has the capability to generate insights, discover problems worth solving, and rapidly prototype solutions. The fourth role of the leader is to remove barriers to change and install systems to facilitate the fast experiments required to test the team's hypotheses—and resolve the uncertainties—at each step.

Be the Chief Experimenter

In traditional management, managers are decision makers. You analyze information and make decisions that will affect the future of your organization. In a way, you're trying to predict the future, and position the company to succeed. For many managers, decision making is the essence of what it means to be a manager.

But when you're acting under uncertainty, the available information is too scarce, or even absent, for you to predict the future with any confidence. The best you can do is guess, and you may be wrong more often than you're right. But if you aren't making decisions, what is your role as a leader of innovative teams?

The innovator's method enables you to make effective decisions about the future—but you must first define a new role for yourself. You must learn a new way to be right. For Intuit's Scott Cook and Brad Smith, it's often a matter of reprogramming new hires. "Unfortunately, you know how big companies and hierarchies make decisions," says Cook. "They tend to rely on politics, PowerPoint, and persuasion."

> So to fix that, you've got to change how and where decisions are made . . . enabling decisions to be made by the best idea you can validate in the market. This means moving decisions from bosses voting their opinions, to enabling and measuring customers

voting with their feet. This goes against what people have been taught in business school. Most leaders in business have been successful because of analysis. They see themselves as decision makers and their job is to do great planning and analysis. That's the kind of change that we are trying to create at Intuit.[6]

Rather than becoming great planners and power decision makers, the company's new leaders are taught to champion experiments. Similarly, at Google, founders Larry Page and Sergey Brin have always supported the notion that decisions should be made by rich data from experiments—so much so that in 2002 they experimented with a completely flat organization, eliminating engineering managers. That experiment lasted only a few months, until too many people went directly to Page with questions about expense reports and interpersonal and career issues.[7] But the philosophy that even top Google executives must back their ideas with data lives on. To illustrate, in one instance Larry Page and Marissa Mayer (former VP at Google who is now CEO at Yahoo!) supported the idea to develop a massive digital archive of books. But rather than simply use their positions to make the decision to proceed, the two went so far as to clamp a three-hundred-page book to a piece of plywood, manually photograph each of its pages, and run the images through character recognition software, all to establish that it would take only forty minutes to digitize a book.

How do chief experimenters differ from decision-making managers? They focus on three things:

- Forming leap-of-faith assumptions with their team

- Rapidly testing those assumptions through experiments (mostly with customers)

- Letting the data (mostly from customers) make the decisions

As a leader, you don't have to do everything yourself: instead, decisions move downward in the hierarchy to small teams, where data reveals what the decision should be—or what the next experiment should be.

Says Cook, "[Intuit CEO] Brad Smith and I have changed the questions that we ask. We used to ask things like, 'Well, what's your answer, and what's your analysis behind it?' And now we ask, 'OK, what's the fastest way to get an experiment to test that idea?'"[8]

Jeff Bezos of Amazon manages in a similar style using similar questions. A few years ago, Bezos charged a team with analyzing the supply chain to come up with recommendations for an overall design of the company's logistics. The goal was to ensure that fulfillment could be done fast and economically. As one team member recalls, "When we presented our analysis, while all other executives were happy with it, Jeff was not. He insisted on being more rigorous and envisioned everybody in the company making decisions based on simulation outputs. So a team was formed to build supporting supply chain simulations—simulations that allowed us to see the results of different kinds of decisions. These simulation tools are now currently used throughout the company to make decisions."[9] The simulations allowed Bezos to experiment under uncertainty before building solutions.

This leadership style is working at Amazon, Google, and Intuit because the leader walks the talk. Says Cook, "Brad and I have to live by the same rules. So we end up asking ourselves questions like, 'I have got a fundamental belief of what we should do. Now, what are the leap-of-faith assumptions on which it is based? And how are we going to test the leap-of-faith assumptions that are crucial to my beliefs?' We need to do this just like we would do for anyone else . . . Experiments will be nothing but window dressing until you change who and how decisions are made."[10] So a key step in becoming a great leader of innovation is to change how decisions are made—and that starts with you.

Set the Grand Challenge

In a now famous 1979 visit to Xerox Palo Alto Research Center (PARC) in California, Steve Jobs recalled seeing a rough graphical user interface. "It was incomplete, some of it wasn't even right, but the germ of the idea was there," he said. "Within ten minutes, it was so obvious that every computer would work this way someday."[11] Jobs then took his engineering team on a tour of PARC—and returned to Apple focused on developing a personal computer that incorporated, and improved on, the PARC technologies.

Jobs assembled a team of brilliant engineers, gave them the needed resources, and infused the Macintosh team with a vision of creating the world's easiest-to-use personal computer. That's what an innovative leader does. In contrast, the executive team at Xerox lacked the discovery skills necessary to exploit technologies developed in their own company. As PARC scientist Larry Tesler observed, "After an hour looking at demos they [Jobs and Apple programmers] understood our technology and what it meant more than any Xerox executive understood after years of showing it to them." Jobs agreed with Tesler, saying, "Basically they were copier heads that just had no clue about a computer or what it could do. And so they just grabbed defeat from the greatest victory in the computer industry. Xerox could have owned the entire computer industry today."[12]

Years later, when Apple was considering offering a portable music device, Jobs and his leadership team set the vision with the tagline "1,000 songs in your pocket." That's why the first iPod was the size it was—small enough to fit in a pocket. These examples illustrate one reason Steve Jobs was a great leader of innovation: he had a nose for opportunity, and he set the grand challenge. You don't have to be Steve Jobs in terms of identifying the right opportunity, but you do have to set the grand challenge for your team.

To do that, says Intuit's Cook, "Leaders should ask questions like these: 'What is the most important problem, the biggest pain point, that we can solve? How does the customer measure the gain? How can we move the needle the most for the customer?'"[13] You don't necessarily have to articulate the solution (for example, the number of songs on a device), but you need to push people to search for opportunities. For example, when Intuit considered the Indian market as an opportunity,

Alex Lintner, the executive overseeing Intuit's Indian operations, asked his team to "create new businesses that will improve the financial lives of Indians." This grand challenge led the Mobile Bazaar team to identify an opportunity for the 150 million farmers in India to improve their financial lives by getting better prices. The Intuit team then sought to create a product that would do that.

Another dimension of setting the grand challenge may be even more important: giving the team and organization permission to break free of traditional management and use entrepreneurial management. This is extremely difficult. If you're like most people, when you started kindergarten you were assigned a desk and given clear instructions on what to do and how to do it. Most of us have been in those assigned desks ever since, completing our assigned tasks. To break that pattern, leaders must set a different grand challenge for the organization, saying something like, "I expect you to go figure out where your desk should be, and discover which assignments will create the most value for customers."

At Valve Software, a multibillion-dollar company that has already revolutionized the video gaming industry, founder Gabe Newell sets a radical vision to ruthlessly pursue customer value. To enable employees to do that, he has torn down all the bureaucracy.[14] He instructs every new hire, "Your desk has wheels. Your job is to figure out where you create the most value for customers, and move it there." Valve's leaders argue that as a company Valve has "spent the last decade going out of its way to recruit the most intelligent, innovative, talented people on Earth; telling them to sit at a desk and do what they're told obliterates 99 percent of their value."[15] Recent innovations include creating the platform on which 80 percent of all PC games are sold and making the first foray into the video game console market by a new company in more than a decade.

Similarly, Amazon's Bezos uses the slogan "It's Still Day One" to remind employees that Amazon is still a start-up—and there is lots of runway ahead. It's such a central motivating idea that Bezos named one of the company's buildings Day One. Asked when Amazon will reach

"Day Two," Bezos responded, "Day Two will be when the rate of change slows . . . And that's the sense in which I believe it's still Day One, and that it's early in the day. If anything, the rate of change is accelerating."[16] A key role for Bezos is to set the grand challenge for Amazon: to behave like a start-up.

Build Broad and Deep Expertise

When Ricardo dos Santos joined Qualcomm, a *Fortune* 100 manufacturer of semiconductors used in wireless devices, he was confident he could transform the company's failing "idea management program" (effectively a suggestion box) into a corporation-wide innovation program. Dos Santos had the support of a visionary CEO, a mandate to create disruptive new products, and the freedom to design a sweeping program to kick-start new ideas. Because prior efforts had flailed, dos Santos searched for ways to teach people how to transform their ideas into experiments to test their validity but with the caveat that the program had to be integrated with existing business units where people continue working full-time on their current projects.

Dos Santos built a three-phase program called Venture Fest. In the first phase, employees submitted ideas, which were then reduced to the twenty best ideas based on peer review. Then Venture Fest trainees took part in a three-month, part-time boot camp, where they tested their ideas with customers and developed prototypes. In the final phase, they presented their ideas to top executives in a competition for funding, after which they attempted to convince an existing business unit to adopt the new idea. Generally Venture Fest was a success, with ideas submitted increasing from eighty-two in the first year to more than five hundred five years later. Moreover, Venture Fest participants identified many potential breakthrough ideas.

But although Venture Fest fostered some truly transformation ideas, a few organization members outside the program began to question, and even attack, the program. Some managers weren't happy releasing some of their best people to work on projects not under their control. And from a more traditional management perspective, the Venture Fest projects seemed too open, fluid, and flexible, clashing with Qualcomm's rational, deadline-driven culture. Perhaps more dangerously, some R&D managers, many of whom felt they owned innovation, argued that the emerging new ideas fell outside the scope of existing R&D programs or didn't have as much intellectual property as usual. Despite the best intentions of many inside Qualcomm, Venture Fest encountered the kind of allergic reaction to implementing innovation that we have observed at many other companies that excel at execution. After five turbulent and exciting years, Venture Fest was quietly folded into R&D.[17]

Build Broad Expertise

The Qualcomm experience is similar to those in many organizations that try to "do innovation" by creating pockets of entrepreneurial management and experimentation expertise without generating broad awareness of the processes and goals associated with successful programs. This lack of understanding and appreciation for goals and methods can lead outsiders to misinterpret the innovator's methods as well as its output. Dos Santos recalls that Qualcomm made great strides in igniting new ideas on the "sell" side (the innovators) and increased the start-up spirit in the company overall. But if he were to do it again, he would focus on one more crucial goal: educating the "buy side"—the rest of the organization—"so that we could all be using the same language and match discovery efforts."[18]

The greater the awareness and appreciation in your organization that innovation requires a different set of management tools, the easier it will be to apply the innovator's method. We aren't saying that everyone needs deep expertise in these principles, but simply that everyone needs some training to understand that managing uncertainty requires a different approach. Of course, if your organization faces greater uncertainty, you may choose to extensively train everyone. At Intuit, Cook and Smith make sure all new hires are trained in design for delight principles, completing a weeklong design training program within the first three months. The goal is not to make everyone an expert but to make sure everyone understands lean experimentation principles and knows the steps for generating insights and nailing the problem and solution. Employees gain a common language to describe the efforts to bring new ideas to market. Having the language to explain your actions gives people immense power in overcoming the inertia that often impedes change. In our interviews with dozens of innovators, they often cited the common language as one of the most important reasons for training everyone.

But there's another reason smart leaders want everyone to understand the innovator's method: it generates ideas. Almost every study shows that searching broadly is the best way to uncover novel ideas that are worth pursuing.

Build Deep Expertise

Building broad understanding is necessary but not sufficient. It's also critical to build deep expertise within your organization. We've seen it done effectively in a couple of ways.

One option is to create a lab or SWAT team that applies the innovator's method to new ideas. In addition to relevant engineering and technology experts, the lab has experts in design thinking and lean experimentation. For example, AT&T—not known for innovation in the past twenty years—recently created five labs (AT&T calls them "foundries"), each employing forty to fifty interdisciplinary experts. Their task: testing new insights generated inside and outside AT&T. The foundries house marketing experts from the business units, experts in telecommunications technologies, and experts in design thinking. What's more, AT&T has invited start-ups and established companies from many industries to participate in rapidly developing and experimenting with new technologies. Each new idea is run through a twelve-week project, where a team applies the kinds of tools we describe in this book to produce virtual or physical prototypes.

Where do the ideas originate? A team of senior leaders across AT&T selects ideas from three sources:

- An internal idea board called The Innovation Program (or TIP), where ideas are posted and voted on

- A "fast pitch" program, where individuals and companies, most of them from outside AT&T (suppliers, start-ups), make ten-minute pitches to key AT&T decision makers

- The business units, where lead marketing executives who are assigned to the foundry full-time are charged with polling their business units for new ideas

Each of the most promising ideas is funneled to a team of experts—a SWAT team—that applies elements of the innovator's method to generate a prototype.

Although AT&T has been at this for less than five years, the foundries are credited with developing ideas that have helped push the company's innovation premium from minus 13 percent in the mid-2000s to almost 10 percent today. "As the foundries have proved their value, we're now using the term *foundry* as a verb," says John Donovan, SEVP of AT&T technology and network operations. "We've proven we get from prototype to product three times faster."[19] Other companies have developed similar labs and credit them with increasing their innovation output, including Hyatt Hotels and Hallmark as well as lesser-known companies like Banco Davivienda, a leading bank in Latin America.

A second option is to build expertise in a great many individuals who assist start-up teams. As described in chapter 1, Intuit has trained more than two hundred innovation catalysts (see "Why Designers Excel: Synthesis"). Each year, an additional twenty to thirty people are selected to join them. Many catalysts are trained as part of a team selected to attend a "Lean Start-In" workshop. Employee teams bring an idea for a significant unmet customer need, and in two days the team goes through the entire cycle of validating a customer pain, prototyping a solution, and testing it with customers. Ben Blank, a founder of the workshops, proudly highlights that many Intuit employees have been kicked out of Home Depot stores or removed from the Caltrain while testing ideas with customers.[20] More than twelve hundred Intuit employees have been through Lean Start-In workshops, building deep expertise in the innovator's method throughout the organization.

Why Designers Excel: Synthesis

If experimentation and analysis are key, why does Intuit train employees in design thinking? At the core, design thinking teaches people how to observe the world, make a guess, and then, through art and science, combine disparate pieces in a way that creates value—in other words, to synthesize. Whereas analysis breaks things into their component parts, synthesis identifies the connection between a problem and a solution, thereby identifying an opportunity. As Roger Martin writes in *The Design of Business,* synthesis is the marriage of intuition and analysis.[21]

Stanford University created an entire interdisciplinary d.school to teach these principles. Intuit, which borrows heavily from Stanford's d.school, teaches its employees about design as a complement to the analysis embedded in lean experimentation, because, as Design VP Kaaren Hanson argues, "The winning companies in the future will be 'design-driven'—because of the importance (and rarity) of synthesis capabilities . . . I also suspect that 'winning' will come from being clever about who to put into what positions (versus assuming anyone can go into any position and play well)."[22] Hanson's point underscores why we believe the innovator's method has unique importance for leaders, managers, and entrepreneurs. Each discipline has developed its own approach to managing uncertainty and innovation (design thinking is engineering's approach), and each offers valuable insights into parts of the process. In this book we've synthesized these similar, but different, perspectives to provide you an end-to-end guide to the entire process, from idea to commercial success.

Remove Barriers and Support Experiments

Your final role is to remove obstacles to experimentation and provide the tools people need to accelerate experiments. What are the key barriers, and what kinds of tools are needed? Let's take a look at what we found when we interviewed dozens of individuals in large organizations.

Allocate Time for Innovation

We've often asked people who work for large companies, "What prevents you from moving more new ideas to market?" The most common answer? "I just don't have time. I have too much on my plate." That's what it's like to work in large organizations designed to execute routine tasks and processes. Good managers work to remove all slack in the system so that human resources (indeed, all resources) are fully utilized.

But innovation takes time. We've seen companies specify 10 percent unstructured time for every employee (Intuit), 20 percent project time for engineers (Google), and, at the extreme end, as much as 100 percent self-defined time (Valve Software). According to Valve's employee handbook, "We've heard that other companies have people allocate a percentage of their time to self-directed projects. At Valve, that percentage is 100. Since Valve is flat, people don't join projects because they're told to. Instead, you'll decide what to work on after asking yourself the right questions. Employees vote on projects with their feet. Strong projects are ones in which people can see demonstrated value; they staff up easily."[23]

Although many companies have innovation boot camps or other innovation events, few provide ongoing time devoted to generating and testing ideas—even though it can make a significant difference. How much time companies allocate depends on the level of uncertainty they face and the importance of innovation (for example, Valve competes in a high-uncertainty market and believes it creates all its value through customer-focused innovation). Time has the power to let people explore new ideas that may not make sense at first; but the greater the variation in new ideas you test, the higher the probability that some will prove valuable. In fact, Google's "20 percent" projects have produced hits such as Gmail, Google AdSense, and Google Docs. One senior executive estimated that roughly half of Google's new products are generated in this way.[24] Such projects account for more than 25 percent of revenues.[25] Sadly, like other maturing companies, Google recently put constraints on the program, a move that many observers predict will shrink its innovation pipeline. However, Google appears to be pouring significant resources into its Google X lab with projects like Google Glass, Google Express, Google Loon, and Google Self-Driving. Just as Google is doing with Google X, some companies, such as Amazon, identify opportunities and form teams to generate solutions to the challenges of uncertainty. Innovation time is explicitly built in.

No matter how it's done, leaders must make sure that employees are given the time—and the expectation—to conceive and test new ideas. It helps if leaders set an example. Facebook's Mark Zuckerberg tries to spend five hours a day on product development, and Scott Cook at Intuit tries to spend one day a week participating on innovation project teams. Ryan Smith, CEO of a billion-dollar survey company called Qualtrics, told us, "Every leader is a player and a coach. You have to get into the trenches if you want to innovate."[26]

Provide Customers, Specialists, and Tools

Another obstacle for start-up teams is a lack of tools. For example, teams need to run experiments with potential customers if they hope to discover the job-to-be-done and then nail the solution. Providing quick and easy access to various types of customers can facilitate rapid experimentation.

Amazon provides employees a list of customers (and merchants) with which they can quickly test new ideas. Intuit invites customers to its headquarters one day a week for experiments. It also provides a list of nearby customers who have agreed to accept visits. These actions have doubled teams' face-to-face interactions with customers.[27] Numerous people told us that until Intuit started regularly bringing customers into headquarters, they didn't realize how easily they could test solutions with them.

To help start-up teams generate a broad list of solutions, Intuit developed a technology palette. The company identified and hired experts in technologies related to mobile devices, social media, user interaction, collaboration, data, and the like. These experts are valuable for broadening solution searches, and they help teams identify what is technologically feasible.

Google's leaders also provide tools for rapid prototyping, such as digital tools for making prototypes and mock-ups as well as flexible code structures for rapidly prototyping software. Google X's "design kitchen" was created to build simple prototypes for big ideas. Located in a building next to Google X's main offices, the design kitchen is a large-scale fabrication shop filled with 3D printers, high-end lathes, and other sophisticated prototyping machinery. These tools can have a profound impact on the productivity of start-up teams.

Remove Organizational Barriers

For employees at companies that have ossified around execution, experimenting feels risky, unnatural, even against the (unwritten) rules. And because of the division of labor and accountability, employees need leaders' permission to test ideas that go beyond the scope of their business units.

At Valve Software, leaders provide permission in a radical way: there are virtually no managers or formal titles among the software designers.[28] "Everyone is a designer," according to the employee handbook. "Everyone can question each other's work. Anyone can recruit someone onto his or her project."[29] Not surprisingly, Valve's approach to minimizing obstacles frees employees to pursue any start-up idea that interests them.

Large companies also try to protect brand image and limit the liabilities of market experiments. In such companies, how do leaders give employees permission to take risks and freely run experiments? At Intuit, the legal team has assembled a list of guidelines; if you follow them, you're free to experiment without asking permission. For example, you don't need permission when these conditions are met.

- Testers (customers) understand they're participating in research.

- The experiment does not involve more than thirty thousand testers over two months.

- The experiment is labeled "Intuit Labs" to signal to testers that it is an experiment.

- The prototype does not actually complete transactions or collect user data.

- Intuit's data stewardship principles apply.

- Participants learn about the pilot via communication to the general public (and not targeted to government employees or agencies).

- Testers may be given a small token, if applicable, for their time.

- Intuit does a complete patent brainstorm before results of the experiment are shared publicly.[30]

These guidelines serve as a signal to employees: "We expect you to run experiments! Don't ask for permission, just do it!"

The I-School Leadership Curriculum

If you attend business school, you take classes in finance, accounting, operations, organizational behavior, and similar topics, all of them drawing heavily on the logic introduced by Frederick Taylor. Rarely do you have a class on product development or the innovator's method as a core course (although many forward-looking professors teach some of these principles, mostly in elective courses). In most business schools, leadership is seen as the set of skills needed to manage mature organizations focused on executing under conditions of low uncertainty.

But when you face uncertainty, you need a different set of management principles. Some of these principles are taught in design schools, led by Stanford's d.school. But we think that beyond d.schools we need an innovation school—curriculum connected to B-schools that teaches innovation leadership across all of an organization's main functions. An I-school, in contrast with the B-school, would deal with the emerging science of managing uncertainty. Entrepreneurial leadership falls under the umbrella of the I-school, as do each of the other functional areas, which you also must manage differently when you face uncertainty. Figure 2-3 shows the differences.

For example, in B-school, when you study marketing, you typically learn the importance of building and protecting your brand, or doing quantitative analysis to identify customer segments and get customer feedback. But in an I-school we argue that you should initially ignore your brand and obtain all customer feedback through direct interaction, observation, or interviews. What's more, rather than emphasize building brands by satisfying a broad range of customers through perfected products, I-school emphasizes the need to test low-fidelity prototypes with small groups of customers, embracing errors as opportunities to learn.

In B-school, when you learn finance you're taught about marginal cost logic: the importance of leveraging prior fixed-cost investments with new initiatives. But this approach biases you toward incremental innovation efforts. In I-school you learn about the dangers of marginal cost logic and other financial tools.[31] In a world of uncertainty, leveraging investments can often be a bad practice, because it may lead to building a workaround solution instead of one that nails the job-to-be-done.

We aren't saying that one approach is good and the other is bad. Both are good. The key to management success is to recognize when to apply a more familiar B-school approach and when to apply I-school thinking—a decision that rests primarily on the degree of uncertainty. When uncertainty is high, apply an I-school approach. When the uncertainty has been resolved, use a B-school approach. After all, there's no

FIGURE 2-3

Differences between the innovation and business school

	B-school (traditional management)	I-school (entrepreneurial management)
Core focus	Execute in certainty.	Experiment in uncertainty.
Strategy	Protect existing resources. Leverage existing resources. Sustain competitive advantage.	Circumvent resources. Discover or build new resources. Temporarily ignore advantage.
Organizational behavior/HR	Hire experts (I-shaped people). Hire for divisional roles. Hierarchical organization	Hire generalists (T-shaped people). Hire for multifunctional roles. Flat organization
Leadership and teams	Vertical team Manager-supervisee structure Maximize and optimize.	Horizontal team Peer group structure Minimize and suffice.
Operations	Efficient routines for execution Longer cycles Avoid error	Flexible routines for search Radically short cycles Embrace error
Marketing	Full-featured, appealing product Quantitative market segmentation Build and protect brand.	Minimum feature set product Qualitative customer interaction Temporarily ignore brand.
Finance and accounting	Marginal cost logic Fixed costs to lower average cost	Full cost logic Avoid fixed costs to be flexible.

reason to waste time running an experiment when there is a low probability that your choice of action is wrong.

That being said, in our discussions with executives we see a rapidly increasing need for an I-school management approach. As Intuit's Cook observes, "We need to use these new leadership practices in our core business, because we face so much uncertainty and need to continue to reinvent ourselves."[32] For those of you reading this with a business degree, we have two questions: How many A/B experiments did you run in your classes before getting a business degree? How many prototypes did you build? For most of you the answer is: zero. That's got to change.

The "I-school" label describes a group of emerging practices for managing uncertainty, especially in start-ups. But in the future, as uncertainty continues to grow, we will see changes in how we organize and manage all businesses. As the science of managing uncertainty develops, the I-school approach will need to be taught side-by-side with traditional management disciplines in B-schools.

3

Insight: Savor Surprises

If you want to innovate, savor the surprises.
Too often we overlook the surprises.

—Kim Clark, Former Dean of Harvard Business School

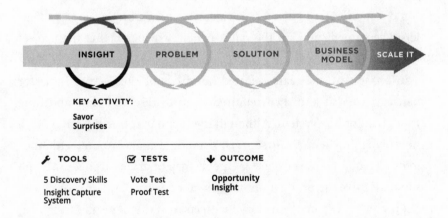

| INSIGHT | PROBLEM | SOLUTION | BUSINESS MODEL | SCALE IT |

KEY ACTIVITY:

Savor
Surprises

🔧 TOOLS	☑ TESTS	⬇ OUTCOME
5 Discovery Skills	Vote Test	**Opportunity Insight**
Insight Capture System	Proof Test	

FOR TEN YEARS (2000–2010) Hindustan Unilever (HUL), subsidiary of one of the world's leading consumer goods companies, experienced declining revenue growth, a flat stock price, and a falling market share. Efforts to improve execution and efficiency led to increased margins but little growth and even less innovation. Few new ideas bubbled up, and even the few that did seemed to struggle and disappear. As CEO Nitin Paranjpe and the management team wrestled to find ways to turn the company around, they hypothesized that the only way to save the company was to generate new ideas and insights. But how could it generate new ideas after ten years of the status quo?

Fortunately, Paranjpe recognized that when you're in the routine of doing your current job well, you're not likely to have epiphanies. So to change course, the management team decided that the company needed to better understand their customers' needs and challenges. In 2010 Paranjpe launched a three-phase initiative called Project Bushfire, with the goal of getting every employee—more than fifteen thousand people in India alone—to visit customers in their workplaces and homes.

In the first phase, HUL launched an internal campaign to create awareness, sending e-mails and hanging posters asking, "When was the last time you really listened to the customer?" Paranjpe also e-mailed employees to explain the program and to ask for ideas, adding that he would respond personally to every idea. But even with this appeal, skepticism remained high. In the halls, people whispered that the project was a "flavor of the season."[1]

In phase two, the team selected hundreds of sites across India for managers to visit and then required them to reserve a date and time through an online system. Although the top management team made a show of logging in on the first day, resistance began to mount, with hundreds of requests to be excused. One factory manager argued, "My job is to maximize the production in the factory every day. I am convinced that my absence from the factory for an entire day will result in a greater loss for the organization than any observation or insight I might have from meeting customers, who meet with our sales and brand managers quite regularly."[2] Despite the protests, Paranjpe held firm, requiring 100 percent participation (he had assistants call and assign recalcitrant managers to observation sites).

For the observations, managers were sent to shadow a frontline sales-person, meet consumers in their homes, or visit shops and ask questions. Each manager was given a sheet with questions such as, "What did I see that confirmed what I already know?" and "What did I see that was totally unexpected or surprising?" The goal was to capture the information in a central database.

Then, as managers visited the field in phase three, their early observations proved transformational: some had never met customers before and were surprised to see the issues they struggled with. Others had such limited interaction with the real problems of their customers that they had overlooked many opportunities. As the stories poured in (the Bushfire team made it a point to quickly share success stories), the recalcitrant attitude among many managers began to change. Just as important, ideas—small and large—began to flow in.

Some of the insights prompted smaller initiatives. For example, when Paranjpe himself stood on the sales floor discussing the new Soya drink with customers, a woman asked why a "health" drink contained sugar. At that moment the CEO realized the team had overlooked a critical factor in the way most customers evaluate health products. Other insights had greater impact. For example, one manager was surprised to find that *Shakti Ammas,* women who sold HUL products in rural areas, couldn't sell other, noncompeting products. This led to an expansion in what the *Ammas* sell, including telecomm and banking services from other providers, as well as new HUL products, such as a low-cost water purification system called Pureit. Yet other insights led to the company's expansion into five thousand additional retail outlets and the adoption of a zero-inventory model.

Other changes had a deeper impact on HUL's culture. For example, the project refocused HUL on generating insights from customers at all levels of the organization. Every member of the management team spends at least two hours every two weeks interacting with customers, and managers are expected to visit at least five customers per month.

In addition, HUL captures insights differently than in the past: when an idea is proposed, a member of the management committee acknowledges it, and when ideas go into pilot testing, the person who generated the idea is acknowledged and invited to participate.

The rewards for these efforts have shown up in HUL's financial performance. After a decade of a flat stock price, in 2012 shares climbed 34 percent (double the Sensex index), and sales spiked 40 percent.[3] Moreover, HUL's innovation premium climbed to 44 percent, making it the top-ranked consumer goods company (and number twelve overall) on the 2012 *Forbes* list of the world's most innovative companies.

Generating insights represents the first step in our end-to-end innovation process. In this chapter, we show that insights are not the result of magic or of simply hiring "creative" people. Rather, they result from behaviors or processes you can apply. You'll learn how successful companies generate insights and how to effectively capture and select them.

Four Key Actions That Generate Insights

Innovations are only valuable if they solve problems. So the first step is to generate an insight about a problem worth solving. The insight could be finding a problem that others have missed or perhaps uncovering a potential new solution to a well-understood problem. We've found that the catalyst for an insight is a "surprise." A surprise is the clue that you've learned something new that might be a valuable insight—because if you are surprised then others may be as well. For example, when Intuit's Mobile Bazaar team was watching farmers conduct their business, they were surprised to find that crop prices could fluctuate by as much as 50 percent in a single day. This was a symptom of a problem that farmers were facing in their attempt to get fair prices for their crops. Similarly, when Michael Dell had purchased all of the components to build a PC in his dorm room, he was surprised to discover that they cost only $600 or $700 when an IBM PC was selling for $2,500. Dell told us this surprise raised a question: "Why does it cost five times more to buy a PC in the store than the parts cost?"[4] Intuit's Scott Cook teaches employees at Intuit to "savor surprises" and says that "at Intuit we teach our people to ask these two questions: What is surprising? What is different from what you expected? That is where true learning and innovation starts."[5]

Our earlier book, *The Innovator's DNA*, explains how great innovators uncover surprises and generate new insights.[6] It describes four behaviors that provoke *associational thinking*: the ability to connect seemingly unrelated information or ideas and put them together in new ways—for example, crossing a kayak with a surfboard to come up with the idea for a paddleboard. Associational thinking happens as the brain tries to synthesize and make sense of information gleaned from questioning, observing, networking, and experimenting. As figure 3-1 shows, the four key actions of questioning, observing, networking, and experimenting are the key to triggering new insights through associational thinking.

FIGURE 3-1

The innovator's DNA behaviors

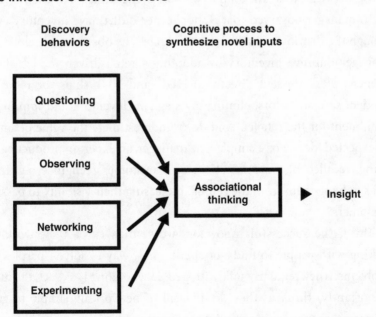

First, people generate insights through questioning, constantly challenging the status quo with "why" and "why not" questions to turn things upside-down. They often ask "what if" questions to envision a different future. Questioning gives you the fuel to power new associations and insights.

Hindustan Unilever's Bushfire project is an excellent example. The HUL team members started with a list of questions as they went out into the field, including "What surprises you?" and "What should HUL be doing that they are not doing?" These questions often acted as a catalyst. The manager of an HUL factory in Mangalore asked why he couldn't buy HUL products at the local store. The observation was a symptom of problems in the distribution network that, after study, led the company to expand into new retail outlets. Questions help you see things in a new light and open new avenues and possibilities.

Second, managers garner new ideas by observing the environment as if they were anthropologists. They get out of their cubicles to closely watch the world around them—especially customers, products, services, and processes—to spark unique ways of doing things. For example, an HUL manager observed that a shopkeeper didn't have inventory even though the distributor had a large stockpile. The observation helped the manager improve inventory by adopting a retail-driven model: shopkeeper orders are sent directly to HUL, and HUL ships the required product to distributors, eliminating stagnant inventory and improving fulfillment for the retailer. And don't underestimate the value of small, unexpected ideas. For example, one manager, an expert in product packaging, recalled his surprise at seeing a customer reengineering Tetra Paks to hang them from the ceiling, increasing their visibility to passing customers.

Third, the successful innovators we studied excel at networking, talking with people to find—or spark a new way to solve—perplexing problems. They regularly talk with people who don't look, act, or (most importantly) think as they do. Instead of networking simply to gain resources, they interact with diverse people to get new ideas. Although the HUL initiative started with field visits, as managers met with people outside their discipline, they established new relationships that led to new ideas; for example, the managers in marketing and sales realized that a supply chain manager could solve a sales problem. As one manager put it, "You would be making a huge mistake by assuming that a Ph.D. in Organic Chemistry has no value to add to the selling process wired into a tablet PC."[7] Another noted, "A couple of years ago, a brand manager wouldn't be caught dead asking his finance counterpart for an opinion on a piece of advertising. Today, it is common."[8]

Fourth, you generate insights by constantly experimenting. Innovators try out new experiences wherever they go. They take apart products or processes to see how things work—and how to improve them. Moreover, as you'll see in chapter 5, they rapidly pilot or prototype various solutions to find one that works. For example, when an HUL factory manager visited a shopkeeper, he was amazed to hear about a myriad of problems that could have been resolved by calling the factory's published help line number. So the manager tried an experiment: he printed the help line number on the outside of every box. Immediately, the number of calls increased dramatically, and the number of long-term issues plummeted.

We studied a sample of founders and leaders of companies that enjoy a high innovation premium (those ranked in our *Forbes* list). We found that they spend 31 percent of their time engaged in the four discovery behaviors in pursuit of new insights. In contrast, leaders of companies having a low IP spent only 15 percent of their time thus engaged.

What kinds of things can leaders do to facilitate the process? And how can they make sure that insights are captured and the best ones are selected to be put through the innovator's method?

Search Broadly

As you engage in the four behaviors, it's crucial to search broadly: look for ideas across countries, industries, companies, technologies, functions, and so on. Einstein called this "combinatorial play." A broad search leads to variation in the knowledge you gain—and that leads to more combinatorial thought trials, increasing the odds of discovering an insight. And we've found that people who searched broadly are much more likely to have an epiphany—an insight that seems to come from nowhere.

Amazon's Jeff Bezos is an excellent example. Before deciding to sell books over the internet, Bezos researched the top twenty mail order products. He hypothesized that people would buy standard products (those that vary little) via the web. To his surprise, books—certainly standard—weren't in the top twenty products. Then he discovered why: there were so many books in print that no one catalog could cover them all. It would be huge and expensive to mail. As Bezos saw it, the internet was the ideal vehicle for offering such a catalog.

Although rooted in books and positioned as a leading book retailer, Amazon has a track record of searching broadly for new business ideas. It has expanded into a wide variety of products and services, from electronic readers and tablets (with the Kindle) to cloud computing services (Amazon EC2) to video streaming services (through Amazon Prime) to daily grocery delivery (AmazonFresh). Amazon has recently moved into merchant lending (Amazon Lending) and reportedly is considering entering categories such as smart phones and TV set-top boxes.

Bezos encourages employees to search broadly despite criticism that Amazon is not focused enough. "Every new business we've ever engaged in has initially been seen as a distraction by people externally, and sometimes even internally," says Bezos. "They'll say, 'Why are you expanding into media products? Why are you going international? Why are you entering the marketplace business with third-party sellers?' We're getting it now with our new infrastructure web services. 'Why take on these new developer customers?'"[9] Bezos adds that most companies' big errors have been acts of omission and not acts of commission: "It's the opposite of sticking to your knitting. It's when you shouldn't have stuck to your knitting and you did," he says. "It's very fun to have a culture where people are willing to take these leaps. It's the opposite of the 'institutional no.' It's the institutional yes. People at Amazon say, 'We're going to figure out how to do this.'"[10]

Most people naturally search narrowly, because they're told to leverage their expertise. Although this strategy makes sense for expanding into known territory, it limits you to only incremental insights. Searching broadly might include exploring new industries for your product, taking apart products from different industries, or asking yourself challenging questions that force you to look elsewhere ("How would we make money next year if we were legally prohibited from selling any of our current products to our existing customers?"). Searching broadly for new knowledge or new possibilities greatly increases the probability of uncovering a breakthrough insight.

Capture the Insight

In the past few decades, many companies have initiated processes to capture new ideas, such as idea repositories and knowledge databases, but many of them are glorified suggestion boxes that simply do not work. Successfully capturing ideas is a critical part of innovation, and managers need to use the right tools and the right process.

A popular process we studied is the *American Idol* model. You challenge employees to submit ideas to be screened and selected by a panel of judges. For example, Google holds an Innovator's Challenge four times a year. Employees submit ideas for top management review; winning ideas receive the resources to be pushed forward (we discuss selecting ideas in the next section). Marissa Mayer (former director of consumer products at Google and now CEO of Yahoo!) championed regular brainstorming sessions during which engineers had ten minutes to pitch their ideas to Mayer and a group of as many as one hundred others. The goal of these sessions was not only to capture the insight but also to build on the initial idea with at least one new complementary idea.

A second approach is to use a digital collaboration platform, sometimes called an idea management system. Google refers to its platform as an idea board, at Intuit it's called Brainstorm, and at AT&T it's called TIP. Many companies, such as Cisco Services, source from an outside company like Brightidea (Spigot and AHHHA are other popular tools). These tools allow employees (or outsiders) to post, view, sort, and filter ideas; vote and provide feedback; and use other social networking features like notifications and tagging. These tools use *crowd-sourcing* (outsourcing tasks to individuals or organizations) to encourage, refine, and advance ideas in ways that a static, centrally controlled suggestion box cannot.

That being said, you must overcome challenges to encourage employees to participate. At Intuit, use of the Brainstorm platform is robust because it's embedded in the culture, but it's still necessary for innovation catalysts to pull out promising ideas to nurture and champion. Other companies, such as Cisco and Qualcomm, create engagement by using a batch-type process to focus everyone's attention on the idea platforms at particular times. Yet other companies, such as HUL, assign teams to respond to and develop each idea. The lesson is to marry crowd engagement with encouragement and cultivation from a trained team.

AT&T's TIP is the largest idea board we've seen, with more than half of AT&T's two hundred thousand employees participating. It helps turn the company's typical innovation weakness—a vast employee base—into a strength. It's egalitarian; frontline employees participate in early stages with a voice equal to those of senior managers. The online platform allows employees worldwide to vote, comment, and collaborate on ideas. At the end of a designated time period, called a "season" (à la *American Idol*), the top ideas are evaluated by "angels," a group of high-level executives, who then select ideas to be presented in a live pitch session. Chosen ideas receive seed funding. Selected projects are managed by innovation champions: employees who act as "CEOs" of each project. They shepherd the idea through the proof-of-concept phase and receive additional funding if a business unit will match the investment for a second round.

To illustrate, a call-center employee who lost a close friend in an accident caused by a distracted driver conceived of an app to help prevent texting while driving. Within one week of posting her idea on TIP, peers were providing helpful guidance on improving and implementing it. Ultimately, she was asked to present her idea to AT&T leadership, including CEO Randall Stephenson. Executives provided funding and moved the idea to an AT&T foundry, TIP's incubation process, where a prototype was developed and eventually released to the market. Dubbed DriveMode, the app has been downloaded hundreds of thousands of times and was a cornerstone of AT&T's "It Can Wait" public service campaign.

Some companies also set up a database to capture ideas. For example, HUL entered all the Bushfire field observations into a database. To keep the ideas alive, it did two things: it promised to respond to every idea, and it assigned managers to probe the database, find strong ideas, and then push them forward with participation of the originator.

Some companies set up processes to capture insights from outside the company. For example, Procter & Gamble has deployed seventy "technology entrepreneurs," who spend all their time searching for new ideas that will make a difference for P&G. These senior people help identify key customer needs and write the technology briefs that define the problems the company is trying to solve. They create external connections by, for example, meeting with university and industry researchers, and they combine aggressive mining of the scientific literature, patent databases, and other data sources with physical prospecting for ideas—say, surveying store shelves in Rome or attending product and technology fairs. It was a technology entrepreneur, exploring a local market in Japan, who discovered what ultimately became the Mr. Clean Magic Eraser. P&G's technology entrepreneurs work out of six Connect and Develop hubs in China, India, Japan, Western Europe, Latin America, and the United States. To date, they have identified more than ten thousand products, product ideas, and promising technologies.[11]

Select the Insight

Recently the editors at *Budget Traveler* magazine had a great idea to generate new material: Why not crowd-source an entire issue from readers? They sent out a call for submissions and received more than 2,800, including more than five hundred for a single piece on "50 Reasons You Love New York." Although the project generated new material, the editors now faced a monumental task: How to sort through almost three thousand submissions and then, for those chosen, rework and edit them to fit into an article. In the end, editor Erik Torkells reflected on the bittersweet experience, saying, "Let's be perfectly clear, making this issue was neither cheap nor easy."[12]

Leaders at large companies can create similar problems when they succeed at inspiring—and capturing—insights but have broken mechanisms for winnowing them to those that are most promising. To solve the problem, most companies fall back on familiar techniques, usually a competition resembling a business plan contest, judged by senior executives. Unfortunately, this approach may not work well. Recall our earlier discussion of the problems of leaders making decisions under high uncertainty. We've found that leaders are more successful at selecting insights for their organizations to further explore by using either a "vote test" or a "proof test."

Vote Test

How could *Budget Traveler* have solved its editorial problem? What if the editors had used their readers to both source and evaluate the material? People both inside and outside your organization can be valuable for selecting insights through a form of crowd-sourcing we call "crowd-voting." One example is Threadless, an online community of artists and an e-commerce website. Threadless enlists its customers in a member community to submit ideas for T-shirt slogans and designs, tapping in to new artists and generating ideas without the need to hire professional designers. Just as important, Threadless uses crowd-voting (by customers and designers) to select which designs to take to market. By using the crowd, Threadless can better predict which t-shirts will sell. It has developed an enviable track record of never having produced a flop; every t-shirt ever produced has sold out.

Crowd-voting works well when you use a crowd to evaluate an offering or predict uncertain events. However, use it with caution if you're trying to predict complex, technical, or radical problems or solutions. In these cases, expertise matters, and hands-on use can be a more viable predictor than opinions.

As an alternative, you can create a system for choosing insights based on whether the advocate can get others to volunteer time to pursue it. This is what founders of start-ups must do. Similarly, Google and Valve Software, among others, challenge employees to recruit other colleagues to use their self-directed time on the employee's project. Compelling ideas are selected for further development because they draw volunteer resources (See "How to Make Innovation Time Work").

How to Make Innovation Time Work

Researchers asked students at Yale to do something for their own benefit: get tetanus shots. To one group, the researchers gave the time and location for the shots and then tried to scare them into attending. To the other group, they gave the same information but added a map to the building. All the students were familiar with campus, but when they received a map their attendance jumped from 3 percent to 28 percent. Even for students who knew what to do, providing a helpful tool increased participation.[13] Similarly, giving your team members time to innovate will be more effective if you provide a "map" to use it.

For example, when Jeff Zias was put in charge of unstructured time at Intuit, he noticed that few people used it. To create a map, he started by encouraging people to mark their calendars with the days they would use unstructured time. This act increased employee engagement 20 percent. Then Zias recruited volunteers to share best practices and champion innovation time.

Even so, Zias found that people didn't know how to use the time. So he created a series of "hack-a-thons": for twenty-four to forty-eight hours, people blocked out everything else and focused on innovation. At first, employees got together in "idea jams" and brainstormed problems and products. More than a dozen products, including TurboTax on the iPad, came out of the early idea jams. Then Zias created a pipeline of increasingly specific jams: "pain jams" to find problems worth solving, "solution jams" to brainstorm solutions, and "code jams" to develop prototypes or try variations to existing products.

Zias argues that much of Intuit's success in new products can be traced to an overall increase in the use of unstructured time. But the greater benefit may be its role as a myth buster. Six years ago, Intuit was perceived as "an old, slow company," and people said it was too hard to be innovative and agile. The idea jams and code jams busted those myths by telling employees, "Go ahead—just hack that."[14]

Even more radically, Valve Software has created an internal market for ideas—a true network of start-ups—by requiring that the generators of insights recruit others. From Valve's employee handbook:

> Since Valve is flat, people don't join projects because they're told to. Instead, you'll decide what to work on. Employees vote on projects with their feet (or desk wheels). Strong projects are ones in which people can see demonstrated value; they staff up easily. This means there are any number of internal recruiting efforts constantly under way. People are going to want you to work with them on their projects, and they'll try hard to get you to do so. But the decision is going to be up to you...
>
> There's no rule book for choosing a project or task at Valve. But it's useful to answer questions like these: Of all the projects

currently under way, what's the most valuable thing I can be working on? Which project will have the highest direct impact on our customers?[15]

This approach is unusual. As Valve employee Paul Kirschbaum (a former Amazon employee) observes, "It's different at Valve. You have to figure out where to allocate your time—which projects you think will create the most value. And if you want to pursue an idea, you've got to convince others that it's worth pursuing. No manager is telling you what to do. Ideas draw resources if others think they have merit."[16] The freedom to choose is critical for innovation success, because research shows that creative ideas come from folks who are intrinsically motivated to generate and pursue those ideas.[17]

This approach also has the benefit of creating an environment where folks are happy and motivated because they work on things they care about. "We want innovators, and that means maintaining an environment where they'll flourish," say Valve's leaders in the employee handbook. "That's why Valve is flat. It's our shorthand way of saying that we don't have any management, and nobody 'reports to' anybody else. We do have a founder/president, but even he isn't your manager. This company is yours to steer . . . You have the power to green-light projects."[18] That's a powerful vote test for an organization to use to select ideas to work on.

Proof Test

It is possible that individuals (or teams) who are passionate about an idea but lack the "votes" may be on to something. How do you sort them out from the passionate individuals who lack votes because their idea is bad? Give them the tools we describe, and ask them to run a quick experiment. If the insight has merit, they'll return with data—the proof—that the idea is worth further exploration. For example, when Paul Buchheit, an engineer at Google, came up with the idea for a system that would read keywords distilled from your Gmail message and automatically find a related ad to display next to it, Marissa Mayer told him to drop the idea. "I was like, 'Paul, Paul, Paul—ads are never going to work,'" Mayer said in a Stanford University podcast. "We'll never make any money, or we're going to target the ads at their e-mail, which is just going to be creepy and weird. People are going to think there are people here reading their e-mails and picking out the ads and it's going to be terrible."[19] Luckily for Buchheit, empirical results trump opinions in Google's culture. So even after Mayer made him promise not to build a prototype, he stayed up all night and built one anyway, gambling that it would prove Mayer wrong. He released the prototype of his system, called AdSense, at 7 a.m. right before Mayer came to work. When Mayer first saw the prototype, she was annoyed. But when she checked her Gmail she saw there was an e-mail from a friend who invited her to go hiking—and next to it, an ad for hiking boots. Another e-mail was about Al Gore visiting Stanford University for a speech—and next to it was an ad for books about Al Gore. Mayer grudgingly admitted that AdSense was more useful, entertaining, and relevant than she imagined.[20] More importantly, the data from the prototype won out. (Buchheit's prototype led to additional prototypes, and AdSense was adapted to identify advertising opportunities through keyword searches, website content, and browsing that led to $10 billion in annual revenues.) In fact, Google CEO Eric Schmidt would often advise Googlers to get "100 happy users inside of Google" as proof of concept before launching a product to the market.

In similar fashion, Regeneron, an emerging biotech star, has achieved a lofty 63 percent innovation premium (number 4 on our most recent *Forbes* list of most innovative companies) by placing many small bets in lots of places—and letting the experiments reveal which ideas are best. According to a *Forbes* analysis of 220 drugs approved over the past decade for publicly traded companies, the companies that invented three or more medicines spent an average of $4.3 billion in R&D per drug. Regeneron's cost per drug? Only $736 million. Setting criteria for success and then letting fast and frugal experiments show which bets to make is a far better way than having senior managers pick the

Watch Out: Innovators Innovate, Customers Validate

Most of your insights into problems to be solved will come from watching and interacting with customers and others. But don't fall into the trap of asking your customers to innovate for you. In later chapters we emphasize the importance of asking for feedback, but don't expect them to tell you what the innovation should be. Customers have a hard time imagining the future or resolving contradictory demands. For example, when customers told Kimberly-Clark they didn't want their toilet-trained children to wear diapers but they also didn't want them to wet the bed, those same customers couldn't imagine the solution: disposable underwear with the absorbent features of a diaper (called Pull-Ups, they became a multimillion-dollar category). To avoid this trap, as we will teach in the next chapter, focus on the customer's job-to-be-done, come up with a variety of prototyped solutions, and then, using tools of the innovator's method, rely on customers to validate the solution.

insights to test and develop. According to Regeneron CEO Leonard Schleifer, having leaders pick the ideas to focus on is a bad idea. "'Focus' is a dirty word for us, OK? It's a big mistake to think that you can pick the very best thing that you should focus on and then ignore all the other things."[21] The point: picking winners under conditions of high uncertainty is extraordinarily difficult: let experiments validate the best insights to pursue.

The Insight Business

You cannot expect to see a flood of insights by doing the same things you've done in the past. But you can generate many new insights by changing what you do. Questioning, observing, networking, and experimenting will increase the probability that you will learn something new that will surprise you. Savor those surprises. They might be the catalyst to something big.

Let us add that you cannot ignite more insights by just throwing money at people. Counterintuitively, some of the most successful innovators we studied offered almost no monetary rewards for innovation. Why did people participate? It's because many people, once they get a taste of it, find innovation the most fulfilling activity in their lives. People typically want to be acknowledged and want to be a part of taking their insights forward and turning them into real businesses, including taking time off to push the idea forward (many companies we observed offer three to twelve months of sabbatical for originators of the most promising ideas). You shouldn't forget to reward people, and it's a good idea to provide financial participation to retain your best innovators. But ultimately, giving people the time and opportunity to pursue their ideas may be the most important thing you can offer. And changing your behavior in simple and easy ways can make all the difference in helping trigger insights that can make a difference.

4

Problem: Discover the Job-to-Be-Done

No problem, no opportunity. No one will
pay you to solve a nonproblem.

—Vinod Khosla, Founder, Sun Microsystems
and Khosla Ventures

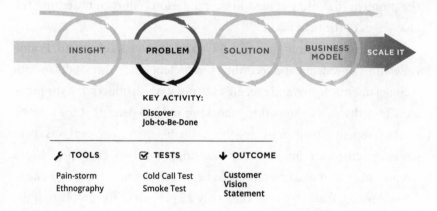

W HEN MIKE MAPLES JR., an experienced executive who had worked in telecommunications, decided to start a new venture with some colleagues, the problem was that they didn't know what type of venture to start. So Maples and his team made an unusual agreement: they would not start building anything until they found a problem that was worth solving. Maples and his friends began meeting several times a week to discuss problems they had seen. Then, then during the week they met individually with people in the industry to test their ideas. Although the group generated many interesting insights, Maples and his team kept pushing, recalling that they were looking for a problem so big that "you needed a tourniquet, or you were going to die."[1]

Eventually, the team focused on the problem of the rapidly expanding help desk, a $70 billion problem bleeding the IT industry dry. Research revealed that as software solutions had become more complex, the help desk required increasingly knowledgeable staff to resolve customers' technical challenges. Help desk functions then consumed 80 percent of Microsoft's head count, and growing. Not surprisingly, several companies had developed solutions, usually knowledge databases of answers to frequently asked questions.

Maples's team members felt that they, too, should develop a knowledge database—but it would need to be a better solution than competitive products. But because they had committed to deeply understanding the problem first, they agreed to devote serious effort to observing the challenges of the help desk.

So the team went into the call centers and observed technicians, timing calls with stopwatches and recording the content. They also sat down with technicians, managers, and executives to discuss and understand the problem. They discovered something shocking: only 25 percent of the time on a call was spent actually resolving the problem. Up to 75 percent was spent gathering customer information, confirming whether customers had a support plan, and diagnosing simple items such as the operating system; knowledge databases were tackling only 25 percent of the problem. If the group could automate the simpler tasks, it could solve a problem consuming more than half the productivity of a $70 billion industry. Using this deep insight into the problem, Maples and his colleagues launched Motive Communications, a company that reached a multibillion-dollar market capitalization by providing a better solution to the real problem.[2]

Maples's experience reinforces the importance of deeply understanding the problem before trying to solve it. Although such an observation may seem obvious, in fact, most managers actually start with the solution first, before ensuring that they've discovered a problem worth solving. As a result, although they develop highly innovative solutions, the product or service fails because they developed a solution that no one wants to buy. Therefore, the most important thing you can do next in the innovation process is to start by deeply understanding the problem you are solving—the job-to-be-done.

Deeply Understand the Job-to-Be-Done

Clayton Christensen argues that customers—people and companies—have "jobs" that arise regularly and need to get done. When customers become aware of a job, they look around for a product or service they can hire to help them get the job done. As well-known marketing professor Theodore Levitt once observed, "People don't want to buy a quarter-inch drill. They want a quarter-inch hole!"[3]

For example, customers may purchase an iron and ironing board to help them remove wrinkles from clothes. But they don't really want an iron and ironing board. They really want wrinkle-free clothing. By understanding what the job is, you can generate various insights about the problem or solution. Instead of thinking about ways to improve the iron or ironing board, you might consider creating a wrinkle-release spray for clothes, or perhaps a product to be used in the dryer, much as a fabric softener sheet is used. Or perhaps you could develop a product to be attached to a washer—or put in a shower—to steam out wrinkles. We've found that stepping back to deeply understand the job-to-be-done is a useful technique, not only for spawning ideas but also for laying the foundation to nail the problem and solution.

Furthermore, it is important to recognize that every job has a functional, a social, and an emotional dimension—and the importance of these elements varies from job to job. For example, "I need to feel like I belong to an elite, exclusive group" is a job for which luxury brand products such as Gucci and Versace are hired. In this case, the functional dimension of the job isn't nearly as important as its social and emotional dimensions. In contrast, if you want to hire a delivery truck you're probably focusing on functional elements, such as the size of the truck or ease of loading. But even when a job looks purely functional, pay attention to hidden emotional or social dimensions. For example, even though a Harley-Davidson is highly functional, many people choose it for social reasons; they want to join the Harley Owners Group and be part of a club that rides motorcycles together. Understanding the functional, social, and emotional dimensions of a job is the most critical element of really nailing the problem you are trying to solve and setting yourself up for a successful innovation. It will lead you to solutions that you may never have considered but that will be much more successful.

Another way of thinking about the job-to-be-done is to ask yourself, What outcomes do my customers want? Anthony Ulwick describes the efforts of Cordis, a struggling medical device manufacturer, to gain a foothold in the market for products related to angioplasty (a heart procedure in which doctors thread a device through an artery to reach the heart, where they inflate a balloon to place a stent, reducing blockage in a compromised heart artery). In the effort to improve their fortunes, Ulwick helped the Cordis team shift their focus from features to outcomes. Interviewers approached a sample of customers (surgeons and nurses) and asked them to talk through an angioplasty from beginning to end. As the customers talked, the Cordis team asked them what they would like, ideally, without focusing on existing solutions. Then they translated those desires into outcomes.

For example, when surgeons said they wanted a smooth balloon, interviewers asked why; the surgeons wanted to avoid accidentally cutting a blood vessel. So the team translated this description into the outcome (the job-to-be-done). They then compared all the jobs to be done in the procedure and developed a hypothesis of the biggest unmet need (the most important outcomes having the least satisfaction): minimizing

recurrence of artery blockage, which was rated 9.5 out of 10 on importance, but 3.2 on satisfaction. They then redesigned the stent to accomplish that job. Within one year, Cordis increased its market share from
less than 1 percent to more than 10 percent.[4]

In your search for jobs to be done, it is worth remembering that not
all jobs are created equal. The world is full of opportunities; the only
real question is which ones are worth solving. So how do you know if it's
worth solving? Search for what we call a *monetizable job:* a significant
need or problem for a large group of customers who: (1) have money and
(2) will readily pay you to solve it. Too many innovators have chased
very intriguing jobs but for very few customers or for customers who
don't have money or aren't willing to pay! For example, while many
elementary schools have a multitude of jobs to solve, they are often so
budget constrained that they cannot pay to solve those jobs, unless you
can find a way to also solve their budget constraint at the same time.

As you think about different monetizable jobs, also consider that occasionally there can be multiple customers for a single job. For any particular job there may be up to three customers: the economic customer (the
person who pays for it), the technical customer (the person who installs
the solution), and the end customer (the person who uses the solution).
Naturally you want to understand the jobs to be done for each customer
type to avoid solving one customer's job while creating a problem for
another customer. For example, if you solve a health care problem for
a consumer (end customer) but insurers or administrators (economic
customer) refuse to pay, you can't actually tackle the job. So remember
that you may need to find creative ways to solve the job-to-be-done for
multiple customers.

Lastly we recommend that you search for a monetizable job to
customers' problems that can be described in terms of shark bites—
and not mosquito bites. Many of us are bothered by mosquito bites,
but we rarely buy the anti-itch cream. We just live with it. But if a
shark bites you, then you will pay any amount of money to solve that
pain—immediately. Your goal should be to look for shark bites that

you can solve—the kinds of problems or needs that keep your customers awake at night, consume their time, engage them deeply, or cause them stress.

When we are talk about shark bites, we're referring more to the degree of customer emotion and engagement than the size of the market. Of course, you want to solve a problem with big markets, but often the markets for new ideas are very small at the beginning. One of the biggest traps managers fall into is shooting down new projects because they're too small to satisfy the growth needs of large corporations. But seeds are small before they become trees—and they take time to mature. For that reason, even though you may be encouraged to start by sizing the market, we encourage you to pay more attention to the emotion of your customers. Strong emotion often leads to attractive markets. For that reason, don't be fooled. Some things that may appear to be a mosquito bite may be a serious customer need worth solving (see "Is Instagram a Shark Bite or a Mosquito Bite?").

Is Instagram a Mosquito Bite or a Shark Bite?

To find a monetizable job, you can focus on what causes your customers stress, what keeps them awake at night, where they spend their time, or what they hate to do: things we might label problems. But what about simple pleasures? Although we use the language of "problems" in the chapter, many important jobs are actually needs or pleasures sought by customers. When you explore customer needs, just think carefully about the difference between *nice* to have and *need* to have.

Many of the things we see as simple pleasures actually solve a deep human need. Psychologist Abraham Maslow identified a hierarchy of human needs, arguing that beyond our basic needs for food and shelter, we have intense desires for belonging, love, friendship, and feeling important. Once those needs are met, we have a need for self-fulfillment, including the need to create and experience new things. If you can solve one of these needs, something that looks like a simple pleasure may actually be solving a big unmet need.

Consider Instagram, the photo-sharing application for smart phones. What problem is Instagram solving? Think of this question in terms of nice to have and need to have. Instagram solves a deep human need for self-expression, social connection, and prominence. But that's not all: the kicker is that it solves this need better than prior solutions. For example, internet blogs took off because they, too, solved a deep social need for self-expression and prominence. The problem with blogs is that writing them takes a great deal of time. Twitter solved this problem by reducing posts to 140 characters, allowing people to share their thoughts and achieve social prominence more quickly and with less work. Now consider the saying, "A picture is worth a thousand words." In some ways, Instagram allows users to share a thousand words with only a few clicks and, on top of that, receive social feedback.

As you look for jobs, sometimes providing a simple pleasure may be solving an important customer problem, defined broadly. To find needs, you can also explore what customers love, want, and feel compelled to do. Only customers can reveal what's important. What looks small initially can sometimes be big. Even mosquito bites can be serious problems, especially if they carry malaria.

Three Tools to Find the Monetizable Job

To really discover the job-to-be-done, don't count on traditional marketing studies, analyst reports, news articles, surveys, or even focus groups. That may sound heretical, but in our opening example, if Maples had relied on an analyst report or a news article, he would never have discovered the job-to-be-done. Even if he had run a survey, he wouldn't have asked the right questions. Clearly these familiar tools have value under conditions of certainty, but they fail when you face uncertainty. So much so that Gianfranco Zaccai, the designer behind P&G's billion-dollar Swiffer product, said, "In my 40 years working in design and innovation, alongside some of the most brilliant minds in the business, I have never seen innovation come out of a focus group. Let me put it more strongly: focus groups kill innovation."[5] These tools fail because you can't get deep enough to observe real customer problems. For this reason we introduce a different set of tools to discover the job-to-be-done.

Pain-Storming

In chapter 1 we describe how Intuit started using "pain-storming" to ensure that the team had nailed a customer's biggest pain points before jumping to building solutions. The purpose of pain-storming is to gain clarity on what you think the problem is so that you can test your hypotheses. We've found that effective pain-storming involves five steps.

> Step 1: Generate a problem hypothesis identifying the customer and the job-to-be-done.
>
> Step 2: Create a journey-line for the customer and identify pain points and emotions.
>
> Step 3: Select the biggest pain points, and conduct a root-cause analysis.
>
> Step 4: Pick a root cause that you think is most important to customers.
>
> Step 5: Identify assumptions behind the root cause, and then test them with customers.

Let's look at each step. First, you create a problem hypothesis of the customer and the job-to-be-done. This involves identifying what you think is an important problem for a specific type of customer. For example, Motive Communications' problem hypothesis was that it could reduce the time (and costs) of help desks to solve customers' technical problems at large software companies like Microsoft. To identify a customer segment for your project, write down at least three identifying characteristics (for example, large software companies, with large numbers of unsophisticated customers, that have large customer support budgets, who want a reputation for good service). These are descriptors of the types of customers with the same job-to-be-done (see "Develop a Customer Profile to Segment Customers"). It may be helpful to fill in the following template from the perspective of the customer.

I am _____ (customer, with at least three characteristics)

I am trying to _____ (outcome/job trying to solve)

But _____ (problem I am facing)

Because _____ (the deeper root cause for why the problem is happening)

Develop a Customer Profile to Segment Customers

To effectively nail the problem, it helps to build a profile for each customer with a different job-to-be-done. Grouping customers based on shared needs or problems is a familiar marketing tool called *customer segmentation*. But in contrast to more familiar customer segmentation, the purpose of customer profiles is to build a deeply empathetic, intimate portrait of customers and the jobs they struggle to accomplish.

To build customer profiles, you might start by first segmenting customers by the job-to-be-done, rather than more familiar metrics like age or income. The job is the critical unit of analysis, and your customer profile should aim to describe your initial hypothesis about the emotions around the job and how customers currently solve it. Then test your hypothesis by observing customers to understand their motivations (likes, dislikes, aspirations), behaviors (how they spend their time; how they purchase new products or services), demographics (income, industry, age, education, and available budget), and, most important, how they currently think about and solve the job-to-be-done.

After these observations, you will see the world in a new way and will need to recreate a new set of customer profiles based on your observations. Each customer profile should be divided by the job-to-be-done, and describe all the elements above (emotions, current solutions, etc.) for that particular job. This profile will provide you the map of what problem to solve and how to solve it. But it will also provide your team focus and motivation, helping you avoid the trap of trying to solve every job, and in doing so, solving nobody's. To illustrate this danger, in one humorous example, the television show *The Simpsons* featured the main character, Homer Simpson, asking customers what they most wanted in a car. Homer then builds a car that includes every feature for every customer desire, such as "power like a gorilla, yet soft and yielding like a Nerf ball." Not surprisingly the car fails in the market, because, in trying to solve every customer's problem, the car actually solves no one's problems. The humor helps us see the absurdity of trying to serve every customer need, but it is inspired by real events. The failed Ford Edsel and Pontiac Stinger were designed to serve too many customer needs (see figure 4-1).

FIGURE 4-1

The Ford Edsel and Pontiac Stinger

Source: Time.com and Carstyling.ru.

Step 2 is to create a customer journey-line: an in-depth visual portrait in which you identify pain points to understand how your customers do the job today and how they feel while doing it. Visually map out the steps customers take to achieve an outcome. It helps to assign a customer emotion to each step to identify how the customer is feeling. For example, Motive Communications first had to understand the journey taken by desk workers, including the tedious process of identifying a customer's software version. You may choose to develop a more simplified "storyboard" after completing your journey-line to share at a later time with customers for their feedback.

The third step is to select the biggest pain point and do a root-cause analysis (see figure 4-2). It's helpful to apply a "five whys" questioning process (developed by Taiichi Ohno, father of the Toyota production system). In most cases, we've found that asking "Why does this happen?" three times (going down three levels) is sufficient. As the Motive Communications team observed people working at the help desk, they measured the time taken by each step. They then broke out each step as a contributor to the overall time, and cost, required to serve a customer, asking, Why does this happen? They thus found out why the technicians

FIGURE 4-2

Root-cause analysis

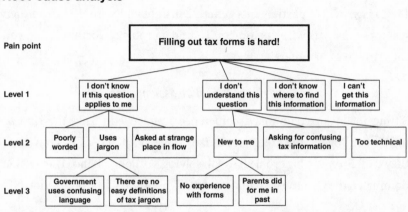

had to gather the customer information, why they had to verify a support plan, why they had to search certain knowledge databases, and so on. You can brainstorm this information as hypotheses to be tested later, but ultimately you will need to gather it through observation (as we describe in the next section).

The fourth step is to pick a root cause to explore in greater depth because you think it's a critical reason for the customer's problem. As you develop a root-cause tree (the map of root causes uncovered by asking "Why" multiple times) for various problems, you may see that a particular root cause shows up in multiple places. This indicates an important root cause to explore. If you include customers in your pain-storming session, they can also help you identify which root causes are most important—and why.

Step 5 is to create a list of questions about (or assumptions behind) the root cause—questions you need to answer through customer experiments. You can use the question-storming technique to develop the key questions, along with the customer activities or experiments that will answer the questions and validate your assumptions.[6] Motive Communications used help desk observations and stopwatches to answer their key questions.

Intuit excels at pain-storming, and we've seen other companies use variations on the process we've just outlined. For example, Mondelez International (Kraft) has a site dedicated to this process, called the FlyGarage, where participants generate insights into problems and then test these insights with customers. To find a problem worth solving, you must involve customers.

Ethnography to Explore Assumptions

Sitting in an air-conditioned conference room overlooking the sprawling city of Bogotá, the executives at Banco Davivienda became convinced they'd discovered a big problem worth solving. Although Banco Davivienda dominated the Colombian banking market, almost half the population had no bank account. Executives realized that if there was a way to tap in to this market of nonusers, they could dramatically grow their market share and help the Colombian people at the bottom of the income pyramid.

They formed a cross-disciplinary team to develop an offering that would appeal to nonusers—a streamlined, easy-to-use version of existing bank accounts. After several months of hard work the bank launched the new product, and the optimistic team celebrated. Despite aggressive promotion, however, few customers adopted the new accounts. Even after several months, the team saw little growth, and by year-end they concluded that the project had failed.

As team members analyzed the initial failure, they came to realize that although they had commissioned a market study and talked to a few customers, they hadn't understood the jobs to be done for the "unbanked." Rather, they had let their knowledge of existing customers and solutions distort their understanding of the problem. So the team decided to try a different approach: to go themselves into poor neighborhoods to interact with, and create profiles of, the target customers. They spent weeks living in various neighborhoods as they observed people's daily activities. Said one team member, "We decided to go out and try to understand what people wanted, not by asking directly 'what do you want,' but by trying to understand how people behave in real life without any kind of prejudice."[7]

The team developed customer profiles (as described in the sidebar) of different target customers and the job-to-be-done, along with their motivations, behaviors, and other characteristics. For example, the team developed the following profile for "Martha."

Martha is one of the 3 million low-income subsidy beneficiaries in Colombia. She wakes up at 2 a.m. to get ready to make the line at the bank at 3 a.m. in order to cash out her subsidy. She waits in line from five to six hours to finally get her turn, and cash the money. Then, she uses the cash to send a domestic remittance, paying a 10 percent fee for the service. In order to pay her utility bills, she will then move to a "district collections center" where she will wait in line for another two hours to get the payment done. The remaining cash will stay "under the mattress" because she hasn't had the opportunity to open a savings account due to the distance she lives from the bank and the high costs it will represent to her.[8]

By building these customer profiles, the team at Banco Davivienda quickly identified the root cause of the failure of the mini bank account: it didn't directly solve any of Martha's biggest problems. In fact, Martha's main job-to-be-done was simply receiving money and making payments. Now that the team deeply understood Martha's problems, they were able to imagine a radically different solution: a mobile wallet that would allow Martha to make and receive payments from merchants directly using an account served by a mobile phone. This account, unburdened with unneeded features like an ATM card, would allow Martha to do everything by phone (including create the account) without ever having to visit a branch. Eventually the "Martha" solution that the team developed was adopted by hundreds of thousands of users. The product was then launched in several other countries targeted to customers like Martha.

The Banco Davivienda team leveraged the number 1 tool for testing and validating the root causes of customers' problems: ethnography. This technique, which we might more descriptively call "fly on the wall" because that's how you do it, requires that you get deep into the lives of your customers by watching them in their natural habitat. You aren't trying to sell your solution or push your agenda. Instead, you're trying to deeply understand their activities, likes, dislikes, aspirations, challenges, and so on (see "What to Look For as a Fly-on-the-Wall"). Then, using this data, you build synthesized profiles of a prototypical customer—including his or her job-to-be-done and ways she or he currently solves it. You develop profiles for each customer segment and then use them to crystallize the biggest problem you can solve for each profile.

You can take fly-on-the-wall further by actually doing the job your customers are trying to do, rather than just watching, through what we call *role play research*. This requires, as Intuit CEO Brad Smith suggests, that you "be the customer." Instead of watching, try to do the jobs with the current solutions whether that be riding in delivery trucks or balancing finances using software. We strongly recommend this powerful form of customer research, because you often get the most accurate and surprising insights from living the lives of your customers.

What to Look For as a Fly on the Wall

What are you looking for when you are trying to find monetizable jobs? Start by looking for obstacles that get in the way of the jobs your customers are trying to do. Look for areas where customers are spending lots of time (time sinks) even if they don't realize it, workarounds they may have developed to solve a problem, or things that ignite their emotions. Cussing, crying, wasted hours, abandoned activities, or figurative "duct tape" where customers just make it work are great signs that customers are struggling to do the job. You might also look beyond the obstacles to the enablers that facilitate something customers want. Look for how people spend their time expressing themselves, connecting to others, or creating shortcuts. People invest time to solve needs and you may find a better way to meet that need. Lastly, don't forget to closely examine nonusers as well as extreme users. Although it can seem counterintuitive these users can help you understand the problem more clearly than mainstream users. Most of all, look for surprises. It's easy to overlook them, because our minds try to conform what we see to fit our preexisting beliefs. But surprises provide the clues and bread crumbs to the real job-to-be-done.

"Advice" Interviews

A fast technique for developing your initial problem hypothesis is to interview customers using what we call the "advice" interview. Start by identifying a potential sample of customers that you think have a similar job to do. When you ask for interviews (via e-mail or cold call), always ask for advice about a specific customer problem. *Advice* is the magic word. In fact, you may want to mention that you aren't selling anything, just to put potential customers at ease. Then let them know you want to get their feedback on a problem you're trying to solve. Your goal is to listen and learn.

Once you have interviews arranged, we suggest you ask three questions and then listen, listen, listen. These questions are as follows.

1. *Quickly and clearly describe the problem you see.* Describing the problem will make customers confident that you know something and will serve as an anchoring point to the conversation. Don't go to potential customers with a blank sheet and expect something to happen.

2. *Ask, "Do you face this same challenge, too, or a different challenge? Tell me about it."* This gives you a chance to find out whether customers really have the problem you hypothesized. If they don't, you can explore what challenges they really face.

3. *Ask, "Would something like this solve that problem?" and then describe your theoretical prototype (see chapter 5).* At this stage you shouldn't become too solution-focused, but discussing a potential solution will help you get better feedback on the problem. Customers react to the concrete, not the abstract. So you might think about bringing a drawing, storyboard, or PowerPoint slide to help them visualize a solution. This will help them talk about why the solution might, or might not, work to solve their problem.

After five to ten interviews, patterns and trends will begin to emerge, which will allow you to test your hypothesis and change accordingly.

Have You Nailed the Problem? Two Tests

When ZipDx demonstrated its new teleconferencing solution, observers were surprised by the crystal-clear audio coming from the conference-call speaker. The new solution, which ZipDx described as "broadband audio," worked seamlessly with available Polycom phones and required little setup to achieve similar call quality. Despite the positive reactions, however, ZipDx couldn't seem to close any deals. Potential customers seemed interested but not enough to place an order.

Like most innovators, the ZipDx team felt confident that it had found a pain point: the poor audio of conference calls. But had it really nailed the customer problem? When our team was called in to help close sales, we asked the ZipDx team members what customer problems they felt they were solving. Most answers involved vague responses about the poor audio quality of conference calls projected in a typical conference room. But when pushed, the team admitted that problem identification had come more from the ZipDx team than from customers. This led us to believe that they had built a solution before creating a customer profile and identifying the job-to-be-done.

Because ZipDx had already developed a solution, it faced more constraints than if it had investigated customer problems first. So our team worked with ZipDx to use its existing customer knowledge to pain-storm a few hypotheses about the types of customers who might have a problem related to the ZipDx solution. They came up with three customer profile groups: (1) Polycom phone resellers (the original hypothesized customer), (2) voice over internet protocol (VOIP) service providers, and (3) companies attempting to capture bridging revenues. The team then identified nineteen customers by name (roughly six in each profile group) and cold-called them, leaving a voice mail about the problem ZipDx believed it was solving. Sometimes they left a second message. Then they waited to see who called back. Only five customers called back. But they had returned the cold call of a no-name company with an unknown product. Who were these people, and why did they call back?

As it turned out, four of the five VOIP service providers they contacted returned the call. When the ZipDx team members described the problem and the solution (using the advice-seeking interview) and then listened, the results stunned them. VOIP service providers actually didn't care very much about audio quality—what ZipDx thought was the key feature. Instead, they struggled to differentiate themselves with reliable, easy-to-use conference-call software features. As it turns out, the ZipDx software that accompanied the "broadband audio" had other attractive features that allowed users to schedule, join, and manage conference calls far better than most solutions on the market. These features solved the VOIP providers' most important job-to-be-done.

Using this deeper understanding of the specific problems of a specific target customer, the team quickly refined its solution and the messaging to that target customer. The CEO then targeted key large customers with that profile. Within three days he closed the largest deal in company history. ZipDx was on its way to nailing a customer problem.[9]

How do you know when you have nailed a problem worth solving? We recommend two tests: the cold-call test and the smoke test. In both tests, the measure of whether you have found a job-to-be-done is if customers give you their time.

The Cold-Call Test

One of the best tests of whether you've discovered a monetizable job is whether potential customers receiving a cold call (or e-mail) will give you their time. You start by identifying your hypothesized customer segments and their job-to-be-done. Then you reach out to each customer group via phone or e-mail (it's OK at this stage to use your contacts), briefly describe the problem, and ask for their advice on your theoretical prototype.

Then observe who calls back, why they call back, and what they say. Initial call-back rates tend to be low (less than 10 percent), but we've seen some companies achieve call-back rates as high as 50 percent when they've hit on a monetizable job. Your final goal is to achieve a significant leap in the call-back rate. When people do not return your call or e-mail, it may be that you haven't clearly described the problem or haven't described a problem they care about. It's also possible you contacted the wrong customer profile or target group, or you contacted them at an inopportune time.

As you work your way toward a 50 percent call-back rate, you need to ask yourself, Who returned the call (versus those who did not), and why? (If you're doing business-to-consumer e-mails, you'll achieve lower rates, so compare to the benchmark response rates for that channel.) For ZipDx most of the hypothesized customer groups did not call back. For these groups, the company needs to work through friends to get contacts with these customers and see where they went wrong. However, for one customer group, the VOIP sellers, nearly 75 percent called back—an extraordinarily high rate. The information from these customers helped the company understand the real problem it was solving.

Naturally you may have to adjust the threshold depending on your context. For example, B2C e-mail return rates tend to be much lower (we all get a lot of e-mail). But ask yourself whether you're clearly and concisely describing the problem. What are the characteristics of the people who are responding? Remember, the real test that you are discovering a problem worth solving is whether people are giving you their time. The percentage of people giving you time should increase when you have discovered a monetizable job.

The Smoke Test

Smoke tests were first used in the 1800s by plumbers, who pushed smoke through a system to discover leaks. The idea of a smoke test proved so useful that the idea spread to engineering, instruments, and information technology, among others, as a way to test for critical flaws. We've borrowed the concept as a way to test for whether you've discovered a problem worth solving. Rather than use smoke bombs, we use a bit more smoke and mirrors to test whether customers care.

To perform a smoke test, create a website, advertisement, phone number, or other channel that describes the problem, theoretical solution, and provides an option to "learn more," "buy now," "reserve now," or some other call to action. Find a way to get your smoke test in front of customers, perhaps by using Google AdWords, a print advertisement, a poster at a trade show, or another venue where you suspect customers will see the call to action.

When customers activate (click, call, etc.) the call to action, they don't actually get to buy a product, but they effectively identify themselves as having an interest in the problem you are investigating. You can then follow-up to learn more about them and why they took the action. The test itself looks at the response rate (the conversion rate on the call to action), with anything higher than 5 percent suggesting that you've identified a real problem worth solving (although your early efforts won't achieve nearly this rate). But people's willingness to spend time with you and their general excitement about a potential solution will be the key indicators.

You can easily use the smoke test for software or online products, but you can also use it for other services and products. For example, one of our students wanted to start a food truck, the latest rage in mobile cuisine. After learning about the regulations, including needing an inspected commissary, he wondered whether there might be a business opportunity to help would-be entrepreneurs jump this legal hurdle. Rather than write a business plan or rent a commissary, we encouraged him to conduct a smoke test. So he placed an ad in the local newspaper: "Want to start a food truck? We can help. E-mail or call …" That was it. Within one day our student received three calls, and by the end of the week had received more than a dozen e-mails. Perhaps more surprising, in conversations with these customers, he learned that people wanting to start food trucks didn't need his help finding a commissary or jumping through the legal hurdles. Instead, he found that the critical obstacle was affordable, lease-based access to the truck itself. His smoke test was key to discovering the problem and the opportunity.

Develop a Vision of the Customer Problem You Will Solve

Lastly, writing a clear statement of your *vision* of the customer problem can serve as a guide and an anchor as you begin to search for the right solution. It can also help unify your team and your organization around the big problem you're solving. A *vision template* helps you develop the articulation of your vision. To use it (see figure 4-3), assemble the data you've gathered, using the tools described in this chapter, to fill out the template from left to right.

First, identify who the customer is—and who the customer is not. Use your customer profiles to define a narrow customer segment for which you will solve a big problem. Second, describe this big problem—the most critical job-to-be-done—that you hope to address, with supporting data and insights about that problem. Third, create a short, focused vision statement for the job you will do, with supporting data.

Consider the development of Amazon Lending. As described in chapter 2, Jeff Bezos has set himself up as Amazon's chief experimenter

FIGURE 4-3

Vision template

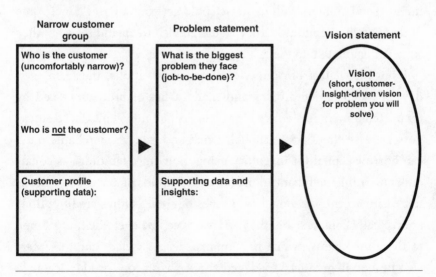

and has vocalized the grand challenge. As a result, everyone in the company recognizes the importance of searching for and generating insights. For example, every spring, the company sets aside time when any employee can propose new ideas for customer problems to solve. One new business, described in the *Wall Street Journal*, is Amazon Lending.[10] The original idea came from the front line: customer service representatives assisting small merchants noticed a common theme: small merchants complained about their capital constraints leading to early stockouts. The discussion of this potential problem made it all the way to Bezos, who asked a small team to explore the problem.

The team started by examining the customer feedback and then talking with customers. While as a general rule, "we always put ourselves in the shoes of customers," another observer noted that "The team's goal was to understand the biggest customer need that was not being met. Once they confirmed their belief regarding what customers wanted, then they thought about how they could implement a solution to solve their challenge that will work for Amazon." To explore the need, the team conducted advice interviews and also employed ethnography: "They would call up small merchants and ask, 'Hey, would you be willing to spend an hour with us so we could get your advice?' Since some of them are here in Seattle, they would go visit them and see what they were doing and talk to them."[11]

Using the data from interviews and observations, the team then developed customer profiles and made a list of problems faced by them. Team members noticed that many small merchants faced stockouts because they lacked capital. Brick-and-mortar merchants often can borrow capital for inventory using their store buildings as collateral, but online merchants don't have these kinds of assets and so cannot easily access traditional bank lines of credit. Other credit options are typically complex, and the paperwork can be overwhelming. Some of these merchants, which the Amazon team labeled "curators," carried unique items that broadened the Amazon.com product catalog.

By contrast, other merchants, labeled "resellers" by the team, focused on identifying a low-cost source of common items and then providing these lower-cost options for Amazon.com buyers. These different merchant groups had some needs that were similar, and others that were different.

Recognizing that Amazon could not solve every customer problem, the team wanted to focus on a specific customer group. Based on the size of the problem, the team decided the target customer was not low-volume merchants (including curators) and low-volume resellers. Rather, it was high-volume resellers that repeatedly stocked out. Their biggest problem was limited (or hard to access) capital for short-term inventory financing, as the team learned from customer interviews and observations and by examining data on how often these customers lost sales because of stockouts. Having created a clear problem statement, the team then moved to creating a vision of the job-to-be-done: quick, easy-to-access inventory financing (see figure 4-4).

FIGURE 4-4

Amazon Lending vision template

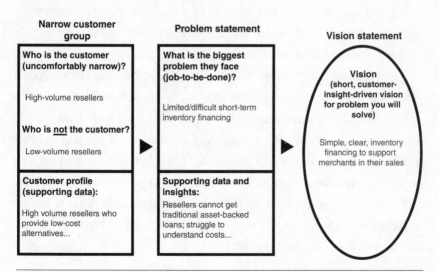

With the clarity and energy of this vision statement, the team moved to the next stage: prototyping the solution. It started by brainstorming a wide variety of potential solutions, including lines of credit, loans, private label cards, and so on. Then, after exploring the challenges, and legal limitations, of each solution, the team went back to customers with a series of prototypes. The team started with theoretical prototypes to quickly get initial customer reactions, then virtual prototypes mocked up in Amazon's web lab, and finally minimum viable prototypes tested with actual customers (we discuss these tools in chapter 5). With each test, the team discovered many surprises about the features customers wanted most (for example, customers wanted financing only for four to six months and not a few years; furthermore, most customers struggled initially to understand the program and the true cost of lending).

Ultimately the team iterated, tested, and validated an invitation-based loan program in which Amazon uses existing data to preapprove loans and eliminate the tedious paperwork of a typical loan. After receiving the invitation, a merchant can quickly accept the loan and have funds transferred to its account with only a few clicks. Although we cannot reveal specific performance figures, the new business has provided a significant lift in sales to resellers (and transaction fees to Amazon), and the team has discovered a solution and business model (discussed in chapter 6) that has allowed it to operate as a profitable, independent business unit within Amazon.

Having nailed the problem and solution for the original customer group, the team is now working to nail the biggest problem for a different customer segment, beginning with the vision statement. "Right now the team is exploring another group of customers," said another observer. "But I can tell you they haven't touched the solution yet, not until they get more feedback from customers to make sure they are going down the right road first."[12] This Amazon Lending team understands the importance of deeply understanding the biggest problem for a specific customer segment before spending time developing a solution.

Watch Out: Incremental, Urgent Problems Create Limited Growth

Large companies fall into traps when it comes to finding jobs to be done. Their existing customers often come to them with incremental problems related to their core activities. They want fewer defects, a new feature, faster service, lower price, and so on. There's always something more that customers want—and it's always urgent. So large companies—in an attempt to be responsive—try to listen to customers and end up solving their incremental problems. This creates a dilemma: Should you focus on solving the urgent problems of your existing customers? Or should you try to solve a problem for noncustomers that could create growth in the future? We all tend to choose the urgent over the important.

This is a big watch out. It's not that the urgent problems of existing customers aren't important, but solving these concerns usually gives you less bang for the buck than bringing a new solution to new customers (or even a new solution to existing customers). It's a matter of diminishing returns: after you've solved the most important problem that affects the greatest number of existing customers, you then work on solving a problem for a smaller set of customers. So you must carefully consider the criteria you use in selecting problems. Disruptive innovation projects must be in the innovation project portfolio—and that means trying to solve the problems of noncustomers. Unfortunately, it's hard for prospective customers to tell you that their problem is urgent, too.

First Things First

Although it may feel "slower" to start with the customer problem rather than the solution, you save time by deeply understanding the customer's job-to-be-done. You avoid wasting resources in pursuit of a solution that doesn't solve a monetizable job. Your first task as a manager is to deeply understand customers and the problems you're trying to solve for them. You cannot ask customers what innovations they want, or rely on their feature requests. Instead you have to observe their jobs to be done, propose a solution, and then watch their reaction. As we like to say, innovators innovate, customers validate, and not the other way around.

5

Solution: Prototype the Minimum "Awesome" Product

*If you can increase the number of experiments
you try from 100 to 1,000, you dramatically
increase the innovations you produce.*

—Jeff Bezos, CEO, Amazon.com

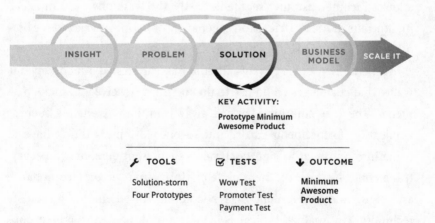

KEY ACTIVITY:

**Prototype Minimum
Awesome Product**

🔧 TOOLS	☑ TESTS	⬇ OUTCOME
Solution-storm	Wow Test	**Minimum Awesome Product**
Four Prototypes	Promoter Test	
	Payment Test	

I N CHAPTER 4 WE describe how Banco Davivienda (BD) tried—and failed—to reach the large "unbanked" population in Colombia by creating simple bank accounts with lower fees. After its initial, solution-first approach failed, the bank sent teams into poor neighborhoods to understand the problem through ethnography. This fly-on-the-wall approach gave managers a deep understanding of the job-to-be-done and a vision of what the solution would have to do for customers. But how did they actually develop a solution?

To get outside the box, the BD team tried some unusual things. First, the team members listed the key elements of a bank account, such as branches, accounts, debit cards, forms, signatures, paper, fees, and so on. Then they subtracted one item at a time and asked, "Can we build a business around this one item?"[1] Initially most team members scoffed. How could you build a solution using only one element? But when they suspended their disbelief, they realized that, for the unbanked, a simple solution to a specific problem might be the best approach. During their field research, teams noted that virtually everyone, including the unbanked, had cell phones. So the team studied wireless service providers and found that some companies had developed products that the unbanked would pay for, such as virally adopted games or a joke of the day. The team also began looking at other industries, such as internet retailers, to see how they provided solutions through mobile phones to a lower-income customer segment. Lastly, the team observed financial institutions in Asia, Africa, and other areas of Latin America to see how others were solving similar problems.

As mentioned earlier, eventually the BD team tested a mobile phone wallet that customers could use to do one thing: receive and make payments. The new solution stripped away traditional elements such as application forms, debit cards, and so on. Customers didn't have to come into a branch to sign documents or present personal ID; everything could be done on the mobile platform. To overcome compliance and regulation issues, Banco Davivienda borrowed emerging big-data techniques to analyze typical behaviors for similar customer groups and monitor or reject atypical usage.

When the team hit a substantial roadblock—how to let customers withdraw cash without adding an expensive and cumbersome ATM card program—the bank tried something highly unusual in banking but common among internet retailers: a one-time password, which, in this case, let customers withdraw cash from any ATM. Banco Davivienda's solution produced significant growth, with BD quickly enrolling more than a million users in various countries.[2]

Solution-Storming to Generate Solution Options

To develop its novel solution, the team at Banco Davivienda used a tool we call *solution-storming* (brainstorming multiple solution options) to help it search broadly for solutions before using customer tests to help it narrow the options to a single solution. Going broad in the search for a solution is a foundational principle for solution-storming—and for innovation generally. It leads to more options and combinations, and that in turn leads to novel solutions. For example, most people credit Henry Ford with developing the modern production line—an invention that allowed him to make the automobile affordable. Ford radically transformed the auto industry and American life. How did he do it?

We see the production line as a "solution," but Ford actually developed it by searching broadly, borrowing ideas such as interchangeable parts (used in sewing machines, firearms, and watches); continuous-flow manufacturing (used in processing flour, canning food, and making cigarettes); and assembly-line techniques (used in meat-packing plants and breweries).[3] In similar fashion, the BD team generated solution options by first searching broadly, in part by observing practices in other industries and other countries.

Starting Solution-Storming

Start your solution-storm with a problem and customer vision statement like the one described in chapter 4. As with all kinds of brainstorming, a key principle of successful solution-storming is that you don't shut down any proposed solution or solution process too early.

Recall that Banco Davivienda was skeptical that subtracting the elements of a familiar solution would work. We can top that: we once had a participant in a solution-storm for Leatherman, a manufacturer of multitools and pocket knives, propose shipping a live monkey with each tool to assemble the product. It took all we could muster to not shut down that idea immediately. But then the idea turned out to be pivotal in helping the team discover a super-simple assembly—one even a monkey could do easily.

To help you brainstorm solutions, we suggest you choose from a menu of techniques (see figure 5-1). You won't use all these techniques at once; instead, think of them as choices or options.

Analogs: Close and Far Away

Think about the possible solutions around you on a spectrum from those that are close to your industry to those that are far from your industry. Closest to you, check to see whether one of your customers has already developed a workaround. Usually, these make-do solutions are held together by figurative duct tape, but they provide insights into ways you could solve the problem. For example, one entrepreneur we interviewed initially felt discouraged when he discovered a potential customer had already developed a workaround to solve the problem. But then he licensed the solution for a small royalty and used it to build a solution and company that eventually reached a market value of well over a billion dollars.

Look for analogs and complements to your existing solutions that can suggest alternative solutions (be aware that there may be novel solutions in adjacent industries). For example, one fuel cell company we studied borrowed newspaper printing techniques to print fuel cell membranes. These examples of borrowing demonstrate the power of analogs of what to do or what not to do. For example, Rent the Runway borrowed analogs from Netflix and from airline reservation systems, and Banco Davivienda borrowed analogs from internet retailers and financial institutions in other emerging markets.

FIGURE 5-1

Tools for solution-storming

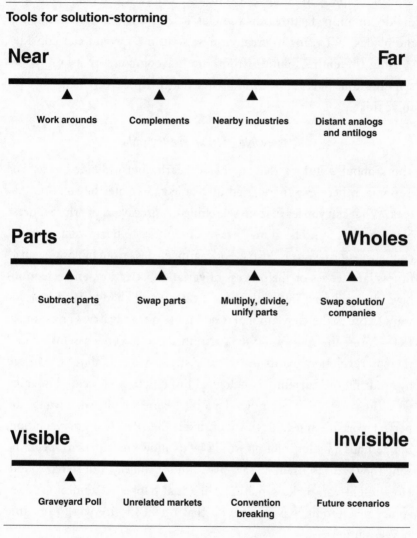

Near   Far

▲   ▲   ▲   ▲

Work arounds   Complements   Nearby industries   Distant analogs
                                                     and antilogs

Parts   Wholes

▲   ▲   ▲   ▲

Subtract parts   Swap parts   Multiply, divide,   Swap solution/
                                unify parts   companies

Visible   Invisible

▲   ▲   ▲   ▲

Graveyard Poll   Unrelated markets   Convention   Future scenarios
                                       breaking

Elements: Parts and Wholes

Consider solutions in terms of parts and wholes. At one end of the
spectrum, as with Banco Davivienda, subtract one element of an
existing solution and try to build on it as the essential component.
Or consider how you could swap in or swap out parts of a solution,
as the iPod did by swapping in the movement of a combination lock

to search rapidly for songs. Also think about how you could multiply, divide, or unify features. In the classic example, Gillette multiplied the blades in a razor to create a new solution. Or you can consider stealing the entire solution from another company by asking yourself questions like, "How would Amazon (or Apple, or Disney, or . . .) solve this?"

Observables: Visible and Invisible

Think about solutions that might be nearby but difficult to see. For example, others may have tried and failed to create the solution you seek. What can you learn from searching the graveyard of prior failures? Next, consider unrelated markets or disciplines to borrow an idea that could transform your industry. For example, ideas from biology (such as fitness landscapes or the process of variation, selection, and retention) have changed how we think about strategy and change. And look for ways to break the conventional wisdom of your industry. For example, IKEA broke the convention that furniture had to come assembled and thereby revolutionized its industry. Lastly, daydream about the future by ignoring the current technological limitations you see and imagine what the perfect solution might look like. For example, what would the perfect portable music device look like? The iPod is a great solution, but perhaps a better solution would be to allow customers to speak the song they want to listen to, say "play," and then hear it in stereo sound. How might you make something like that happen? Examining "awesome" new products is an activity that might inspire you to imagine novel solutions.

Selecting Solutions to Prototype

After you've generated a range of solution options, you're ready to select the most promising ideas to test with customers. Recall Intuit's experience from chapter 1: when the team voted on the "best" ideas, they tended to pick those that were easiest to understand and implement. Wendy Castleman, the innovation catalyst community leader at Intuit, comments:

> Project teams had truly mastered "going broad"; they were good
> at generating lots and lots of ideas . . . But teams did a bad job of
> picking the best ideas to work on because our selection criteria
> were generally faulty. The problem stemmed from the team
> voting on ideas, a classic design thinking approach . . . The ideas
> with the most votes get explored further. But it turns out that
> people often vote for what is easy to implement and familiar, and
> that rarely yields ideas that will surprise and delight customers.[4]

Based on our observations at Intuit and other companies, we recommend you post the solution options on the wall and use the following process. First, think of the different themes or characteristics represented among the solutions, such as "ease of use" or "high performance." Then select an option from each theme to explore so that you can observe how customers respond.

Second, define the proposed solutions along a dimension or spectrum. For example, one spectrum might involve ranking solutions from low to high on dimensions such as "game changing," "bold/risky," "most easily attainable," "technical difficulty to deliver." Then select solutions to test at different ends of the spectrum. This approach will help you to go broad in the solutions you test.

Third, once you've selected solutions to test, write down your leap-of-faith assumptions or list them as questions to be answered. Then prioritize the assumptions based on those that you think are most important to validate in order for a solution to succeed. For example, when the Banco Davivienda team was brainstorming solutions for the unbanked, they wanted to test whether customers would sign up for bank accounts through their smart phones without visiting a branch or speaking to a person. It was critical to test this assumption for target customers, who didn't have the time or means to get to a branch. Once the critical assumptions have been made explicit, the team can design experiments (use prototypes) to test them.

Four Kinds of Prototypes

In a semisecret location, the Google X lab has been exploring crazy new technologies such as flying wind turbines and wifi balloons. These are the kinds of technologies, given the level of technical and demand risk, that most companies don't even consider. The first product, Google Glass, began to roll out in early 2012, with customers lining up to pay $1,500 to try a beta version. Although the success of Google Glass is anything but assured, the product development process offers lessons on prototypes.

The Google Glass team originated with a project by University of Washington professor Babak Parviz.[5] Although initially an interesting technology, it became an interesting solution when the team noticed a problem: How often in social interactions people "check out" to check their smart phones. The Google X team asked, "What if you could use this technology to stay engaged with the world around you while also using the internet?" At the same time, you can imagine the immensity of the technical challenges: How could you allow someone to connect to the internet using a lightweight, touchless device? Given the technical risk, ask yourself, How long should it take the team to create the first fully operational, wearable prototype that projects live images from the internet? Ready? It took one day.

In a recent presentation, Tom Chi, head of experience at Google X, described how the team created and tested the first prototype. How did they do it? Check out the image in figure 5-2.

After creating a wearable device, Chi and the team needed a way to navigate it. If you've seen the movie *Minority Report,* you probably remember Tom Cruise moving his hands in the air to manipulate the

FIGURE 5-2

Google Glass first prototype

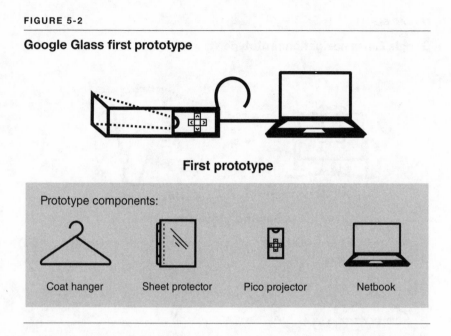

First prototype

Prototype components:

| Coat hanger | Sheet protector | Pico projector | Netbook |

computer. The Google X team also saw the movie and asked, "Why not try it?" Any guesses as to how long it took to prototype the motion detection system? Ready? About forty-five minutes. Chi and the team allowed users to manipulate the device by attaching borrowed headbands (worn around the wrist) to a clicking device (made from a pencil, a binder clip, a chopstick, and a mouse) via a taut fishing line (run over the back of a whiteboard) so that any movement by the user put tension on the line and clicked the device (see figure 5-3).

Right away the team learned that even though it worked for Tom Cruise, it looked and felt strange in practice, so they experimented with other approaches. Despite what at first appeared to be a series of dead ends, each rapid prototype helped the team nail down the final navigation system. And what about the glasses themselves? Although it easily could be overlooked, people hate to wear heavy glasses that press down on their nose. So what should you do about the weight? Chi and his team started prototyping using clay to weight different parts of the

FIGURE 5-3

Google Glass navigation prototype

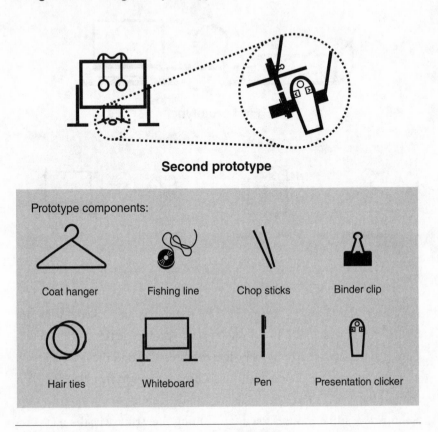

Second prototype

Prototype components:

Coat hanger	Fishing line	Chop sticks	Binder clip
Hair ties	Whiteboard	Pen	Presentation clicker

glasses and discovered that putting the weight behind the ears was quite tolerable (see figure 5-4).[6]

The Google Glass experience shows how quickly a company can move in developing prototypes, whether hardware, software, or services. And Google Glass is not an outlier. Gmail and AdSense (Google's content-targeted advertisement product that has made billions) were each prototyped in a day.[7] Indeed, we have found that at companies like Google, Intuit, and Valve, it is typical to build a prototype in twenty-four to forty-eight hours.

Although many people have heard about prototypes, few people understand the various types or know how to use them properly.

FIGURE 5-4

Prototyping Google Glass weight distribution

Refined prototype

Prototype components:

| Modeling wire | Scale | Clay | Paper |

Managers often go wrong by forgetting that every prototype should answer a specific question or by putting more effort into the prototype than is justified, simply because building stuff feels like progress.

Based on our research and practice, we recommend four types of prototypes. Here they are, in order from the simplest—with the fastest learning cycle—to the most elaborate, and thus slower learning cycles:

- Theoretical prototype

- Virtual prototype

- Minimum viable prototype

- Minimum awesome product

Theoretical Prototypes

The number 1 thing you can do to avoid the trap of building products customers don't want is to not build anything. We're not advocating inaction. But we are advocating a theoretical prototype as a tool to help you survive the early days of innovation ambiguity without falling into the *Field of Dreams* trap (the "build it and they will come" myth portrayed in the film). A *theoretical prototype* expresses your idea as a well-structured mental image in which you outline the general shape of the solution, but not the specifics. An example of a theoretical prototype might be to ask customers, "If you could check on your house visually from your smart phone, would you want to?"

The beauty of a theoretical prototype is that it's fast and cheap. You can test dozens within a week. For example, AT&T recently held a series of workshops with the members of its leadership team to build their innovation skills and consider ways to improve customer service. The attendees took fifteen minutes to solution-storm pilots or experiments to test new ways of delivering the industry's highest-quality customer experience. These were simple theoretical prototypes, such as testing a way for customers to walk into an AT&T store and make purchases without needing to interact with a human. These sessions led to the testing of a number of virtual and minimum viable prototypes during the next twelve months.

By contrast we've watched many teams dive into building products based on their intuition alone before they've even tested whether anyone cared about the solution. In fact, the biggest problem for most corporations is that when they do a prototype, they do it in a complicated, expensive way, using lots of 3-D modeling and other techniques that are inappropriate at such an early stage. A theoretical prototype gives you a cheap and easy way to "test" and adapt solution concepts with customers. Generally when you talk to customers about the jobs to be done, you will use a theoretical prototype (or sometimes a hyper rapid virtual prototype) as a straw man for the conversation. At the point when you're getting enthusiastic, positive responses to your theoretical prototype from potential customers, you're ready to create a virtual prototype.

Virtual Prototypes

Several decades ago, IBM wanted to test an unusual solution to a common customer problem: transforming spoken words into type. A team of computer scientists and executives envisioned highly sophisticated voice recognition software that would transform dictation into text. In addition to the core software, the solution would require high-quality microphones and an adaptive algorithm to parse differences in dialect and diction. Although the technical risk seemed high, the team believed that if it could overcome the technical challenges, it would solve a huge customer problem.

But before it made a big investment, how could IBM test whether customers cared about the solution? At a minimum, it seems that some primitive beta software would be needed to test whether the solution would be worth building. Instead, the IBM team hung a sheet across a room, and, when the customer spoke, a hidden typist on the other side of the sheet captured what was said and projected it on a computer screen for the customer to see. Essentially IBM "pretended" to have the solution to answer the question, "Do customers care?"[8] Like IBM and the Google Glass team, most successful managers use *virtual prototypes* (VPs)—"pretend-otypes"—to answer key questions while avoiding the costs of developing expensive, unwanted solutions.

To develop a VP, ask yourself a simple question: If I had to sell the solution today, how could I fake it in a way that feels realistic? The answer should be a good guide for what you could develop and how fast. Our favorite VPs use PowerPoint, sketches, off-the-shelf components, or other mock-up tools. For example, PowerPoint can mimic software by creating invisible click-through hot spots to quickly simulate what might take months in development. Similarly, Kaiser Permanente faked various service innovations through a combination of storyboards and rehearsed service simulations. One observer said, "There's something magical about low-fidelity ways of trying something out. It automatically allows people to feel like they can put their fingerprint on it. The more polished, the more people feel like it's already done."[9]

Whatever tool you use—including advanced tools like 3-D printers, video, or flash demos—remember that all prototypes should be designed to answer specific questions. Your VP will likely be an imperfect representation of the product, but the goal is to start answering your key questions, or hypotheses, about what customers want. By doing only the minimum to get feedback on the most relevant uncertainty you face, you speed up your learning and preserve your flexibility. The ability to learn quickly through prototypes (especially VPs) may be your most important advantage over slower rivals. In the words of one innovator, "A chess novice can defeat a master if moving twice each round."[10]

Minimum Viable Prototypes

When someone at social gaming giant Zynga has an idea for a new game, no one starts the process by building the game. Instead, the team members boil the idea down to five words and perform a smoke test, as described in chapter 4, to see whether there is any customer interest. For example, suppose someone has an idea for a game about running a hospital. She would put up a low-cost ad on a high-traffic web page that simply says, "Ever fantasize about running a hospital?" The users who click on the link receive a brief description of the theoretical prototype and are told they will receive an e-mail when development is complete.

If the ad produces enough response, Zynga designers then spend a week or less building a minimal, stripped-down version and launch it to the e-mail list. Then they see what they can learn about the solution: How many users sign up, how long they play, what features they like, what they hate, and so on.[11] This one-week test, or what has been called a *minimum viable prototype* (MVP), helps them learn crucial lessons about what customers actually want and guides them in deciding whether to perform another iteration or go explore different ideas.

A minimum viable product has been defined as a product having the minimum feature set required to work as a stand-alone product while still solving a "core" problem (we use the word *prototype* rather than *product* as used by Eric Ries in *The Lean Startup*, to emphasize that your objective is to test your assumptions rather than build a product).[12] You build an MVP to rapidly test which features are most likely to drive customer purchases. It's like an exercise in archery: your goal is to hit the bull's-eye features that drive purchases and put other features on the back burner. Why? It's easy to be swamped with feature ideas that could add value. Adding features feels as if it will increase the chances customers will like the product, but actually it can decrease customers' ability to recognize how your solution solves *their* problem (see "Don't Forget to Go Narrow"). Worse, you waste time building features that don't motivate customers to purchase. You may not fully identify the bull's-eye in the beginning, so use the VPs and MVPs to identify those features that matter most to customers. At first, the process may feel haphazard and random. But remember that you can use many MVPs to test minimal feature sets, as quickly as you can, to get multiple points of useful feedback from target customers.

Don't Forget to Go Narrow

When the cofounders of an educational software company first met with the chief technology officer at the University of Southern California, his feedback on their beta product seemed fairly positive. Earlier conversations with other faculty and university officers had established a significant problem with existing learning management software. But to get a sense of how well they were solving the problem, members of the team showed the CTO their minimum viable prototype: essentially an inexpensive flash-based version of the software that highlighted the top twenty features they believed would be most valuable for educators. Then they asked a critical question: "How much would you be willing to pay for a solution like this?" Despite the CTO's early enthusiasm, his response—$2,500 per year—dimmed their hopes of building a sustainable business.

But before leaving the room, they tried a tool we recommend called the $100 R&D game.[13] You ask customers to allocate $100 of an R&D budget to the features they most want. When the developers asked this question, they were surprised that the CTO allocated $80 to a simple drag-and-drop feature and then split the remaining $20 between two other features, a pattern repeated in visits to other universities.

Using this data, the team crafted a new flash prototype and returned to the first CTO, this time with a minimum viable prototype that contained only three features, the most prominent being the drag-and-drop feature. What does your intuition tell you about how the CTO responded to the stripped-down prototype? In fact the CTO liked the product more and offered to license the product for $12,500 per year. By focusing on the minimum feature set, the team sold an early product with only one-tenth the features for five times the original expected price.[14] Throughout the book we emphasize the importance of diverging and going broad first, but as you develop MVPs, don't forget to converge and go narrow to really nail the solution.

In addition, rather than add many features to a single prototype, it's a good idea to develop several prototypes that emphasize different key features, and see how customers react (see "Won't an MVP Hurt My Brand?"). Even testing a solution missing the key feature has power. Remember, the goal is to learn, and it's easier to learn when you're testing fewer dimensions in a single MVP. One team we worked with tested a medical device lacking the key feature they felt added value (which was also slowing FDA approval) and discovered an entirely new market that didn't actually want that "critical" feature.

Won't an MVP Hurt My Brand?

Some folks are concerned that offering a low-fidelity MVP to the market might damage the company's brand. For products in mature categories where customers have a developed understanding of the product and clear expectations (conditions of lower uncertainty), it's true that MVPs can be dangerous because customers will demand what Geoffrey Moore calls "the whole product solution."[15] But when companies launch new products that are not well understood, they're often adopted first by innovators who have lower expectations and are more forgiving of an MVP. Therefore, when you test your MVP with a sample of customers, you can get away with a minimal prototype. Of course, you will be embarrassed about it. In fact, as Eric Ries argues, if you're not embarrassed, you've done too much work. You didn't develop an MVP.

To help allay this concern, we recommend several tactics. First, create a separate brand or sub-brand that clearly communicates the preliminary status of the product. For example, Intuit launches all MVPs with the "Intuit Labs" brand, and Google uses "Google Labs."

Second, flip the liability of testing an MVP on its head by providing higher levels of service and satisfaction for the MVP test. For example, when Samsung launched an experimental refrigerator in Southern California, it offered customers a hotline with white-glove service (the company would replace the fridge and all its contents within twenty-four hours if something went wrong). An acquaintance actually participated in this experiment, and his fridge had a problem. He told us, "They responded so well to my problem that I'm only going to buy Samsung products from here on out."[16]

And remember, you are testing the MVP with a sample of customers and not the entire population. You may think of a sample in terms of limited geography (e.g., a particular town), type of customer (e.g., early adopters), or a limited number of customers.

Minimum Awesome Products

Once you have a minimum viable prototype and have validated your core assumptions, your next step is to develop something that customers cannot resist, something that customers love, something awesome. We first heard the term *minimum awesome product* (MAP) while spending an afternoon observing Intuit's globally broadcast training session for all the product designers, developers, and user-interface architects in the company. The training was focused on a single issue: What is "awesome"?

Intuit had presented lean start-up training, and everyone was familiar with the concept of a minimum viable product. However, founder Scott Cook was uncomfortable with some aspects of the concept. "When you say 'minimum viable product,' engineers naturally focus on the word *product*. So they want to jump to building a product," says Cook. "At the early stages of a new product idea, we want our engineers to just be experimenting, answering their leap-of-faith hypotheses."[17] We agree with Cook, and that's why we prefer to substitute the word *prototype* for *product* in our use of the term *minimum viable prototype*. But once the MVP has revealed which features are most likely to drive a customer purchase, it's time to go beyond viable and reach for awesome.

The goal of a minimum awesome product is to deliver a solution that is so extraordinary on the most important dimension that it inspires positive emotion in your customers. As Scott Cook explains, "You don't want to be *viable* in the dimension that matters—you want to be *awesome* in the dimension that matters, all while maintaining an uncomfortably narrow focus." In other words, you want to identify the minimum feature set possible and then relentlessly focus on making your solution awesome on those dimensions. But what is awesome? And how do you get there?

Customers describe products as awesome when they inspire positive emotions, such as creating deep satisfaction, calming anxiety, or giving confidence. Often "awesome" solutions do unexpected things that inspire positive emotion. When a product or service surprises you by doing something you didn't expect—something you may not have even thought was possible—it can evoke positive emotion and prompt you to say, "That is awesome!"

Apple has often achieved awesomeness in this way. When the first iPod launched, customers said, "Wow! I can really carry my whole library of songs with me everywhere I go. That is awesome." When the first iPhone launched, many customers said, "Wow! I can do this (listen to music, take a photo, find an address, etc.) on my phone. That's cool."

Steve Jobs was known to say that Apple's job was not to give custom-ers what they wanted. It was to give them what they didn't know they wanted (or needed). That's when you evoke positive emotion.

Of course, that's a high hurdle. What if the product just nails the job-to-be-done perfectly but doesn't do it in an unexpected way? For example, Dyson vacuums are touted as having "twice the suction of any other vacuum." Can better suction really create positive emo-tion? The answer: absolutely. But the solution must be noticeably bet-ter than alternative solutions (and of course, the customer must care about suction). The solution evokes positive emotions because the cus-tomer is surprised by how much better the offering is than competitive offerings.

To illustrate, Intuit identified what it thought was a problem for a large group of Americans: simple tax filers struggling to fill out their com-plicated tax forms. One thing Intuit learned from early experiments—using theoretical and virtual prototypes—was that simple filers often had trouble figuring out which information from their W-2 statement to plug in to their tax form. (For tips on getting the most from your experi-ments, see "How to Run a Good Experiment.") So the Intuit designers tested an MVP that let filers take a photo of their W-2 form with their cell phone or camera and upload it to their computer; then the software pulled the data from the W-2 into the right location on the tax form. Tests showed that filers loved the idea of taking the photo and having the data magically appear at the right location. But they didn't like the ensuing steps of uploading it to their computer, because it was both time-consuming and complex. "Why can't I just take the picture of the W-2 and finish my taxes on my phone?" many asked.

Intuit listened, creating a prototype that took the W-2 photo, plugged the data into a tax app, and quickly completed the taxes (after asking the user a few basic questions) on the smart phone. This dra-matically cut the time and complexity of tax preparation for the simple filer. Initial tests revealed that the app, dubbed SnapTax, let simple filers take the photo and finish and file their taxes in less than ten minutes (something Intuit touted in ads). That was unexpected. And it evoked strong positive emotional responses from users. One early user of SnapTax gave it a five-star rating, gushing that it was so easy to use he literally completed his taxes during a Valentine's Day date. The couple were so happy to be finished with their taxes they had one of their best dates ever. Can you imagine a tax preparation product inspiring that kind of a response from a user?

To develop a minimum awesome product, Intuit focused on simple filers (some 59 million people), identified the key pain points, and then persisted in searching for a solution to that pain in an unexpectedly easy way. Of course, minimum awesome products start out as satisfactory MVPs. In fact, with the first smart phone version of SnapTax, more than 90 percent of users abandoned the app after three touches on the phone. Why? It was because "the first screens required people to create an account with name, password, et cetera," says SnapTax product development head Amir Eftekhari. "But users just wanted to check out the app to see how it worked. They didn't want to create an account."[18] So Intuit redesigned the app so that within three touches, users could see the three steps to complete their taxes and capture a photo of their W-2 to start the process. Account setup, and payment, wasn't necessary until the user was ready to file—but that was typically within ten minutes. The point is that you use the MVPs to quickly improve those dimensions of your solution that can inspire emotion—and turn your MVP into an MAP—a Minimum Awesome Product.

As you refine your prototype, remember that your customers are hiring your solution to do a job for them—and that every job has functional, social, and emotional dimensions. Your solution may inspire awesome by doing the unexpected on any of these three dimensions of the job. But beware: it can be difficult to be awesome to everyone. Stay "uncomfortably narrow" as you build your minimum awesome product.

How to Run a Good Experiment

Most people believe they understand experimenting, but when we teach executives and students, 90 percent of the time they get it wrong at first. What are the mistakes they make?

- **No hypothesis or metrics.** Don't conduct an experiment without a clear hypothesis or without defining how you will measure what you learn.

- **Wrong tools.** Don't rely on focus groups. They tend to get stuck in groupthink. And avoid starting with surveys. You don't yet know what questions to ask.

- **Bad samples.** Make sure you talk to a relevant sample of customers. Often experimenters pick the wrong people (for convenience), or they talk to everyone (the population). Also, don't reformulate your solution between every conversation; wait for a pattern to emerge, and then reformulate.

In contrast, good experiments test the most important assumptions quickly, reliably, and affordably on a relevant customer sample. And they measure the results. Consider the following simple experiment at Intuit. The finance operations team wanted to retain small-business subscription customers whose credit cards were about to expire. It had been sending e-mails to these customers, but a large percentage didn't respond and when credit cards lapsed, the income stream from a customer was typically lost. So the team, looking for a better way, wanted to verify that customers were receiving the e-mails and whether the e-mails were effective at triggering a response. "The idea was to call customers to see if they had received our communication and get them to take action immediately, instead of putting it off—small-business people are busy folks who forget about things that aren't urgent," said Wendy Castleman, an Intuit innovation catalyst. So the team ran an experiment to test the hypothesis that many customers weren't getting Intuit's e-mail. When team members called a dozen customers selected because they represented different customer segments, they discovered that about a quarter had an outdated e-mail address and weren't getting the e-mails. Others didn't feel the urgency with an email communication. The team then tried another experiment: they hired a small team of temp workers to call businesses as their credit cards came due for renewal. The new communication process resulted in more than $8 million in recovered revenues in FY2013.

This experiment quickly tested a clear hypothesis, using customer behavior as the data, with clear metrics of success. Although this experiment worked out, Intuit has conducted hundreds of experiments in which the team quickly learned what doesn't work and why, and pivoted to explore other ideas.

Have You Nailed the Solution? Three Tests

Using virtual prototypes and MVPs can be an illuminating but ambiguous process. How do you know if you have it "right," the kind of solution where people say, "Wow, they really nailed it"? There are a few tests we recommend that you can use to "nail it, then scale it" rather than the other way around.

The Wow Test

If you're in the early days of theoretical or virtual prototypes, we recommend the *wow test* to measure how excited customers are about your solution. The wow test has two parts. First, qualitatively, when you show customers your prototype, can you see their enthusiasm, or are they only being polite? If you can't see the enthusiasm in their faces or hear it in their voices, then you probably need to make a change.

Second, quantitatively, ask customers, on a scale of 1 to 10, how excited would you feel to own the solution (10 being "extremely excited" and they're ready to buy the solution, and 1 being not at all excited)? You should be aiming to improve the wow score over time, shooting for an average greater than 7. Anything significantly lower than 7 may suggest customers are only being polite and you need rethink your solution.[19]

The NPS Test

Once you have an MVP or MAP that customers can start using, you can apply the promoter test. There are a few variants on this test, our favorite being the net promoter score (NPS). Recall that NPS is based on a single question: how likely are you, on a scale of 1 (not at all likely) to 10 (extremely likely), to recommend this product or service to a colleague or friend? "Promoters" answer 9 or 10, "passives" answer 7 or 8, and "detractors" answer from 1 to 6. A company's (or product's) NPS is the percentage of promoters minus the percentage of detractors (see figure 5-5).

Your ultimate goal is to score 9 or higher with your core customer group. But you won't start there, so don't get discouraged. Instead, use the prototypes we've discussed to iterate there. When 80 percent or more of your core customers rate a solution 9 or 10 and your average NPS is higher than 60 percent, then you've not only nailed the solution but also created evangelists for your product. Notice, too, that we said "core" customer group, and not all your customers: one of your greatest challenges is to stay narrowly focused on a customer group. Ten customers may ask you for dozens of features that can pull you in multiple directions. As mentioned earlier, if you try to please everyone, you will

FIGURE 5-5

Net promoter score

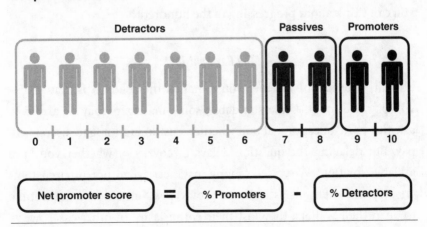

never nail the solution or turn your customers into evangelists. As you get feedback on your prototypes, look for the themes that segment customers into groups based on the functional, social, and emotional dimensions of the job-to-be-done, and then remove some customers from your focus (tell yourself you'll serve them later). For example, when Google engineer Paul Buchheit was building a prototype of Gmail he was told to find one hundred "happy" users. "I was like, 'Oh, that's easy, Google has like thousands of employees,'" said Buchheit.

> But it turns out that happiness is a really high bar, and to get people to say they're happy is actually sort of challenging. We literally did it one user at a time. We would go to people and ask, "Okay, what's it going to take to make you happy?" And in some cases they would ask for something really hard, and we'd be like, "Okay, well, you're not going to be happy with Gmail, quite possibly ever." But with other people it turned out there would be something really small we could do and then they'd be happy. So we'd do the really easy things until we got 100 people who were happy. And 100 doesn't sound like a lot but it turns out people are pretty similar to each other so if you can make 100 happy, you can usually make more [happy].[20]

So start by shooting for a 9 or 10 NPS score with ten people, and then you can think about progressing to the hundredth.[21]

The Payment Test

The ultimate test of whether you've nailed the solution is that people will pay you for it. Understandably, some managers may be afraid to ask the hard questions about whether customers (or end users) will pay. But delaying the question delays discovery of whether you have a viable solution. We've seen many instances when potential customers responded enthusiastically to prototypes, but when it came time to open their wallets, they lost their enthusiasm. In other cases, we've seen customers prepay for a product that doesn't yet exist. In one of our favorite examples, Coin (a single card device that stores multiple credit cards) presold millions of cards that weren't delivered until a year later. In truth, its story is nothing special: crowd-funding—which resulted in more than $5 billion in transactions in 2013—employs a form of the payment test in which funders prepay for an item.[22]

At the core, the payment test involves asking customers to pay for your solution, whether or not you actually collect the money. In most cases you conduct the payment test during the MVP stage or later. During the test, you need to get a credible commitment from customers. Just asking customers whether they will pay yields weak results. Actual behavior counts. For example, Intuit gives testers of its prototypes the opportunity to preorder or purchase using a credit card. After testers enter the first four numbers, a message pops up saying their contact information has been registered and they'll be contacted to purchase the product after it has passed final testing.

At this point, we should clarify a critical point: we are not asking you to go out and sell. Although that may sound contradictory, selling often reinforces a one-way communication pattern that shuts down your openness to feedback. Rather, when you conduct the payment test, keep in mind you're actually seeking customers' feedback. If your customer prepays, wonderful! But if customers hesitate or stall, then view that as a good outcome, too: it gives you the opportunity to directly ask customers what is still missing from the solution.

Don't wait too long to apply the payment test, because it's the ultimate test of whether your solution does the job. We've heard too many stories from managers who delayed the payment test, only to realize much later that their solution was neither viable nor awesome.

A Solution Process Template

To map the process you'll use to nail the solution, consider applying the solution process template shown in figure 5-6. The template reflects the approach we've suggested, starting with a solution-storm that generates a wide range of solutions. Then select several solution options to rapidly

FIGURE 5-6

Solution process template

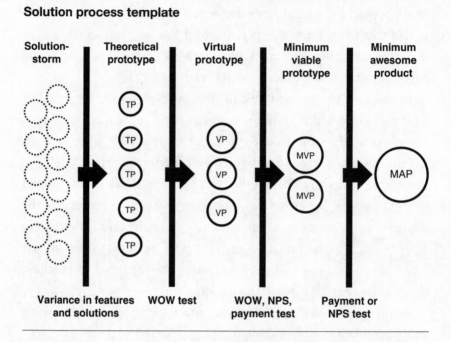

test with customers using theoretical prototypes. Then use the wow test to identify which solutions attract the most attention. Next, develop at least three virtual prototypes that embody different aspects of the solution, and test them with customers. Eventually you will converge to one virtual prototype using the tests described here, and you can develop it into a minimum viable prototype. Once you reach the MVP stage, you should use the NPS or payment test to determine which key features to highlight and perfect as you iterate your way to a minimum awesome product.

Watch Out: Don't Get Trapped by Your Capabilities

Large companies develop core competencies that are key to their success. And executives are often encouraged to stick to their knitting—to apply the competencies that got the company to where it is now. But large companies that stick to their knitting face a big watch out. Although there are a handful of companies that have strayed from their core competencies and failed, there are mountains of cases in which companies, in times of uncertainty, stuck to their knitting and missed a huge opportunity or were killed by innovation.

Going beyond your current competencies is important for another reason: people typically develop new solutions by combining technologies and ideas from different fields. This means that a broad search typically outperforms a narrow search in generating solutions. While it feels more efficient to search narrowly within the company, it tends to result in incremental solutions that don't delight customers. Searching a broad range of technologies and firms (possibly through alliances) is critical for large companies if they hope to solve new problems and enter new markets. Amazon is one of the few large companies we know that has developed a broad range of technologies internally—and with other firms in partnership—that it draws on to generate solutions to help it enter new businesses.

Getting to Awesome

Some 90 percent of initial proposals don't nail the solution to a significant problem. This explains why it's folly to start by building a product or service before you've discovered how it falls short. It also explains why it's important to know how to test many options by using prototypes. Adopting solution-storming and prototyping will minimize your investment, accelerate your learning, and allow you to test the assumptions that can kill your idea. We encourage you to use the cycle of searching broadly and then creating theoretical, virtual, and minimum viable prototypes, along with a minimum awesome product, to test your hypotheses and answer crucial questions. Remember to design your prototypes to answer specific questions and to use clear metrics to assess them. Embrace the freedom of using prototypes to validate your solution as the key to success under conditions of uncertainty.

6

Business Model: Validate the Go-to-Market Strategy

The scale and speed at which innovative business models are transforming industry landscapes today is unprecedented.

—Alexander Osterwalder and Yves Pigneur,
Business Model Generation

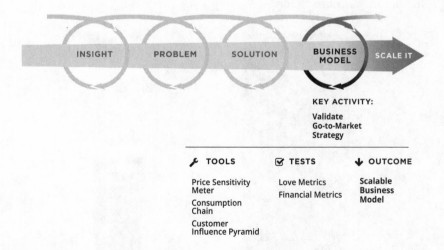

ODREJ & BOYCE MANUFACTURING is a 115-year-old company that sells consumer goods in India, most notably household appliances. For years it succeeded by bringing technologies developed abroad, such as refrigeration, to the wealthiest segment of the population. But as low-cost competitors from elsewhere in Asia entered India, Godrej's market share began to erode rapidly. As company leaders looked for ways to respond, they discovered a surprise that had the kernel of a problem worth solving: 80 percent of Indian households lack refrigeration. As a company run for more than a century according to the best B-school thinking, it immediately leapt to developing solutions. As Navroze Godrej, director of special projects, recalls, "We imagined we would be making a shrunken-down version of a refrigerator. Make it smaller, make it cheaper. And we had preconceived notions of how to build a brand that resonated with these users through big promotions and fancy ad campaigns" (see figure 6-1).[1]

The Godrej team, with the help of Innosight (an innovation consulting firm cofounded by Clayton Christensen), quickly learned the error of a solution-first approach and instead decided to first try to understand the problem. To start, team members traveled all over India and

FIGURE 6-1

Initial refrigeration vision

Source: "ChotuKool: An Innosight Impact Story," Innosight, 2013.

were shocked by how wrong their initial guess had been. As Navroze Godrej recalled, it was a "long and fascinating journey. We were surprised by many things, we were shocked by many things."[2] As they talked to customers they realized that women managing households in rural India faced many challenges. One was that they could not store food, so they had to buy and prepare it every day, something that was time-consuming and expensive. Moreover, most potential customers had intermittent power, and that would rule out a standard refrigerator like they initially imagined. Furthermore, if the refrigerator broke down, the cost of repair would likely be prohibitive, because there were few local repair shops or servicers, especially in rural areas. As Navroze Godrej recalled, "[W]ith all this information we realized our original hypothesis was quite wrong. We knew we couldn't just repackage and reconfigure an existing refrigerator and just pass that off."[3]

Based on their understanding of the customers' jobs to be done, the team decided to tackle the problems faced by lower-income women. As they explored solutions, they tested a number of virtual prototypes and minimum viable prototypes and discovered the crucial features for any solution. For example, the customer group they were targeting needed much less space than that found in a traditional refrigerator. The target customer simply couldn't afford to buy, and store, large amounts of food. They also learned that the refrigerator needed a battery to operate during power outages, and given the 90 degree or higher heat in some regions of India, it would be critical to minimize cooling loss when the door was opened.

So the team iterated to a solution more akin to a cooler: the chotuKool opened at the top, preventing cold air loss, and cooled by using solid-state thermoelectric technology rather than the familiar refrigerator coolant. Furthermore, they placed all components, including the battery, in the lid so that they could easily be removed for servicing (see figure 6-2).

Because the team appeared to have nailed the problem and solution, most companies would assume it had succeeded and would assimilate the product into its existing business model—its approach

FIGURE 6-2

Prototypes of the chotuKool

Source: "ChotuKool: An Innosight Impact Story," Innosight, 2013; and G. Sunderraman, "ChotuKool: Innovating at the Bottom of the Pyramid," *Japan International Cooperation Agency*, 2010.

to communicating with and capturing value from customers. Unfortunately, such an assumption often kills innovations. For example, Godrej originally assumed that it could simply "launch the product the way we used to with a big advertising campaign."[4] But as team members talked to customers, they realized that for their women customers, their local community and support groups played a much more powerful role in their purchasing decisions. If the chotuKool team was to succeed in convincing women to buy the product, it needed to find out how to communicate with these women.

The team conducted a number of business model experiments. In one test of the business model, it "launched" the new chotuKool (which means "little cool" in Hindi) at a village fair attended by more than six hundred women and the local support groups. It was in the discussions at the fair that the team discovered how best to communicate with this customer segment (which message, which channels). They also discovered that, given the low household incomes among their target customers, the price of chotuKool would probably need to be less than $50 USD—and even then a large percentage would need financing.

This pricing constraint meant that the traditional appliance supply chain (which had been operating for fifty years) did not work well for distributing a low-cost, low-margin product to customers in rural areas having few appliance stores. The team experimented with several approaches, talking to as many people and experts as possible to find ways to solve the problem. Finally, the team had a breakthrough when G. Sunderraman, Godrej vice president and leader of the chotu-Kool project, sat next to a university vice chancellor on an airplane. As Sunderraman talked to the vice chancellor about obtaining application forms for his youngest son, the university official pointed out that Sunderraman could get the forms at any post office. The next day, when Sunderraman went to the post office and asked for the forms (which the post office offered for a fee), what surprised him was the helpful clerk, who then promoted several other universities and their accompanying application forms.

It dawned on Sunderraman that the post office—which had offices in every area of rural India—might be an ideal distribution channel for chotuKool. In further discussions in the field, the Godrej team also learned about the central importance of the post officer in rural villages, where the postal representative is treated like a trusted friend and may even be invited into the house for tea. At this moment the team realized that it could effectively turn postal officers into the sales channel and leverage the post office to create an entirely new distribution chain, which, in combination with a novel microfinancing scheme, would allow Godrej to distribute, sell, and make money from chotuKool, all while improving the lives of local villagers.[5]

The chotuKool story shows that even after nailing the problem and the solution, the team's job was not finished. They had to develop the business model that would allow them to successfully take the solution to market. In this chapter we will focus on how to validate the unique go-to-market strategy for your innovation projects.

Validate Each Component of the Business Model

The term *business model* refers to a firm's overall strategy for delivering value to—and capturing value from—customers. The most important dimension of a business model is the solution—the value proposition—that a firm offers to a target segment of customers. Once you've nailed the solution to an important problem for a particular group of customers, you're ready to test and validate the other critical components of a business model to build an effective, data-driven go-to-market strategy.

Several tools are available to help you think through the dimensions of a business model. One of our favorites is the Business Model Canvas template, developed by Alex Osterwalder and Yves Pigneur. The template shows nine business models components, starting with the value proposition. We highly recommend these authors' excellent book *Business Model Generation* for a deeper exploration.[6] From our experience and research we've identified six business model components—a subset of the template—that you need to validate when you're taking your value proposition to market. We refer to this as a business model *snapshot* (see figure 6-3).

The six components of the business model snapshot are as follows.

1. *Value proposition (solution).* What is the solution that you're offering to provide value to your target customer segment?

FIGURE 6-3

Business model snapshot

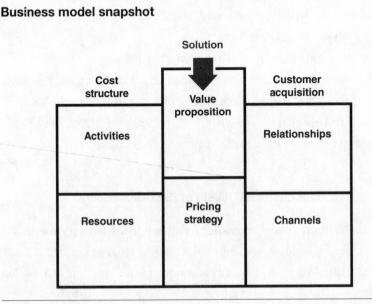

(The value proposition emerges from your earlier efforts to nail the problem and solution.)

2. *Pricing strategy.* How should you price your solution to optimize revenue streams and generate profits? How much are customers willing to pay? How do they prefer to pay?

3. *Customer acquisition: relationships.* How can you communicate with and convince your target customers that they need your solution?

4. *Customer acquisition: channels.* How do you make it easy for customers to access your solution? Through which channels do your target customers most want to be reached?

5. *Cost structure: activities.* What key activities do you, or your partners, need to perform well in order to deliver your solution?

6. *Cost structure: resources.* What resources or assets are most critical for delivering your solution?

Fortunately, once you've developed an awesome solution, you know the value proposition you want to offer. Now you're ready to explore and validate the other five components. We recommend starting with pricing strategy so that you can figure out your customers' willingness to pay and the kinds of revenue streams you will likely generate to cover your costs.

The next step is to figure out your customer acquisition and education strategy and the channels you will use. Succeeding here requires a deep understanding of the customer consumption chain (described later). Then you turn to figuring out which activities are most critical. These activities may be conducted internally or with partners. You also need to determine which resources (assets such as brands, patents, installed base, physical locations, plant and equipment, etc.) are most important and how you can effectively access or build them.

The emergent chotuKool business model snapshot would look something like figure 6-4. The chotuKool product required a different business model because it targeted a new customer—low-income women—with a value proposition that solved a significant problem. This new business model demanded a low price, paid either at purchase or under a microfinanced payment plan. It also required new customer acquisition, using women as a communication channel and the post office as a distribution and communication channel. Finally, it required new activities (low-cost manufacturing) and resources (solid-state thermoelectric cooling and batteries). The completed business model snapshot describes how chotuKool creates and captures value.

To underscore the importance of validating each of your assumptions with customers in a world of uncertainty, in launching the chotuKool, the team actually discovered a new customer segment: vendors of items like cold soda or chocolate in hot climates. Many sales have shifted to this new customer segment. Serving these customers uses some of the same resources but requires a new approach to customer acquisition.

FIGURE 6-4

ChotuKool business model snapshot

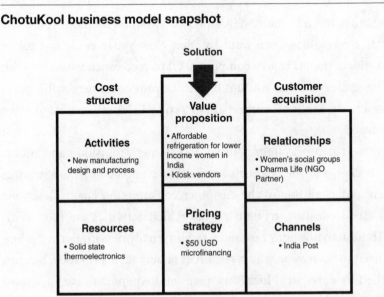

The business model snapshot is a template to capture your hypotheses: what you believe to be true about the business model. Writing down your hypotheses at the beginning, as at any other stage of the innovator's method, will help you focus on asking the right questions, running the right tests, and recognizing whether you've validated the assumption. Your goal should be a validated business model snapshot like the chotuKool example.

Nail Your Pricing Strategy

We recently advised a team that was developing wireless pulse oximetry socks, which allow parents to monitor their infant's breathing during the night in hopes of preventing tragedies like sudden infant death syndrome. The team members followed our process to identify the problem, first interviewing and observing nurses and mothers to understand the problem and then using a smoke test to gauge customer interest. In the smoke test, the team posted a video on its website describing how the product—which didn't yet exist—worked to see whether customers cared about the idea. By accident, the smoke test generated national media coverage, along with e-mails from more than five hundred parents asking to buy the product immediately. Convinced it had found a problem worth solving, the team started prototyping solutions, first using theoretical prototypes to discuss with experts and customers, then using virtual prototypes—simple drawings of the product—to show parents as they came out of stores like Babies 'R Us, and then finally minimum viable prototypes that they tested with infants and parents.

As the team members gained confidence that they were converging on a solution, they asked, "What price can we consistently charge?" As a first step, they sent a survey asking potential customers how much they would be willing to pay. Surveys are not the ideal way to figure out how to price a product, because buyers typically don't tell the truth about their willingness to pay. Because you're facing uncertainty, the sooner you can observe customer behaviors, the better. That being said, what people say they will pay gives you a starting point for your pricing hypothesis, and you can later observe their behavior. For the pulse oximetry socks, most survey respondents stated they would expect to pay around $100.

Unfortunately, given the estimated costs of production and the margin required by wholesalers and retailers, that price would leave little room to produce the device at a profit. Rather than give up, we suggested the team look at customers' actions, rather than their words, comparing what they actually pay for a product that solves a similar problem. So the team members drove to the nearest Babies 'R Us and checked the prices on baby monitors, finding that most were priced higher than $200. Furthermore, when they asked the store clerks which products sold in highest volume, the clerks reported that most parents bought the more expensive monitors. Intrigued, the team then called thirty-one other stores around the nation and found the same thing: most parents bought the more expensive baby monitors.

Using the information from the survey and the price comparison of close substitutes, the team then conducted a payment test experiment. On its website it listed the baby monitor at different prices (starting with higher prices and then moving to lower prices) and displayed a "Buy Now" button. When customers selected the button, they were told they would be put on a preorder list and notified when the product became available. Using data from this payment test, the team estimated the price elasticity of demand (how the number of purchases changes as the price changes) by observing customers' actions—their actual purchase behavior. The team learned that a price around $200 would maximize revenue streams while leaving plenty of margin for profit.

The Price Sensitivity Meter Tool

The team roughly followed a process that we recommend for testing your pricing hypothesis. The first step is to look at the price of current solutions that are the closest substitutes for yours. Potential customers will use those solutions as price reference points, and you can use these prices as a reference point for your initial pricing hypothesis.

Second, create a price sensitivity meter (PSM) using a customer survey to further refine your initial pricing hypothesis. Developed by Dutch economist Peter van Westendorp, a PSM lets you estimate optimal pricing by surveying target customers. We suggest a simplified version of the traditional PSM approach that involves two price-related questions:

1. At what price would you consider the product to be so expensive that you would not consider buying it? (Too expensive)

2. At what price would you consider the product to be priced so low that you would feel the quality couldn't be very good? (Too cheap)

The standard method requires that the percentage of respondents indicating a specific price is "too expensive" or "too cheap" are plotted as cumulative frequencies. Figure 6-5 shows a PSM analysis for

FIGURE 6-5

Price sensitivity meter

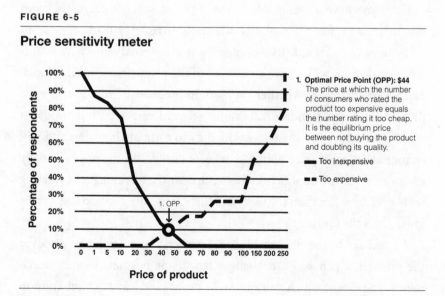

1. **Optimal Price Point (OPP): $44**
   The price at which the number of consumers who rated the product too expensive equals the number rating it too cheap. It is the equilibrium price between not buying the product and doubting its quality.

   — Too inexpensive

   ■■ Too expensive

the innovator's DNA self-assessment, an assessment of an individual's innovation and execution skills that was developed by Jeff Dyer and Hal Gregersen.[7] You graph the "too expensive" line by plotting the percentage of respondents who said a particular price was too expensive. The "too cheap" frequency is plotted starting at 100 percent of those who find a particular price too cheap and then eventually going down to zero at higher prices. The intersection of the two lines reveals the *optimal price point* (OPP). This is the price (in this case, $44) at which the number of consumers who rated the product too expensive equals the number rating it too cheap. It is the equilibrium price between customers' not buying the product and doubting its quality.

The bottom line is that a PSM analysis can give you a reasonable range of prices to test with your payment test and a proxy for your ultimate goal: discovering the demand curve where you can garner the greatest revenue and profit. In the case of the innovator's DNA assessment, the estimated optimal pricing was $44. Although this example is for product-based pricing, it can be done for subscription pricing, licensing, upsells, and so on.[8]

Once you have a reasonable range of prices, you conduct a payment test to validate your hypothesis. The pulse oximetry team conducted a payment test through its website, but it also tested simply by standing outside Babies 'R Us with pictures of the product, including prices, and asked customers whether they would preorder. If you do this with three sets of one hundred randomly selected target customers using three price points, you will have the data to estimate how demand will change at different price points, what economists call the *price elasticity of demand*. As you conduct the test, consider the advantages of starting with a price higher than the OPP and then gradually move to test a price lower than the OPP.

As you apply the pricing tool, remember you're trying to discover the price at which you can create a repeatable business model, which requires a price at which you can make profit (and leave extra margin in that price for the inevitable errors). So try to get a sense for what your costs will be at different levels of demand. But the point of the tool is to find an accurate way to develop and then test an appropriate pricing hypothesis.

Nail Customer Acquisition

Scott Cook generated the insight for Quicken, Intuit's first product, while sitting at his kitchen table while his wife complained about the hassle of manually keeping track of their finances. (The table is now at Intuit's headquarters, and Cook regularly sits there to meet with employees.) With an insight into a potential problem, Cook spent the next several months exploring the problem by discussing his hypothesis with potential users.

When he became convinced that easing the tasks of bill payment and personal finance was a big problem to solve, he partnered with Tom LeFevre to develop a solution. The duo did an excellent job of testing multiple prototypes with customers to nail the solution. For example, Cook famously lugged a computer to a meeting of the Junior League of Palo Alto and challenged the participants, many of whom had never used a computer, to write a check in less than fifteen minutes using his prototype software. Some users were so unfamiliar with computers that they had to be told where to find the Enter key. But when even these users were able to print a check using Quicken, Cook felt he had nailed the solution and was ready to take it to market.

At the time, consumer software was sold primarily in large retail outlets like CompUSA, and the typical customer acquisition strategy was to mount a big advertising campaign. With this typical model in mind, Cook went to venture capitalists in Silicon Valley to raise money. To his surprise, the venture capitalists turned him down. Even though initial tests showed that Quicken was far easier to use than other financial software solutions, the doubters pointed out that Quicken would be the forty-third financial software package in a crowded market.

Not dissuaded, Cook approached retail outlets directly. He recalls the ominous feeling as he approached the door of one store and noticed a large bin of software titles marked "90% Off" just outside the door. When he asked the retailer to sell Quicken, the manager simply pointed to the discount bin and said, "These were the titles I decided to sell."[9] Increasingly desperate, Cook tried to stir up PR for the new PC-based software and succeeded in generating several articles, but few sales resulted. Finally, as company funds dwindled, in a bid to sell some software Cook approached a friend at Wells Fargo about selling Quicken in its branches. Although this did generate some sales, it was not enough to cover costs, and soon Intuit's CFO approached Cook with the bad news: they had less than $100 in the bank. It was over.

Cook returned all the office furniture and, for desks, used pieces of plywood on top of stacked copies of Quicken. When the landlord began nosing around, asking why they didn't have furniture, Cook dodged the question, saying they were redecorating. Cook then tried, and failed, to place Quicken in more retail banks while LeFevre raced to code an Apple-based version of the software in hopes of selling a few more copies. The end of the company seemed imminent.

Then a surprising thing happened: when the Apple software hit the Wells Fargo branches, Cook started to get phone calls from customers wanting to buy the software. Surprised, he asked how they found out about it, and callers replied they had read about it in a magazine featuring new Apple software titles. Call by call, Cook pieced together what he and LeFevre had missed: although they had put a good deal of effort into promoting the PC-based version, most PC customers used their computers in their businesses. In contrast, people who wanted personal finance software used Apple computers at home. Furthermore, these users found out about, and were influenced to purchase, new software based on reviews in a few key software magazines.

With this deeper understanding of customers and their preferred way to learn about and purchase software, Cook scraped together $125,000 and ran a big advertising campaign in the Apple software magazines his target customers read. The phones soon rang off the hook, and Quicken quickly became the number 1 personal financial software in the United States.[10]

The Consumption Chain Tool

Intuit's experience is not unusual. Like Intuit, many companies develop an innovative solution to an important problem, but they have a hard time communicating and distributing the solution to customers. Because established companies already have a familiar business model, they often fail to realize that, for an innovative product, they often need a different business model—one that includes new ways to communicate with customers.

It's critical to develop a relationship with, and a channel to, customers. Success usually requires testing a number of messages, at different points in the consumption chain, with different channel options. Channel options include a direct-to-customer website or a sales force, distributors (such as pharmaceutical distributor McKesson), focused retailers (Wells Fargo, Best Buy, Zappos), mass merchandise retailers (Walmart, Amazon), original equipment manufacturers (such as General Motors), or value added resellers (e.g., system integrators like IBM and Accenture). Fortunately for Intuit, Cook was persistent in experimenting with different channels and different customer acquisition strategies. His initial guesses about the best channel to the customer were wrong—and it almost killed the company. But as he continued to test channel options, he developed a deeper understanding of how customers find out about, decide to use, and purchase personal finance software.

A tool that can be extremely helpful for understanding your target customer and developing a customer acquisition strategy is the *consumption chain*—a term popularized by Ian MacMillan and Rita McGrath.[11] The consumption chain is the series of steps through which customers pass from the time they first become aware of a need for your solution, to evaluating your solution (relative to others), to purchasing,

FIGURE 6-6

The consumption chain

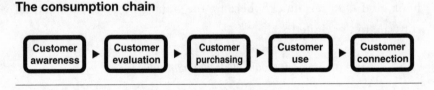

using, and even staying connected to it (see "Ten Questions to Ask about the Consumption Chain"). Products or services may have somewhat different consumption chains, some with more or less steps,[12] but in general five steps (awareness, evaluation, purchase, use, and connection) are common to all consumption chains (see figure 6-6).

Ten Questions to Ask about the Consumption Chain

To help you understand the factors that influence customer acquisition, here are ten questions you should ask.

Awareness

1. How do customers become aware of a need for your product or service? Is there a way to make it easier or more convenient for them to find your offering?

Evaluation

2. What is your product really used for? What job is the customer hiring your product to do?

3. What does the customer ultimately consider the most important features when making a final product selection? (If they had 100 points to allocate across all the features they consider important, how would they allocate them?)

4. Which influencers (reference customers, critics, experts, press, media, peers, direct referrals) are most likely to influence the customer's evaluation of your product?

Purchase

5. How do consumers order and purchase your product? Is there a way you can make it easier, less costly, or more convenient to buy? How is your product delivered? Can you do it faster, cheaper, or in a different way?

Use

6. What frustrations do your customers have when trying to use your product? Do they use your product in ways you didn't expect?

7. What do customers need help with when they use the product?

8. Do customers do things that hurt the longevity or reliability of your product?

9. How is your product repaired, serviced, disposed of? Are there opportunities to make this easier or more convenient (or teach the customer how to use the product so that it requires less maintenance, or do self-maintenance)?

Connection

10. How might customers connect to and promote your product? How could you leverage customers' connections to each other to influence parts of the consumption chain for your customers and noncustomers?

Scott Cook's experience with customer acquisition at Intuit illustrates the importance of understanding how target customers become aware of and evaluate new products, which lies at the heart of your unique go-to-market strategy for your innovation. Just getting Quicken into various channels wasn't enough. The consumption chain reminds you that you first need to generate awareness and favorable evaluation before you will acquire a single customer (see "The Customer Influence Pyramid" for more about how to create awareness, and positive evaluation, of your product through influencers).

Even if you have the right channel, it can be challenging to create awareness, positive evaluation, and purchase. Consider Merck, which launched a new serotonin reuptake inhibitor (SSRI), an antidepressant. In the crowded market, the new drug, although performing essentially the same task as Prozac via the same chemical mechanism, fared poorly, and initial revenues were disappointing. Merck returned to the drawing board to explore the customer need from the perspective of physicians who prescribe the product as well as consumers who felt depressed, worried, or anxious. Through extensive interviews with physicians and customers, the company learned that before the decision to prescribe or purchase, physicians as well as consumers associated certain products with certain labels. For example, Prozac was closely associated with the "depression" label. As a result, when patients came into the office complaining of depression, physicians often intuitively leaped to prescribing Prozac (in part because patients requested it based on the recommendations of friends and family).

In researching the consumption chain, the company also discovered that many consumers sought physician assistance for anxiety, rather than depression. Although SSRIs also help treat anxiety, the research revealed that the "anxiety" label was not clearly associated with any one particular product. Merck regrouped around the "anxiety" label, launching a new marketing and sales campaign describing the product as the "new" anxiety solution. Using the same channels, but a different communication strategy with the customer, sales leapt from tens of millions to billions of dollars.

What's more, sometimes you can't use an existing distribution channel. You need to create a new one, as Godrej did for chotuKool. But note that Godrej didn't create the distribution channel from scratch. Instead, it piggybacked on the activities and resources of the Indian post office. In other cases, companies have built their own distribution channels. For example, Cemex did this in the late 1990s when it discovered that its distributors were not effectively meeting the needs of its poorest customers. After adopting a radical approach to understanding customers—literally living with the poorest customers for several months—the Cemex team realized that customers didn't really want the solution it had been selling: bags of cement. Instead they wanted houses built with cement, which Cemex distributors either could not or did not want to provide (many distributors actually engaged in corrupt practices that damaged product quality). The Cemex team developed its own distribution channels to deliver cement, advice, and financing to customers—products and services that allowed customers to do the job of building a house. In this way, Cemex achieved significant growth in what had appeared to be an unattractive market.

The Customer Influence Pyramid

Most managers who have a marketing background understand that we rarely directly influence customers; their purchase decisions are influenced by many other forces. The customer influence pyramid complements the consumption chain by mapping influence forces.

The forces closest to the company represent those you have most control over, and those closest to the customer represent forces that have the most influence over the customer purchase decision. At the level closest to you, partners include channel partners, resellers, and complementors that sit on your side of the table and attempt to sell to customers. Although you have greater influence over their message, the message typically has less impact on customer purchases compared with other influences. For example, Godrej could have worked with appliance stores as partners in selling chotuKool, and

FIGURE 6-7

Customer influence pyramid

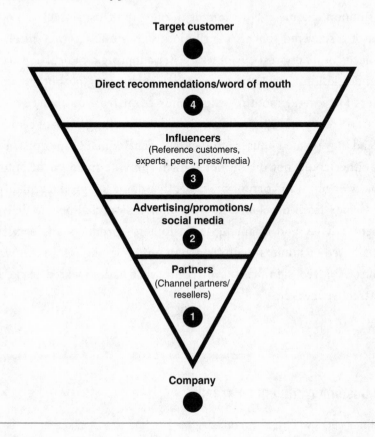

together they could have marketed the benefits of the product to customers, but this likely would have been less effective than getting respected women to be advocates.

Next, as a company you may construct marketing messages in the form of advertising, promotions, and social media blasts, but they typically have a modest influence on the customer purchase decision. We cannot cover the science of optimizing these campaigns, and it may be irrelevant; when you face uncertainty, the key idea is to understand what your customers pay attention to and the elements of the job-to-be-done (social, emotional, functional, etc.) that they want to accomplish. Using these two elements you can design a customer acquisition strategy that works because you target the customer's job-to-be-done in the channels they pay attention to.

Influencers can profoundly shape customer decisions. Influencers fall into four categories: *experts* such as product reviewers, thought leaders, or product evaluators; *peers* such as bloggers, customer reviews, and forum discussions; *media and press,* whose attention shapes customer perception; and *reference customers,* who create legitimacy and comfort with your solution in customers' minds. For Godrej, the key influencers proved to be prominent women in the local community—socially central individuals. For other companies, these influencers may be online or in the real world. For example, Skull Candy made a successful business of branding headphones and then sponsoring extreme athletes to wear them, thereby influencing other customers to buy them. Understanding and managing your influencers can be keys to success.

Everyone understands that word-of-mouth recommendations from someone you know and trust have the greatest influence on individual purchase decisions. Having a solution that delights customers is the best way to get word-of-mouth referrals. But you should explore different ways to create word of mouth using the principles we've discussed. For example, Dropbox relied on an intuitive but ultimately costly approach to acquire early customers, paying almost $300 on AdWords to capture subscribers, who ultimately paid only $100 in annual fees. As Dropbox experimented, it discovered it could more effectively acquire customers by offering current users free storage space to invite new users, a promotion that cost pennies on the dollar while increasing the virality of the solution.

As you try to acquire customers, pay attention to your customer acquisition costs. As a rule, customer acquisition costs should be less than one-third of customers' lifetime value, leaving plenty of room for the inevitably inaccurate assumptions one makes under uncertainty. As your innovation matures, you can move from simple metrics such as customer acquisition costs or virality to an optimization approach, measuring the funnel of customer acquisition, activation, retention, referral, and revenue.

Cost Structure: Key Activities and Resources

Once you've figured out your value proposition (solution), pricing strategy, and customer acquisition strategy, you're closing in on a scalable business model. The final challenge is to determine the right cost structure—the key activities and resources—for delivering your solution. *Key activities* are those processes the firm or its partners must engage in to operate successfully—from software design to manufacturing to product delivery or service. These are the activities that are most critical to delivering your value proposition. *Key resources* are those assets that are most important to your value proposition. They could be physical resources (land, plants, equipment), intellectual resources (brands, patents, databases), human resources (scientists, engineers, salespeople), or financial resources. Understanding your cost structure is critical, because if you can't figure out how to deliver your solution at a cost that is lower than the customer's willingness to pay, then you aren't ready to launch and scale your product.

Webvan, an online grocery-delivery start-up, represents a spectacular cautionary tale, having racked up losses of almost a billion dollars before flaming out after the dot-com crash. The Webvan team assumed there was proven demand for grocery delivery, so the Webvan team's plan was to replace the expensive brick-and-mortar grocery retailers with centralized distribution centers that delivered groceries to the customer's door. The company spent a billion dollars developing the distribution centers and networks, only to discover that it had made critical untested assumptions. For example, it assumed that the average customer order would be $100 and that it would generate enough orders to operate its expensive distribution centers at full capacity within three months of opening. But demand turned out to be much lower, orders were much smaller ($81 on average), and the real killer—delivery—ended up costing about $27 per order. In the end, executing on the plan rather than testing the overlooked uncertainties killed Webvan.

How could Webvan have tested the uncertainties about customer demand and the cost of delivery without investing the money? The answer: borrow, defer, or pretend rather than build the resources. Webvan could have partnered with local grocery stores to do the distribution as it figured out the actual sizes of customer orders (thereby validating demand). It could have experimented with various ways to most efficiently pick and deliver customer orders, thereby learning about the challenges of delivering ice cream on a 100-degree day during rush hour. At the very least, it would have learned the true cost of delivery. By leveraging the activities and resources of other firms to experiment with the cost structure—essentially making all of its costs variable instead of fixed—Webvan could have resolved key uncertainties about the cost structure before making huge fixed-cost investments.

Webvan didn't figure out, until after it spent the money on expensive resources, that its cost structure was too high for customer demand and willingness to pay. It's interesting that Amazon.com has recently moved into grocery delivery with the AmazonFresh service in the Seattle area. At this point it appears to be a limited experiment. But Amazon, as the largest online retailer, has now had years of experience in the activities of fulfillment: managing the supply chain, using robotics, picking inventory, packing products, and shipping. Amazon understands the activities required to be successful at grocery delivery in a way that Webvan could not.

Moreover, Amazon has critical resources that Webvan didn't have, including large fulfillment distribution facilities, equipment, a trusted brand, and employees who have deep knowledge of the technologies that are critical to effective fulfillment. It has even experimented with delivering products via drones. Even with all this going for it, Amazon is experimenting with the business model (in particular, the activities and resources required for efficient grocery delivery) before a full-scale launch. If anyone can make it a success, we expect AmazonFresh to have a serious chance.

Stay Variable, Stay Flexible

One of the first steps toward nailing your cost structure is to make a list of the key activities and resources and estimate the cost of each. Traditional management thinking would then encourage you to lower your per-unit costs by investing in fixed costs (investments such as buying custom injection molds, building a proprietary back end, or purchasing equipment). But fixed costs require more up-front capital and are naturally sensitive to volume, and that makes such investments more dangerous under conditions of uncertainty. We have seen many failed innovators make seemingly logical fixed-cost investments with their precious capital, only to discover demand was lower than expected. Hence, we strongly recommend flipping traditional financial logic on its head: take any fixed cost, and turn it into a variable cost as you experiment.

For example, an acquaintance wanted to launch a snack business, but rather than buy kitchen equipment he leased a kitchen at a restaurant during the off-hours. Only after building a significant revenue stream—when he had enough sales—did he build a multimillion-dollar factory, with cash, for nationwide expansion of the business. As you're testing your business model, if you have to lose some money on each unit sold to preserve your flexibility, it will be worth it in the short term. These are investments in learning. To judge when to accept higher variable costs, recall that the greater the uncertainty, the greater the value of the flexibility.

As a general principle, borrow, defer, or pretend wherever you can. Today, most of the capital-intensive equipment or service resources that companies formerly owned and paid for have become easy to access through outsourcing. For example, companies that need computing and server capacity can buy processing power and storage in the cloud from companies like Amazon rather than set up servers themselves. Manufacturing that used to be capital intensive can now be outsourced on a small scale to local flexible manufacturers or on a large scale to Asia.

IT and services can be outsourced to India, with an equally significant reduction in cost.

The trick is to defer costs while you resolve the uncertainty about which activities and resources are most critical to delivering your solution to customers. Rather than invest in facilities, equipment, leases, rentals, salaries, or any other expense, defer it as long as possible. Use every free tool (e.g., Google Docs, Skype, Quora) that you can find. Also consider outsourcing, crowd-sourcing, open sourcing, licensing, or substituting some component of the solution rather than developing it yourself.

Putting the Pieces Together: Business Model Snapshot Template Example

For an example of how to capture your initial hypotheses about your business model and then record your validated hypotheses, see the before and after snapshots for the chotuKool business model. Figure 6-8

FIGURE 6-8

ChotuKool business model snapshot hypotheses

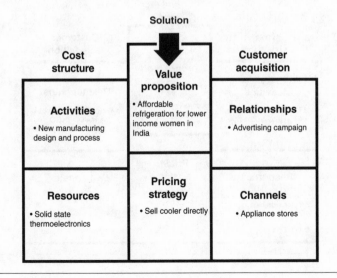

captures the starting hypotheses for the chotuKool, with the value proposition (and resulting resources and activities) being fairly clearly defined but with the pricing and customer acquisition elements being uncertain and in need of validation.

As the chotuKool team tested and validated elements of the business model, they were able to eventually validate their go-to-market strategy. Figure 6-9 shows the business model that eventually emerged from the experimentation and validation process. Notably, even at the late stage of discovering the business model, the chotuKool team discovered surprises to which they had to adjust. Most notably the chotuKool has turned out to be a perfect solution for kiosk vendors because of its extended cooling time, which can be supplemented with a car battery and is now being sold through NGO partners like Dharma Life, which empowers fledgling entrepreneurs to deliver products that improve the quality of life in rural India.

FIGURE 6-9

ChotuKool business model snapshot postvalidation

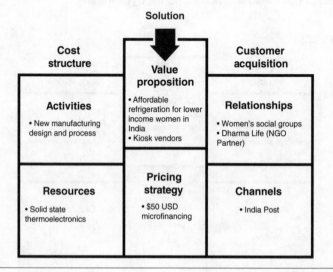

Watch Out: Don't Let Your Business Model Kill Innovation

Large companies love it when they can sell a new value proposition to (a) the same customer, (b) using the same pricing strategy, (c) through the same distribution channel, (d) using the same marketing messages and process, (e) leveraging the activities, capabilities, and resources they already have. In other words, companies always want to do the efficient thing. They want to take any new solution and apply the same business model, preferably in their existing business units.

The reason is that big companies are designed for execution, not searching for new opportunities. This is a big problem for innovation, and here's why. First, it means companies often refuse to consider developing a solution that doesn't fit the existing business model—and this means they miss many new growth opportunities.

Second, most business models have interdependencies among elements, and so if you change one or two, you often must make changes to other elements. For example, when Netflix first shipped DVDs by mail to customers they iteratively discovered and then optimized their business model. In particular, Netflix acquired resources such as distribution warehouses and specialized sorting equipment and developed capabilities for efficiently acquiring and allocating DVD inventory. When video on demand (VOD) first emerged, Netflix experimented with VOD as an add-on, and soon discovered the technology had greater capability and demand than initially predicted. But the new solution also required different resources: distribution warehouses were worthless in a VOD world as were many of their prior capabilities. To Netflix's credit, the executives recognized this and tried to create space for a new business model when they tried to split off mail order DVDs in the Qwikster business. By trying to organizationally divide those two business models into separate businesses, they initially confused and upset many customers. Although they perhaps could have handled the division better (Netflix's stock price dropped from over $300 to $50), in the long run separating the businesses has produced some advantages of being able to focus and align the business models to fit different customer profiles. Today over 75 percent of Netflix's business is VOD and their stock price is over $300. By contrast, Blockbuster, who ignored DVDs by mail and VOD for a long time because it conflicted with their business model eventually went bankrupt.

Large companies prefer to leverage rather than build, but that is a big watch out. As companies like Godrej, Intuit, Cemex, and others have discovered, the right business model for an innovation can be much different from what you expected—and different from your existing business model. Trying to force disruptive innovations into the existing business model will almost certainly destroy them. Don't be afraid to make room for new business models by creating new business units or by spinning off or even creating a separate business unit that incubates new business models themselves.

Making It Pay

It's crucial to nail the six components of the business model snapshot before you're ready to fully scale. As with each phase of the innovator's method, nailing the business model depends on generating explicit hypotheses, in this case about the optimal pricing strategy, customer acquisition strategy (customer relationships and channels), and cost structure (activities and resources), and then testing them by conducting experiments with customers. There are many ways to take your solution to market, so use your business model exploration to test various combinations of approaches. We provide more tips, templates, and tools online at www.theinnovatorsmethod.com to help you in this process.

7

Master the Pivot

I'm so glad you made this mistake. Because I want to run
a company where we are moving too quickly and doing
too much, not being too cautious . . . If we don't have any
of these mistakes, we're not taking enough risk.

—Larry Page, Google CEO, to a Google executive
who made a multimillion-dollar blunder

MAX LEVCHIN, COFOUNDER of PayPal, majored in computer science
during college, where he developed an intense interest in security
and encryption technology. Soon thereafter, Levchin wrote a software
package running on a PalmPilot to replace the handfuls of password-
generating devices that IT administrators carried around (one for each
secure computer or system). After receiving hundreds of downloads and
offers to develop more features for pay, Levchin moved to Silicon Valley
to pursue his emerging dream of starting a company offering compact
security software.

Shortly after arriving, he dropped in on an encryption technology
lecture at Stanford University. Only six people were there, so it wasn't
hard to start a conversation with Peter Thiel, a hedge fund manager
who was interested in using encryption technology to secure financial

transactions. The two immediately hit it off and soon started a company based on security software for handheld devices like the PalmPilot.

As Levchin and Thiel discussed what security product would have the biggest impact, they decided to create security software that would allow corporations to securely access their IT systems. But rather than develop programs themselves, they began developing security software libraries to be licensed by the coming wave of software developers. Levchin recalls thinking, "'Any minute now, there'll be millions of people begging for security on their handheld devices.' [But] it just wasn't happening."[1] So the team made a major change—a pivot. In the second version of the company, they offered to develop the security software themselves for corporate customers. Unfortunately, despite initial customer enthusiasm, no paying customers materialized. So they changed course yet again. They attempted to attract consumers by offering an electronic wallet that would store credit card numbers and passwords. Unfortunately, the electronic wallet largely solved a nonproblem, because pulling out a physical wallet was a simple (and often necessary) substitute.

This led to a fourth major change in strategy, with the team trying a different solution to a different problem: provide software that would allow a PalmPilot to store money that could be electronically beamed from one PalmPilot to another. This business idea caught the attention of leading venture capital (VC) companies in Silicon Valley, leading to PayPal's first round of financing. At Buck's, a favorite restaurant for many VCs, PayPal's investors showed up with $4.5 million preloaded on a PalmPilot, which they beamed to Levchin and Thiel's PalmPilot. PayPal seemed to be on its way.

PayPal's initial growth was rapid, with downloads reaching three hundred per day, but quickly leveled off because it was limited by the roughly three million handheld PDA users in the United States. As Levchin and Thiel considered options to expand the customer base, they observed that many customers wanted to sync their PalmPilots to their computers and send money through the internet to others having computers and PalmPilots. "We came up with the idea of attaching money to an e-mail," Thiel recalls. "Since there were 120 million e-mail users in the United States, this made it much more viral. You didn't have to meet face-to-face."[2] To test the idea, the team set up a website version of PayPal that included a demo allowing users to send money attached to an e-mail. Despite trying to use the website to push downloads on the technically sophisticated PalmPilot software, by early 2000 the team noticed a large amount of traffic from an unexpected source: users from a site called eBay began requesting use of the PayPal logo.

At first, the PayPal team felt that eBay sellers were scattered and disreputable and so pushed back. As Levchin recalls, "For a while we were fighting, tooth and nail, crazy eBay people: 'Go away, we don't want you.'"[3] But as website traffic continued to grow, the team began to ask themselves, "What if these are our real users?"

The team then made its fifth major change: for the next year it focused on the website, iterating like crazy to improve the site. The number of users exploded. So the team made perhaps its sixth major change: although the PalmPilot version software had attracted twelve thousand users, the website had attracted 1.5 million users, so the team shut down the PalmPilot software and became the company we know as PayPal, which was acquired a few years later by eBay for $1.5 billion.

Looking back on his experience, Levchin recalls that "the company was really not founded to do payments at all."[4] Even though Levchin may be one of the more famous and wealthy entrepreneurs in the world, his innovation started with a faulty guess—in fact, at least four major inaccurate guesses. And he is not alone, as evidenced by some of the other pillars of the modern economy. Microsoft started by selling programming compilers and not operating systems. Symantec developed artificial intelligence products and not antivirus software. Beyond technology businesses, the makers of Listerine tried to sell it as hospital antiseptic, floor cleaner, shampoo, and aftershave before finally succeeding as a mouthwash, and Play-Doh was originally sold as wallpaper cleaner before becoming one of the most widely recognized toys of all time.

Unfortunately, finding out that you're wrong is the very thing most corporations and most managers try to avoid—fervently. Inside and outside corporations, failures are often perceived as a mistake on the innovator's part for not being smart enough to foresee the problem. But this is exactly the wrong attitude. No one can foresee the problem when you face uncertainty. It's all a guess, and there's only one way to discover whether it's right or wrong: by testing it in the market. But because of our perceptions, most managers feel the pressure to avoid mistakes, and so they either do not innovate or try to make their first guess work, something you know by now is nearly impossible. Indeed recent research confirms that because many managers are afraid of making mistakes, established companies almost always delay until they miss the opportunity rather than pursue an opportunity and discover they were wrong.[5]

Our study of successful innovators tells us this: you should *expect* to be wrong much of the time when you operate under uncertainty. That is a fundamental part of the process and completely acceptable. The only failure is not failure itself, but failure to learn quickly enough that you were wrong.

When you do find out that you were wrong, you will need to change— or *pivot*. Many people understand the basic idea of making a change, but one of the big challenges facing any innovator is knowing when to pivot versus when to persist.

What Is a Pivot?

The word *pivot* has recently been popularized among entrepreneurs in the lean start-up movement to mean a specific type of change: as in basketball, to pivot means to adjust or change direction while keeping one foot planted.[6] The word helps you remember that you should accept change as a reality of dealing with uncertainty, but when you do change, keep one foot planted by using what you've learned rather than throwing it away. In pivoting, you change one dimension of your idea. The idea is to discover new insights that you would not have seen if you had changed multiple dimensions at once.

That said, for us the term *pivot* doesn't mean making minor changes to optimize your solution or refine your distribution strategy; that is iteration. You iterate after the data suggests that you've pretty well validated a problem, solution, or business model. In contrast, you pivot when you still haven't nailed the problem, solution, or business model so that you can try a new, more promising approach.

In some instances you want to pivot to a new problem, because the data from your experiments and prototypes reveals that the problem may not be worth solving or is beyond your skills. PayPal's early changes—from security software to an electronic wallet and finally to financial transactions—were pivots to a new problem. Levchin and Thiel discovered from early prototypes that the customer pain wasn't significant enough or the market was just too small.

You might also pivot on the right solution. PayPal's shift from PalmPilot-based to e-mail-based financial transactions was a solution pivot. The company was solving a similar customer problem but in a different way. Soon thereafter, they achieved "pivot takeoff" (we describe this shortly) with the PalmPilot product, and that confirmed it was targeting a problem worth solving. But the new computer-based solution opened the door to many more customers—anyone with access to a computer, as opposed to anyone with a PalmPilot. The change in solution also led to some changes in the business model—notably, target customers and distribution channel. The PalmPilot solution was targeted to higher-income business individuals and required distribution through PalmPilots—preferably having the software preloaded. In contrast, the computer-based solution was targeted primarily at online sellers and buyers, such as users of eBay. This shift required a different distribution strategy, with a focus on online buying and selling sites.

You may want to pivot to a new problem, a new solution (and new customer segments), or one of the key elements of your business model: pricing strategy, customer acquisition strategy (customer relationships or channels), or cost structure (activities or resources). Because of the interdependencies between each of these steps in the innovator's method, a *problem pivot* leads to changes in the solution and business model (except in the case when you try a solution for one problem and find it actually solves a different problem). A *solution pivot* often leads to changes in different components of the business model. Finally, a pivot in one component of the business model often leads to changes in other components of the business model because of the interdependencies between components.

Don't be afraid of such changes. Instead, recognize that the goal of pivoting is to engage in systematic search and experimentation as you test various configurations of problems, solutions, and business models that might prove valuable.

Understanding When and How to Pivot

Pivoting is a powerful and liberating idea. It's liberating to recognize that no human being can guess correctly when you face uncertainty, and that part of the process is making changes to adjust to these inevitable errors. But beyond being a liberating idea, the ability to recognize when and how to pivot is a critical capability.

That being said, the literature reflects a limited understanding of ways to harness this tool effectively. To better address this gap, we conducted a two-part research project.[7] Our research suggests that, on average, change has a significant benefit by allowing managers to adjust assumptions that prove incorrect. At the same time, pivoting has its dangers. For example, sometimes people "overpivot," failing to notice key clues about a valuable opportunity. In other cases, companies "underpivot," holding on too long to an idea in search of those same key clues. Or, in a strangely counterintuitive way, innovators may be paralyzed by constantly asking themselves whether they should change. To help you avoid such traps, let's look at emerging rules of thumb for when and how to pivot.

Pivot Cycles

Our project followed ten companies to observe their innovation process. In one case, we spoke with Dan (a fictitious name), leader of an innovation team assigned to develop new software to help corporate teams improve task coordination. During our bimonthly interviews, Dan agonized over the direction of the project. He understood the importance of pivoting, and each month he made a change or two on some dimension of the customer problem, solution, or business model. Each month the customer engagement metrics either didn't improve or improved only modestly. Dan agonized over each change. He asked us, "Am I doing the right thing, or should I just try something completely new?"

From our vantage point, Dan was making several mistakes. First, he wasn't clear about which assumption he was testing. Without a hypothesis, it was hard to tell whether the idea was succeeding or failing. Dan tended to pull the plug and make a change before really understanding whether his hypothesis was true or false, because he hadn't developed a clear hypothesis. In contrast, most managers who fail to develop a clear hypothesis often have the opposite problem: they persist forever, because they never actually realize that their hypothesis was proven false. This is why Intuit executives Brad Smith and Scott Cook insist that no experiment start until there is a numerical hypothesis; in this way, they can tell whether the hypothesis was proven true or false.

Dan's second mistake was that he was changing too many things too quickly, and thus it wasn't clear what he had actually learned. The pivots and iterations felt good, because he felt he was taking action, and in some instances he saw incremental improvements. But because he didn't have a deliberate approach for when and how to pivot, he overreacted to each piece of customer feedback before he had a chance to learn what customers were telling him.

To make matters worse, Dan expended a great deal of mental energy by constantly asking himself, "Should I pivot?" Like any decision that is overanalyzed, the change decision can paralyze a company that is constantly asking, "Should we change?" Companies that are stuck in this mode waste precious time. In addition, the indecision amplifies the tendency to abandon an idea too early by leading companies to overreact to the first bit of negative customer feedback (and there will always be some)—or underreact because they can't make the decision to change course (a classic challenge in the early stages of design).

How can you overcome pivot paralysis while avoiding changing too early or too late? The solution: use time-bound deadlines framed to answer the most important questions you face. A lesson we learn from PayPal's experience is the need to set pivot cycles—typically, two- to three-month cycles during which you conduct experiments to answer key questions about a problem, solution, or business model. The cycles should be structured to give enough time for testing and going deep, but also be short enough to force rapid development. At the end of a cycle, you assess the answers to your key questions and then decide whether to make a change.

As a rule, pivot cycle deadlines of two to three months or less appear to work best (sometimes they may be much shorter). Although pivot cycles may appear similar to other types of deadlines, such as a corporate product development deadline, a pivot cycle is briefer and more intense. Most product development processes range from twelve to thirty-six months, whereas we argue that you should cram a great deal of that process into a two-month window designed to answer a specific set of questions. This means that as a team you will work with the kind of intensity and focus found in start-ups and that whatever you do will not be perfect (you will have to use virtual prototypes or other rapid experiments). But the brevity of the timeline can give you the focus to work intensely and not get bogged down.

Levchin and Thiel's experience launching PayPal is instructive. In two years they made at least five major changes. This means they tried testing a different solution every two to four months to see whether it got traction with users. However, after roughly three months without getting traction, they didn't just continue to refine the product. Instead, they shifted to a different problem or solution. The changes still involved software security, but they were focused on different problems or different solutions.

Like PayPal, established companies that change effectively use pivot cycles. For example, Mondelez International (Kraft) gives each innovation project a two- to three-month development period and then forces a thirty-day "go or no-go" decision period. AT&T's innovation labs use twelve-week project cycles to test an idea before moving to a decision to pivot or persist. Amazon typically uses six-month timeframes but expects to make major changes to both the problem and the solution during that time (average three-month pivot or persist). At Intuit, most projects have a three-month deadline, after which they face a pivot-or-persist decision.

Pivot Testing

During pivot cycles, how do you determine whether you should change? Recall Dan, who led the task coordination product team and struggled with constantly making small iterations without feeling he had discovered what his customers really wanted. Dan also fell into a different trap, one that we observed among many other managers we studied: applying only one testing mode to try to understand the core problem.

There are three testing modes based on modes of learning under uncertainty: abductive, inductive, and deductive logic. *Abductive* learning is the process of making a guess, usually based on your intuition—for example, you have a guess about the product or service customers want, and you develop your guess by building a product rather than testing whether customers want it. *Inductive* learning is the process of developing a theory, usually based on your guess, using qualitative methods such as fly-on-the-wall or interviews—for example, you talk to customers in face-to-face interviews about the problems they have. Finally, *deductive* learning is the process of testing a theory, usually using quantitative methods, to prove whether your theory is correct—for example, you believe an improvement to a website might increase sales, and you use the quantitative evidence from a parallel test of two versions (called an *A/B test*) to provide evidence about which website version increases sales.

We've observed many managers mistakenly operate in a single mode. For example, Dan was addicted to the deductive mode, using quantitative tools such as user surveys and A/B testing to measure his progress. Such deductive tools are attractive because they let you test your assumptions quantitatively and obtain a statistical measure. Dan used these tests to determine whether he should make a change; then he made the change, saw a small improvement, and repeated the cycle. But where did the theory about the problem, solution, and business model come from in the first place? How do we even know whether Dan had the right theory—the right assumptions? Although Dan used quantitative tools effectively, he used only one method to test his assumptions.

In our research, less effective managers tended to rely on one method to test their ideas, particularly quantitative tools such as surveys. This was particularly true for managers in established companies, where hard data and numbers are more respected than qualitative observations. But these deductive tools are appropriate only to test a theory or assumption and not to develop a theory in the first place. For a manager running an existing business, sticking to quantitative tools can make sense, because the theory is already well established and managers are making refinements under conditions of relative certainty. But for high-uncertainty projects, sticking to one mode has serious liabilities. The most important is that you don't deeply understand the theory you're testing or know the right questions to ask.

In contrast, effective managers cycled between the available modes. They started with a guess (abductive), tested the guess qualitatively to develop a theory (using techniques like fly-on-the-wall, interviews, etc.; this is inductive learning), and then tested the theory more quantitatively (using surveys, A/B testing, etc.; this is deductive). If at any point they discovered they were wrong, they returned to an earlier point. Although it may sound obvious, a remarkable number of managers got stuck in one type of learning, most often deductive or abductive. Innovators who engaged in the complete cycle, rather than stick to a single mode, proved their assumptions true or false months earlier than those who did not.

As you enter a pivot cycle, take stock of where you stand in relation to nailing the problem, solution, or business model. Don't leap to surveys first, but instead make sure you understand your hypothesis; then test your hypothesis qualitatively to build your theory to explain what is going on, and then engage with your customers using quantitative tools.

Broad versus Narrow Pivots

Often managers ask us, "should we focus early or stay broad?" Recall that Dan's team was changing often, but these were narrow pivots (or iterations) around the problem and solution it had identified early on, rather than broad pivots designed to cast a wide net for problems and solutions (see "Pivoting Sequentially Versus in Parallel").

In the early stages of solving a high-uncertainty problem you need to go broad before you go narrow. In a broad pivot, you change the problem or pain point you're trying to solve; change the technology or approach you're using to solve the problem; or, when you get to the business model stage, you completely change distribution channels or pricing strategy—perhaps going from per-unit pricing to subscription pricing. Dan's team focused on a particular approach—a particular software tool—to solve the problem of coordinating team tasks. Each "pivot" was really a small iteration from the initial approach. The team would have been better off making broader changes every two to three months and then narrower changes during the pivot cycle in search of what we call pivot takeoff, as discussed in the following section.

Pivoting Sequentially Versus in Parallel

Focus has immense power and plays a critical role in the innovator's method. You need to focus on the precise customer problem, on the minimum features that drive a purchase, and on the right business model. But somewhat counterintuitively, at the start of each phase, you need to look very broadly before you focus. In this chapter we imply that broad pivots occur sequentially as you test one idea and then move to the next. But your exploration and pivots can also occur in parallel—and probably should when both uncertainty and complexity are particularly high.

For example, when Sony wanted to develop high-power rechargeable batteries, it took a very different approach to managing technical uncertainty. At the time, nickel seemed the only safe solution compared with other compounds having a high energy density, such as lithium—an element that exploded on contact with water. In the race to develop a solution, Sanyo and Matsushita (Panasonic) focused solely on the safer, but lower-energy-density, nickel-based rechargeables.

But Sony decided to take a leap into the uncertainty of simultaneously developing lithium batteries. Instead of working on a single lithium solution, Sony funded six separate projects, each working on a variation of the solution. Furthermore, instead of following the typical long development deadlines at Sony, managers met with the teams every month to assess progress, make changes (pivot), and rapidly respond to obstacles. Each project pivoted sequentially, and the various projects were pivoting in parallel. In the end, one project team found the combination of lithium-based materials that became the world standard lithium-ion batteries.

Sony's unique approach helped it resolve the technical uncertainty faster than its competitors, which eventually were forced to follow suit, but not before ceding a four-year head start and many valuable patents to Sony. Similarly, at the start of each phase of the innovator's method, you might also consider exploring in parallel, searching for multiple pains, solutions, or business models before pivoting to a single, focused option.

Pivot Takeoff

Should pivot cycles go on endlessly? When do you know whether you've arrived, and how do you get there? The answer: look for *pivot takeoff*. Pivot takeoff occurs when, after making a change, you see a significant change in the trajectory of customer interest (see figure 7-1). For example, recall that PayPal made several significant alterations, with only moderate interest, until after the fourth change to the PalmPilot money-transfer solution. This solution led to a dramatic increase in the customer engagement metrics, and this means that potential customers were much more likely to give the company time (the time test) and money (the payment test) and to promote the product to a friend (the promoter test). This led to a much faster rate of usage and adoption among users compared with earlier solutions. Moreover, when PayPal made the fifth change to the website that allowed e-mail money transfers, it saw yet another leap in customer interest and adoption, and this signaled that the team had nailed a solution for a great many people.

Although we encourage you to embrace pivoting, ultimately what you're looking for is pivot takeoff. It indicates that either you've found

FIGURE 7-1

Pivot takeoff

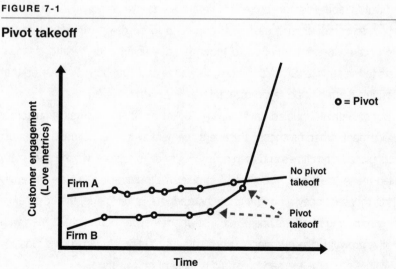

a problem worth solving (the level of customer interest increases significantly) or the solution you're currently testing is at least doing a reasonable job of solving the problem (the level of commitment or payment increases markedly). For more about measuring your results, see "Use Multiple, Robust Metrics for Pivot Takeoff." As a rule, pivot takeoff typically occurs somewhere between the third and seventh pivot for most innovations—although it may take longer for more radical projects.

In contrast, if your pivots seem to yield only small improvements or decreasing returns for each change, you may be hitting the limit of what's possible with your current approach. Every circumstance is different, so use your judgment. If you don't achieve pivot takeoff after six or seven major pivots over twelve to eighteen months, it may be time to abandon your problem and solution in search of something entirely new.

Use Multiple, Robust Metrics for Pivot Takeoff

As an experienced innovator who had developed products and services worth more than a billion dollars, Mike Cassidy had lots of experience in searching for pivot takeoff. His new project, Ultimate Arena, which allowed video game players to compete for a cash pot, appeared to be doing well. The number of registered users continued to grow as advertising and PR efforts drove users to the service. Given the growth in usage and adoption, it appeared that Cassidy's team had achieved pivot takeoff.

But something troubled Cassidy as he looked at other measures of customer engagement. When he checked user engagement over time, he found that most users played a few times and then never returned. To explore why, he personally called these users and discovered a problem: although people were generally willing to lose money among friends, as during a poker game, they didn't like losing money to strangers online, against whom they felt outmatched. Even with positive growth in the number of users, without a set of returning users, Cassidy knew that over time the service would run out of new users.

He first tried some minor pivots—changing the ranking system for grouping players for competition and adjusting the fees charged—to see whether either change would keep users coming back. But in the end, the data won out. With advertising, the service continued to attract new users, but the other pivot takeoff metrics—return users, net promoter score—didn't validate the takeoff as robust. A larger pivot was necessary.

After additional observations and conversations with customers who'd left the service, Cassidy discovered that what most customers really wanted was a way to connect and play games with their friends online. So Cassidy changed the product to an instant messaging service that allowed gamers to connect with friends and then port into their favorite game together. The new solution achieved pivot takeoff as measured not only by the number of registered users but also with return users, net promoter score, and ultimately revenues. In fact, the new solution grew like crazy, eventually becoming a major new initiative inside Vivendi's portfolio of products. But Cassidy might not have achieved such success if he had paid attention only to the single pivot takeoff metric of growth in the number of registered users.

Having multiple types of pivot takeoff metrics helps you make the tough decisions about whether to change. We recommend paying particular attention to growth in users/trials, net promoter score, or growth in users who pass the payment test. However, the data should be appropriate for the pivot. It may be X number of interviews with Y negative statements, or it may be the percentage of users who did not use your solution again. Although we've provided options for customer engagement metrics that indicate pivot takeoff, you must figure out what metrics provide a robust (reliable) measure of whether you've nailed the problem, solution, and business model for your target customers.

Mountains versus Hills: Keep Pivoting

Once you've achieved pivot takeoff, you should focus on maximizing it. After all, you're gaining traction with a solution that's working. However, takeoff doesn't mean you should quit pivoting altogether. Instead, you can move to narrower pivots and iterations as you search for an even higher trajectory of customer interest and adoption. Remember that the first uptick may be only the start of pivot takeoff, as happened with PayPal's PalmPilot application. As you focus, take care to look up periodically and ask yourself, "Is there another change we could make that could increase our trajectory even more?" Never be afraid to use the tools you've gained to explore new opportunities that you may not have previously observed.

Consider the case of Aardvark, a company whose social search engine allowed users to post questions to their social network rather than conduct an internet search. The founders believed that some questions—for example, asking for recommendations for a moving company—might be better answered by people you know than by a generic search request. At the start, the founders did an excellent job of using the tools we describe to test multiple solutions in search of pivot takeoff. For example, although most of us might start such a company by first developing the software, instead the team created a minimum viable prototype that relied on Amazon's Mechanical Turk (an online outsourcing service) to "fake" the functionality of the software by having people manually type answers to questions rather than use a software algorithm.

Although it wasn't perfect, Aardvark was able to test many aspects of the solution by faking it and quickly iterated to a fully functioning solution that achieved pivot takeoff (based on growth in customer satisfaction and usage). As Aardvark's social search solution reached one hundred thousand customers, the customer adoption metrics continued to improve, and increasingly narrow iterations of the solution led to incremental improvements in customer engagement.

All seemed to be on track, except for a recurring nuisance. Customers continually requested two features that Aardvark had not developed: a searchable database of previously answered questions, and a list of questions a user could answer. Although the features would be easy enough to develop or even fake, the Aardvark team resisted, because it contradicted the team's vision of social searches. Indeed the team argued that such features would turn Aardvark into a version of Yahoo! Answers or a similar service. Because customer engagement continued to improve, the Aardvark team decided to stay focused on its current solution and vision.[8]

Aardvark's story has a happy ending—at least for the founders and the team. Aardvark was acquired by Google for $50 million in 2010. However, it might have been an even happier ending. While Aardvark continued to iterate around its solution, another company, Quora, designed a product focused precisely on the features most requested by Aardvark's customers: searchable previously answered questions. The year after Aardvark was acquired by Google, Quora reportedly reached a valuation of more than $1 billion. (As a side note, the ending wasn't so happy, because Google shut down the Aardvark service less than a year after acquiring it.)

The sad thing for Aardvark is that, given its remarkable skills at rapidly testing assumptions, it could have easily tested the product that Quora succeeded with—but it would have required quickly testing a new solution in parallel with the existing solution, one that was not an iteration of the existing product. This is what Sony did as it searched for multiple solutions to the battery problem. For Aardvark, it would have represented a parallel pivot, although not a massive change. Of course, whether Aardvark could have succeeded in launching a product like Quora's is speculation. But comparing Aardvark's approach after achieving pivot takeoff with PayPal's is instructive.

Aardvark fell into a trap we've noticed among many other teams— what we call iterating around a hill when a pivot may lead you to a nearby mountain peak. If you think about a landscape as a metaphor for the distribution of opportunities, then flatlands or valleys represent no opportunities, hills represent small opportunities, and mountains represent large opportunities. Researchers have long observed that companies often get trapped on a smaller hill and fail to see the nearby bigger mountains of opportunity.

In our research we observed that some teams are so excited about achieving pivot takeoff that they feel they've found the solution. After all, it feels great to find a hill when you've been in a valley. Moreover, refinements through smaller iterations will lead to small steps up the hill, and that feels like progress. The challenge is to remember that there are often mountains nearby, perhaps next door. For Aardvark, that mountain was called Quora. For PayPal, that mountain was conducting financial transactions via e-mail instead of by PalmPilot.

Of course, when you achieve pivot takeoff, you don't have to abandon the hill or mountain you've found (see "Popularity Versus Customer-Driven Pivots." PayPal didn't abandon its PalmPilot product when it launched its computer-based product. Instead, use the tools we've described here to test emerging opportunities. Your initial pivot takeoff may be a stepping-stone to an even bigger opportunity.

Popularity versus Customer-Driven Pivots

What should you do when someone powerful, influential, or talented tells you to change course, but the data suggests something else? A Swedish company we studied experienced this when it began to develop a solution analogous to Microsoft Office but for advertising agencies—a tool that would assist them in developing the next wave of dynamic advertising. After working with several global agencies for months to define the problem and solution, the company was invited to TechCrunch50, a conference for the most innovative companies of the year.

But when the team presented to the panel of judges, an extremely successful individual, comparable to the Bill Gates of entrepreneurship, began to criticize the approach, saying the company should not bother to target advertising agencies; it was a waste of time. The Swedish team members earnestly debated: should they pivot and do something different? But in the end, they went back to the data from customers. Ultimately the data proved correct, and the team evolved to become world renowned for its prowess in advertising analytics.

We are all easily influenced by high-status individuals—an executive, an entrepreneur, a mentor, or an investor who may be known for expertise, intellect, or past successes. Sometimes these people are correct in their advice, and they should be listened to. But you need to ask whether they fit the profile of or truly understand your customer. In many cases they are not your target customer—so whatever they say needs to be measured against the data before you make the potential mistake of a popularity pivot. If you need to gather new data, do so. But don't pivot just to be popular. As we've said before, innovators innovate, customers validate.

Right to Be Wrong

Pivots are an essential part of every stage of the innovator's method. You should expect to be wrong and focus instead on learning as quickly as possible and then changing when you discover that a guess was wrong. Pivots liberate you to change mistaken assumptions, and they're a powerful tool in your innovation tool kit.

Like any tool, pivoting needs to be used correctly. Set short pivot cycles that create urgency to explore your key assumptions. Rely on these cycles as key decision points rather than get mired in an endless debate about whether to change. Use the cycle to identify the key themes, rather than the random data points, that can drive the decision to modify your approach. Use multiple approaches to test your assumptions, including abductive, inductive, and deductive approaches. Furthermore, try searching various problems or solutions in parallel during the early stages—when uncertainty is especially high. The key is to be sure to explore broadly before going narrow.

Once you've achieved pivot takeoff, it can be tempting to keep your head down and make incremental changes and improvements. But don't forget to lift your eyes occasionally and ask whether there's a mountain of opportunity nearby that you're missing. Knowing when and how to change is more art than science—but using the guidelines we've offered will help you master the pivot.

8

Scale It

As soon as you start to scale, everything is going to change. Everything.

—Ryan Smith, CEO of Qualtrics

MAGINE HOW EXCITED you will be after you've have applied the innovator's method to nail the problem, solution, and business model and you start to generate revenue. People around you are excited, and they can see that your project has begun to succeed. But now you face a new challenge: scaling your fledgling innovation. In a strangely paradoxical way, if you're particularly adept at applying the innovator's method, you may face great difficulties in making the transition to scaling. Recall in chapter 2 we argue that being a good manager can make you a bad innovator. When it comes to scaling, the opposite can also be true: being a good innovator can make you a bad manager.

Consider the case of Lew Cirne, who founded Wily Technologies to automate the complex task of diagnosing software flaws. Cirne had the initial insight while driving along Highway 17 between Palo Alto and Santa Cruz, California, feeling frustrated about his own challenges in managing the growing complexity of software projects. Early discussions with potential customers confirmed that other developers faced similar problems.

Cirne did an excellent job of prototyping a minimum awesome product, identifying the right business model, building the team, and selflessly sacrificing for the new business. Using the kinds of tools described in this book, Cirne successfully closed initial customer sales that established a multimillion-dollar revenue stream and raised almost $40 million in venture capital. Everything seemed to be going well, and Cirne felt that he had done a great job as founder and CEO. So imagine his surprise when the board of directors replaced him.

Why did the board replace Cirne when he had accomplished so much? He acknowledged that he had not done everything perfectly in recent days. For example, as the team grew beyond twenty-five people, communication had become more difficult, and there had been a number of communication fumbles. Decision making had also become slow and challenging: the consensus decision-making process Cirne favored in the early days bogged down the process of taking action. In addition, Cirne found he needed to repeatedly step in to help close sales calls as the sales force struggled. As a result, Cirne's investors asked to bring in senior executives as advisers on the operational issues that were slowing growth. When the investors eventually asked Cirne to step aside, he wondered what he could have done to show that he could manage the company as it grew.

In fact, Cirne's story is common. Multiple studies confirm that a majority of founders are kicked out of the companies they create, and often just at the moment when revenues are skyrocketing.[1] Why?

Although it may seem counterintuitive, founders are often removed for a simple reason: they aren't well equipped to make the transition from discovering the business model to scaling it. This transition is a challenging management problem, and here's why. As you apply the innovator's method to rapidly resolve the uncertainties underlying your project, hypotheses will become facts, unknowns will become knowns, and uncertainties will become certainties. As uncertainties decline, the reasons for applying entrepreneurial management begin to disappear. You enter the territory where traditional management principles focused on optimizing and capturing value are more appropriate.

As you move from innovating to executing, your project passes through a transitional phase when neither entrepreneurial management nor traditional management alone is entirely appropriate (see figure 8-1). This is the time to learn how to effectively blend the two management practices as you transition to a mature growth business.

Bringing an innovation from a start-up to a billion-dollar business can be compared to the human life cycle: childhood, adolescence, and adulthood. In the Middle Ages, people treated children as little adults, but now we recognize that children are different from adults: they require different training, expectations, and even different medicine than adults. In a sense, start-ups, whether inside or outside the corporation, are like children: they require a different set of management techniques than a mature business (we use the term *start-up* here to refer to your innovation project whether you're pursuing it inside or outside a corporation). But just as children do not immediately become adults,

FIGURE 8-1

The transitional phase

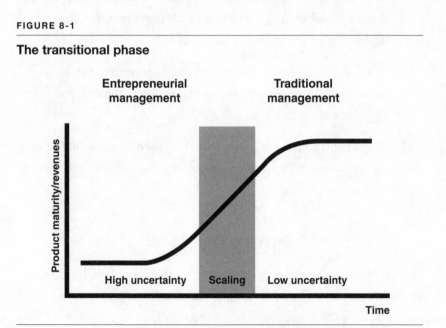

as the innovation takes off and starts to scale, your innovation does not immediately become a mature business that you can manage using traditional practices. Instead, the new product passes through a series of adolescent transition steps. Just as teenagers are neither children nor adults but rather a unique blend of the two, effective scaling requires a unique blend of entrepreneurial and traditional management.

When and how should you make this transition to scaling? First, we help you recognize some of the key inflection points that indicate when it's time to scale the business. Then we discuss how to make this transition in terms of market, process, and team activities. We address how to manage the following key changes:

- *Market scaling.* Recognize when to move from a minimum awesome product to a whole-product solution and how to create the legitimacy to make the transition from early adopters to mainstream customers.

- *Process scaling.* Understand how to shift effectively from discovery processes to execution processes designed to efficiently deliver the whole-product solution without prematurely destroying your innovation capabilities.

- *Team scaling.* Identify how to get the right people with the right skills for scaling the company in place while assigning new roles to people who cannot, or will not, adapt.

Finally, we introduce you to a scaling tool used by many of the most successful managers who have scaled ideas from small teams to effective billion-dollar businesses.

Recognize When to Scale

Qualtrics, an online survey company, recently grabbed headlines as an overnight success: after rejecting a $500 million acquisition offer, it raised $100 million in funding and reportedly is valued at more than

$1 billion as it grows at breakneck speed. In reflecting on his experience, CEO and founder Ryan Smith says that the company is "an overnight success . . . ten years in the making."[2] Smith adopted the title of one of our earlier books, *Nail It Then Scale It*, as the mantra for his company.[3]

Smith emphasizes that Qualtrics spent ten years nailing the problem, solution, and business model before raising millions in venture capital to scale the business. He argues that although it may seem slower at first to proceed through the phases of deeply understanding the job-to-be-done, prototyping numerous solutions, and then validating your business model before you invest to scale it, this process saved the company from failure many times. But Smith also acknowledges that once you start to scale, "everything is going to change." Asked how he recognized when Qualtrics needed to shift, his answer reflects something we've heard from other managers of growing companies: when you feel the pain, then you know you've hit an inflection point that demands a change. But what does that mean?

As a rule, you've hit an inflection point when you see the same types of problems cropping up repeatedly. It becomes evident when the percentage of time you spend solving the same problem becomes disproportionate to the cost of routinizing the problem. The pain caused by a broken process is a symptom of the needed shift from entrepreneurial to traditional management.

For example, consider the sales process for a company over its life cycle: in the early days the founding team closes most sales, and, because the product and business model are still in flux, it makes little sense to create a routinized sales template. But as new salespeople are added, problems emerge: they struggle with how to sell, what to sell (making inconsistent promises to customers that require customization), or how to close the sale (calling on the founder to close deals). As these problems multiply and consume more time, it's a sure sign that the innovation has hit an inflection point. You need to develop a standard sales process template, based on a standardized set of products, with a standardized set of customer promises, all tracked in a system linked to each salesperson.

Of course, you still need room for flexibility—for entrepreneurial management—because at this early stage, you may still discover new uncertainties. That's why the challenge of scaling is to balance entrepreneurial and traditional management.

We've noticed two other indicators that you've hit an inflection point and it's time to scale: solution standardization and team growth. While using the innovator's method, you will pivot frequently, but eventually you should achieve pivot takeoff. Team priorities will shift from discovering what customers want, to improving the features you offer, to standardizing the features customers want. Companies that have hit this inflection point often describe the feeling of having a "haphazard" or "bag-of-bolts" solution that's always breaking. Thus, they feel the need to "redesign" or "rewrite" the product to make it more efficient or more reliable. For example, Qualtrics rewrote the core software code three times as they matured. This shift to standardizing the solution represents a key inflection point because, rather than ask what customers want, managers must ask, "How do we deliver this solution reliably and repeatedly at low cost?"

To make this change effectively, managers often must change their product development processes from search (pivoting on features) to execution (standardizing features) and their resources from flexible (variabilized costs, flexible people who can search, multipurpose tools) to fixed (fixed costs spread over a large number of units, experts who can create better solutions).

A second inflection point occurs as the team grows. Research suggests that early-stage teams are most efficient with four to eight people and become unwieldy at ten to twelve people. We've observed that when a start-up grows to employ more than twenty-five people, it has likely hit a scaling inflection point. Previously, everyone knew each other well and communicated informally, but now communication starts failing and coordination becomes a headache, with balls being dropped.

To deal with this inflection point, managers must establish formal communication processes and coordination tools (described in more detail later in the chapter). Companies must respond to this inflection point by becoming more formal, with set meeting times, tracked information systems, and standard reporting that was previously absent.

Scale the Market

As start-ups begin to scale, they often experience initial growth followed by stagnation, a situation that perplexes the founding team. Why would sales stagnate just as the team starts to improve the product? The answer has something to do with the cornfields of Iowa. As a child in the 1930s, Everett Rogers watched as drought decimated the cornfields, including his father's crops. But not all the corn was destroyed. A few years earlier, drought-resistant seeds (which also produced a 20 percent to 25 percent higher yield) had hit the market. Although some farmers quickly adopted the higher-priced seed, others waited until, convinced by the drought of 1936, most farmers finally adopted the new seed.

Watching the family cornfields die raised important questions for Rogers about how innovations get adopted. Why had it taken so long for some farmers to adopt the seed? Why doesn't everyone adopt an innovation at the same time? In his later work *Diffusion of Innovations*, Rogers synthesized hundreds of studies, including the studies about the adoption of hybrid corn seed, and concluded that the people who adopt any innovation fall into different categories, with different needs and preferences, which affect when and how they adopt the innovation.[4]

Rogers argued that for any innovation, the groups he called the "innovators" and "early adopters" are the first to adopt because they have a higher risk tolerance and like to try new things to stay on the cutting edge. As a result, these customers are willing to overlook weaknesses in a potential innovation in the quest for an advantage. In contrast, the groups he labeled "early majority" and "late majority" have different preferences. For the most part, they want to be safe (e.g., they don't want to get fired for trying an untested idea) and so wait to adopt an innovation (see figure 8-2).

This difference led a later author, Geoffrey Moore, to argue that companies face a significant challenge in "crossing the chasm" from the early customer groups to the later customer groups, because these groups want different things that innovators have a hard time satisfying (see figure 8-3).[5] Whereas early adopters are willing to try something entirely new that may not work perfectly, the early and late majority don't want a minimum viable product: they want a *"whole product solution,"* meaning a full-featured, functional, error-free solution.

Teams often stumble because they don't understand the innovation adoption life cycle. As we've discussed, most of us have the intuition that we need to build whole products that have broad appeal and are error-free in order to be successful. Although this intuition has an element of truth—it holds for the early and late majority—at the beginning of your project you can waste a great deal of time and resources trying to perfect your product based on untested assumptions. That's why we emphasize the importance of using virtual prototypes or an MVP to test the key assumptions with target customers. At first you may have resisted this advice because it seemed counterintuitive, but it was rooted

FIGURE 8-2

The technology adoption life cycle

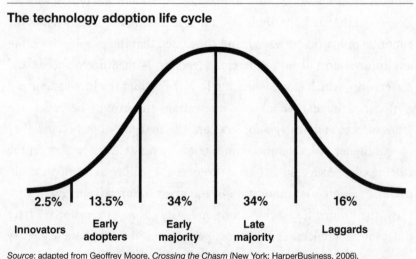

| 2.5% | 13.5% | 34% | 34% | 16% |
| Innovators | Early adopters | Early majority | Late majority | Laggards |

Source: adapted from Geoffrey Moore, *Crossing the Chasm* (New York: HarperBusiness, 2006).

in the fact that early adopters are more forgiving of weaknesses. Thus, you can use them as a sounding board to validate your key assumptions. Then you can use the minimum awesome product to help you to cross the chasm to your first early majority customers on your way to developing the whole-product (error-free) solution that solves the customer need robustly for a broad array of customers (see figure 8-4).

FIGURE 8-3

The chasm in the innovation adoption life cycle

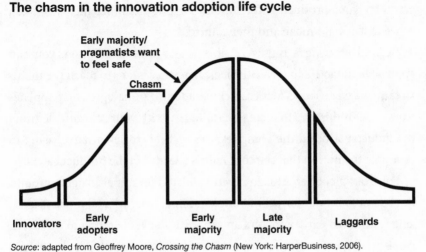

Source: adapted from Geoffrey Moore, *Crossing the Chasm* (New York: HarperBusiness, 2006).

FIGURE 8-4

MVP versus whole-product solution

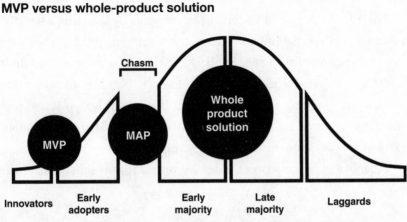

Source: adapted from Geoffrey Moore, *Crossing the Chasm* (New York: HarperBusiness, 2006).

As you scale, you must also adopt the tactics to cross the chasm.[6] To do this, Moore argues that you need to deeply understand why a particular group of customers is attracted to your solution and then focus your resources on that single customer niche. Your objective is to effectively communicate your message and create enough legitimacy in the minds of a few reference customers (among the early majority) so that they feel safe enough to adopt your product. These early majority reference customers serve as touch points, convincing other like-minded customers to try your product. After conquering one customer niche, you can move to a second niche and then a third.

Beyond creating a highly reliable whole-product solution, you can apply several tactics to create the legitimacy necessary to reach the mainstream market. These tactics include adopting analogies or templates from other industries to increase familiarity with your solution, defining the industry around the company, or creating stories or advertising to reinforce the notion that the company is a leader in the product category.

For example, after Amazon.com validated its initial insights around the business model for selling books online, it faced a significant challenge: although early adopters and innovators were willing to buy from Amazon, buying anything online was unfamiliar to most people, including the early majority. To enhance legitimacy, Amazon used a number of tactics. First, it used analogies from off-line retail, such as shopping carts and checkout, to make the site feel familiar and safe.

Amazon also signaled leadership by strategically targeting a few distant customers so that it could claim it was shipping products to forty-five countries and fifty states. Similarly, the online retailer defined itself as the industry leader, claiming to be "Earth's Biggest Bookstore"; that was true in geographic scope or product breadth, although actual revenues were tiny. And Amazon aggressively distributed stories about extraordinary customer service (for example, stories of CEO Jeff Bezos or other Amazon employees obsessively working to satisfy customer requests).

Together, these tactics worked well to create sufficient legitimacy in the minds of the early majority to use Amazon.com and then spread their experience by word of mouth.[7] Then, having conquered the books category, Amazon rolled into other online product categories.

Scale the Process

In scaling a product, a major task is to develop, and then standardize, a company's processes to deliver its whole-product solution to the market. This means adopting a key principle advocated by Frederick Taylor that we rejected at the beginning of the process: task standardization and worker specialization. We've found that start-up managers who are successful at scaling follow a simple pattern as they introduce scalable, standardized processes to the organization.

1. List all the tasks to be done to effectively execute your business model, and assign each task to an individual.

2. Have each team member write a job description for the tasks he is assigned. Then review them together so that everyone can agree on how the tasks are to be done. This also helps everyone understand who wears which hats.

3. Create a visual map of all the critical processes, noting the linkages and relationships. This diagram will help you ensure that someone has responsibility for all the key processes and handoffs. If you don't write down and make the processes visual and explicit, most of the valuable, tacit knowledge the team has gained will be lost.

4. Finally, link the tasks and processes to performance metrics, and assign accountability for those metrics to specific individuals.

Each of these steps will help you create standardized and repeatable processes.

Transparently Communicate the Transition

The best way we've discovered to manage the transition is to employ purposeful, transparent communication. During the early days of a project, communication happens naturally and informally because the team is usually small and in close physical proximity. But as the project scales, team leaders often struggle to recognize the importance of instituting a formal, transparent communication structure. But this structure supports three critical things:

- Communication of the newly adopted execution processes and activities

- Discussion of common mistakes in adopting the new process, allowing the team to unlearn old habits and learn new ones

- Acknowledgment of the tension inherent in blending experimentation and planning, letting team members see where to apply entrepreneurial management and where to apply traditional management

Qualtrics founder Ryan Smith said that in the early days the company was relatively easy to manage: there were few employees, few customers, and few metrics (mainly a couple of love metrics). But as Qualtrics started to scale, keeping track of everything became increasingly difficult. The founders struggled with how to manage the company. On the one hand, Qualtrics faced the same kinds of problems for which business schools were created: it needed to make the trains run on time and optimize its operations. On the other hand, as executives of a young company facing some remaining uncertainty, the founders sensed that they faced significant dangers in becoming too focused on execution.

As they struggled to bridge the teenage years, they adopted a culture of transparency. As Smith observes, "You can't change the way people think. You can only shape how the environment affects their decisions.

It has to be peer group driven, and we do that with total, 100 percent transparency."[8] Qualtrics used a combination of meetings—such as all-hands meetings, skip-level meetings, and daily syncs—to communicate new processes, common mistakes, and ways to balance the tension between discovery and execution (see "Communicating to Shape Process and Culture"). For example, at Qualtrics employees hold all-hands meetings every Friday. Key things happen: after the standard announcements, they highlight sales to emphasize the continued centrality of the payment test. They also discuss new execution processes and explain how to best implement them. They call out mistakes, with an award for the best mistake; then they break down ways to solve the problem for future reference. Finally, they often talk about situations where they're still in discovery mode (e.g., opening the office in Ireland or adopting the new 360-degree feedback tool) as well as situations where they're transitioning to execution mode. This level of transparency has helped the organizational members make sense of and adapt to rapid changes.

Communicating to Shape Process and Culture

Among the innovative ventures we observed, communication always played a major role in surviving and prospering during scaling. Similarly, transparency speeds learning and transition. Here are four types of meetings we observed in ventures that are scaling successfully.

All-hands meetings. These familiar meetings are vital. The best ones have three components: leaders highlighting the key priorities, smaller teams reporting what they're working on, and everyone discussing key challenges and emerging solutions.

Daily sync meetings. Teams or leadership have a stand-up meeting of less than fifteen minutes in the morning to identify the key priorities and then a short end-of-day check-in to measure progress.

Skip-level meetings. The front line often has the best information about key challenges. Skip-level meetings let managers get deep into a team on the front line, rather than hear about it secondhand. At Intuit, Scott Cook regularly skips directly into an innovation team.

Outsider meetings. In a scaling venture, you can't know everything. Don't be shy about learning as much as you can from outsiders. Meet with them individually or as a company, and then interpret their advice in the context of the problems you're trying to solve.

Measure Your Progress

By changing what they measure, growing companies emphasize and encourage a change in activities. Recall Intuit's three designations for innovation projects: H1, H2, and H3, indicating increasing degrees of innovation. In contrast to H1 efforts (incremental innovations that improve core, existing businesses), the key metrics for H3 businesses are love metrics (customer activation rates, customer usage rates, net promoter score), measuring whether you've solved a significant problem. H2 businesses, in our analogy, are teenagers, and the metrics start to shift. In addition to NPS, the innovation is measured by market or margin growth as the team builds out the business model.

Based on our observations with other companies, three categories of metrics are appropriate for the three phases of growth. *Love* metrics (including measuring time, enthusiasm, recommendations [NPS], and payment) are appropriate during start-up. *Growth* metrics are appropriate for the adolescent scaling period, when you're trying to determine whether you're delivering a solution reliably with increasing economies of scale. Growth metrics include detailed measures of users (such as customer acquisition, activation, advocacy, retention, and referral) and revenues. You might also add measures that capture the efficiency of your processes, such as counts of defects, successful delivery, and so on.

Market power metrics are appropriate for a mature stage of the business, when you want to pay attention to measures of market dominance such as market share, return on assets or invested capital, and other familiar accounting measures by which we judge mature businesses.

Scale the Team

During start-up your team should largely comprise people who are good at generating insights using the five discovery skills—questioning, observing, networking, experimenting, and associating—described in chapter 3. These folks generally have a *T-shaped* expertise profile, meaning they possess deep expertise in a particular field (software engineering, anthropology, marketing, biology, etc.) but also demonstrate a breadth of knowledge in many fields. This knowledge profile helps them generate new insights, because they can see problems and solutions from many angles. However, as you start to scale, you need more *I-shaped* people—people who have a specific expertise and excel at applying that expertise to solve routine problems in that field.

As you build out the team during the growth phase, it's useful to think about balancing your mix of innovators (T-shaped) and experts (I-shaped). As you hit scaling inflection points that demand execution, you should add more I-shaped people and possibly replace some of the original T-shaped people. For example, the Big Idea Group, which uses an *American Idol* model to get new product ideas from a network of inventors, carefully manages its mix of T-shaped and I-shaped people. During the first phase of developing new product ideas, the company uses a selection panel with an 80/20 mix of innovation/execution people to meet with inventors. Once a promising idea has been selected for further development, a team with a 50/50 mix refines and tests it with prototypes. Finally, when the product has been proven and is ready to scale, the Big Idea Group moves to a 20/80 balance during the execution phase.

Our experience suggests that as the demands grow from an ever-increasing customer base, you will long for people who can execute. In fact, Corey Wride, the founder of Movie Mouth, maker of a cutting-edge software tool for teaching English, told us, "Right now I just want people who will be like vending machines: I want to put a coin in and have them spit out my request without changing it too much. What I most need now is better execution."[9]

As a general rule, only about half of the original innovation team can make the transition to scaling and execution. You may lose people you don't want to lose. After eBay acquired PayPal for $1.5 billion, Meg Whitman, CEO of eBay, went to the office of PayPal cofounder Peter Thiel to discuss plans to grow PayPal. "I noticed there were plane tickets sitting on his desk," recalls Whitman. "He said he was off to Saudi Arabia. He was ready for a new adventure and wasn't interested in scaling PayPal. Some entrepreneurs fundamentally don't like being in companies with more than about thirty to forty people."[10] Thiel went on to use his entrepreneurial management skills to cofound Palantir Technologies (based on technology developed at PayPal to detect fraudulent activity) and become the first outside investor in Facebook. Although it's not clear what contributions Thiel might have made had he stayed with eBay, be aware that during scaling you want to retain many of the talented people who helped you nail the business model. This may mean you have to find new opportunities for them.

For example, Craigslist, founded by Craig Newmark, used extensive rounds of cocreation with customers to iterate to one of the leading classifieds websites in the world: "Most of what we do is based on what people in the community suggest . . . People suggest stuff to us, we do what makes sense, and then we ask for more feedback."[11] For example, when Craigslist started to be flooded by spam ads from employers and brokers, the community suggested a solution: charge these users fees.

But as the company scaled, Newmark struggled with the management of the larger company. Fortunately, he had the foresight to recognize he wasn't well equipped to manage a large organization and brought in someone else who could. "Jim [Buckmaster] is a much better CEO. And my skills are not management skills," says Newmark. "However, I'm a really good customer-service representative."[12] The transition to a CEO who had experience running a larger organization was better for Craigslist and better for Newmark. What's more, Newmark moved to a position where he could still add value rather than moving to a different company.

Use a Scaling Tool: V2MOM

Every company we studied struggled to manage the changes demanded by scaling. In fact, every manager we studied who had successfully scaled an innovation project used a tool to help in the process. Our favorite approach was developed by Marc Benioff, chairman and CEO of Salesforce.com. This tool has proved so valuable that the leadership team continues to use it to adapt to the rapidly changing environment.[13]

This scaling tool emerged from Benioff's frustrations as a manager at Oracle during the scaling stage. Benioff recalls, "I personally lacked the tools to spell out what we needed to do and a simple process to communicate it. The problem only increased as the teams that I was managing increased."[14] When Benioff later faced the same challenges scaling Salesforce.com, he recalls feeling frustrated with the existing approaches, such as traditional budget-based planning, key performance indicators, and critical success factors. Benioff talked to leadership, personal development, and spiritual gurus and eventually developed a tool that Salesforce.com labeled V2MOM. This tool "has been used to guide every decision at Salesforce.com—from those we made in 1999 to the decisions we make today as the largest high-tech employer in San Francisco," says Benioff. "It is the core way we run our business; it allows us to define our goals and organize a principled way to execute them."[15]

The V2MOM acronym stands for vision (where you want to go), values (what things are important to you), methods (what you're going to do to get there), obstacles (what could prevent you from being successful), and measures (how you know whether you're successful). "A V2MOM is the strategic plan for the company. It can be the strategic plan for a department, it can be the strategic plan for a person's career, it can be the strategic plan for a project, just a framework to get your thoughts down," says Jim Cavalieri, SVP in charge of the V2MOM process. "It's really used to set the direction for the company for the next twelve months."[16]

Every August, Benioff sketches out the vision and values priorities for the coming year, which he shares with the top people in the executive team (see figure 8-5 for an example). The executive team then defines three values that support the vision, and then three or four prioritized methods to support each value. So, for example, if Salesforce.com had a value of "growth," it would support this with about three prioritized methods to support and generate growth, such as specific product plans around its cloud services. In addition, the team identifies obstacles to implementing each method, as well as measures that indicate whether the method is making progress toward achieving the value and vision.

Then the executive team holds a meeting with the distributed senior management team members (currently about seven hundred people), who provide feedback on the proposed V2MOM in small groups and via Chatter, an internal social networking tool. Leaders are asked for their top five recommendations as well as the top five mistakes in the current V2MOM. Then, after integrating this feedback by making changes to the V2MOM, each member of the senior management team is assigned one method for which she has operational responsibility—and for which she will have measures of success. Finally, the new V2MOM is announced to everyone inside Salesforce.com at the beginning of the fiscal year in early February, and each group is expected to create its own personalized V2MOM that feeds in to the larger V2MOM.

Beyond the specifics of how Salesforce.com constructs a V2MOM, consider the steps of the process at a higher level of abstraction. There is an initial period of *definition* of what to achieve and how to achieve it, followed by several rounds of *feedback,* first with senior managers and then with other managers. Using this feedback, Salesforce.com *adapts* its V2MOM and then *delegates* responsibility for a single method

FIGURE 8-5

Salesforce.com's first V2MOM

Vision

Rapidly create a world-class internet company/site for sales force automation.

Values

1. World-class organization
2. Time to market
3. Functional
4. Usability (Amazon quality)
5. Value-added partnerships

Methods

1. Hire the team.
2. Finalize product specification and technical architecture.
3. Rapidly develop the product specification to beta and production stages.
4. Build partnerships with big e-commerce, content, and hosting companies.
5. Build launch plan.
6. Develop exit strategy: IPO/acquisition.

Obstacles

1. Developers
2. Product manager/business development person

Measures

1. Prototype is state-of-the-art.
2. High-quality functional system.
3. Partnerships are online and integrated.
4. Salesforce.com is regarded as leader and visionary.
5. We are all rich.

Source: Marc Benioff, "How to Create Alignment within Your Company in Order to Succeed," Salesforce.com blog, April 9, 2013.

to each individual. Next, it *disseminates* the V2MOM and asks groups to *personalize* the method. Last, the company *measures* its progress and assesses whether it is achieving its goals. Benioff argues that the V2MOM process "works especially well for a fast-paced environment.

THE INNOVATOR'S METHOD

It is challenging for every company to find a way to maintain a cohesive direction against a backdrop that is constantly changing, but V2MOM is the glue that binds us together."

Amazon.com uses a similar strategic planning process but complements it with a separate loop focused on identifying new ideas that can

FIGURE 8-6

Constructing your own V2MOM

Vision

Where you want to go.

Values

What things are important to you?

Methods

What are you going to do to get there?

Obstacles

What could prevent you from being successful?

Measures

How do you know if you are successful?

be used to restart the innovator's method on a new project. During this process in the spring, anyone can propose an idea in the form of a one-page press release, dated in the future, that describes his vision of what he would like to do, complete with fake customer quotes. These press releases are distributed, and if they garner enough attention, a small team is formed to test and validate the idea using a process similar to the innovator's method. This second loop creates space for Amazon to initiate new projects as it executes and scales the existing businesses.

To construct your own V2MOM, ask yourself the key questions shown in figure 8-6.

The Chasm Awaits

If you forget everything else about this chapter, remember two things. First, the process you used to nail the insight, problem, solution, and business model won't help you scale the business. You need to start incorporating traditional management principles. Second, you can't just flip the switch between entrepreneurial and traditional management. You must slowly blend traditional management in to entrepreneurial management as you scale the market, process, and team. As you go forward, you'll always face some uncertainty. In these situations, you can apply the principles and tools we've discussed to quickly resolve the new uncertainties you face. Finally, even as you scale the business, never stop talking to customers. You may discover an uncertainty—and an opportunity—you've previously overlooked.

Watch Out: Timing Counts

Entrepreneurs typically struggle because they rely on entrepreneurial man-agement for too long, failing to introduce traditional management techniques quickly enough to meet the demands of an ever-growing—and increasingly demanding—customer base. The result: communication snafus, decision-making flaws, and process breakdowns. In contrast, managers in established companies typically have a hard time applying the innovator's method, but once they find a business model that works, they sometimes apply traditional management too quickly, killing entrepreneurial management prematurely. The corporate parent squeezes the life out of a promising new project (often an acquisition), killing the innovation and driving away the innovators.

Neither approach works well, because scaling is not about entrepreneurial or traditional management alone. Rather, it's about blending the two during a transition from the start-up to the growth phase.

9

Making the Innovator's Method Work for You

I N CHAPTER 1 WE explain how Intuit introduced the innovator's method from the top down, with support from the CEO and a sweeping, companywide program aimed at training every employee. Few of us are so lucky. If your top management team does not support or is not aware of the ideas in the innovator's method, what should you do? How can you make these ideas work for you, your team, or your organization?

The answer is to adapt the method to your circumstances, particularly if you're acting alone, leading a team, or trying to ignite innovation in your organization. If you're pursuing more radical innovation versus more incremental innovation, it also calls for special adaptation.

Applying the Innovator's Method on Your Own

What if you work in an environment that may not be conducive to, or may even be hostile to, the innovator's method? Even when companies claim they want to bring new ideas to the marketplace, they may really reward execution, leaving little room for innovation. Or leaders may be averse to making mistakes or simply may not see the need for innovation, even if the world around them is changing rapidly. In these environments, can you apply what you've learned in this book?

Even if you're the only one who has read and believes in the innovator's method, you can apply these principles to transform your career and your life. Remember, the key principles are to identify the uncertainties surrounding an insight and learn about them as quickly as possible in a low-cost, reliable manner. The goal is to turn uncertainties—stated as leap of faith assumptions—into facts. One thing you have in your favor is that most managers hate uncertainty and love facts almost as much as they love saving time and money. You can use these tendencies to your advantage by leveraging the power of questions to sneakily propose a rapid experiment to test a key assumption—but in language acceptable to more traditional management.

For example, as a team member, if someone proposes an idea and you spot uncertainty, you can say, "That's a great idea. What are the key assumptions that must be true for that idea to create value for us? I wonder whether there's a way to run a quick experiment to get some data to validate those assumptions." If you need backup, you can use words like *market test* or *use the scientific method to validate*. These terms sound familiar and palatable to most managers, although you now have a new and different appreciation of them. Or you might refer to a prestigious innovator, such as Amazon.com, and talk about how this company might test the new idea.

The basic formula for introducing the innovator's method to your organization in "stealth mode" has three parts, for which we created the acronym VIP to help you remember the steps.

1. *Value.* We are all naturally defensive of our ideas. To put people at ease, start by showing that you value their idea.

2. *Investigate.* Investigate the proposed idea by asking questions to unearth the leap-of-faith assumptions behind the idea. What must be true for the value to be realized?

3. *Propose.* Propose a way to conduct a rapid experiment to validate the key assumptions; if possible, cloak your suggestion

in familiar language. Appeal to the natural desires to save money or time or to avoid embarrassment.

Former students of ours who are managers and executives in established companies have applied the innovator's method but have done it in stealth mode. For example, one former student, Anne (not her real name), had just started working at American Express. In a meeting she attended, a group proposed a new product that would incorporate data and recommendations from customers' social networks to help customers manage their finances and make better spending choices. There were a number of passionate advocates in the room, and they proposed starting product development immediately; they assumed they had sufficient knowledge of customers felt the urgency and of a company-wide innovation imperative.

But Anne could see the fallacy of starting product development based on only a guess; however she didn't want to stick her neck out, especially as a new employee. So she applied the method we discussed, handling the new idea with care by first valuing the effort. She recalls saying, "This looks really exciting and could have an incredible impact. I'm so happy to be in a place where new ideas like these are getting discussed." Then she started the second step to investigate, but in the spirit of building on the innovation, by saying, "I know that social is a huge new space with so much possibility, and there is so much to figure out still, and I'm wondering how we could make this project truly amazing by quickly figuring out the key features that customers really want. I think we have a good idea of what they are, but if we could quickly test those assumptions, we could make this a billion-dollar business."

Then she mixed in an appeal to a prominent company to drive home her idea: "I'm wondering if we could save time and money by doing some rapid, in-the-field experiments to understand exactly what customers are looking for so we can build those features from the start. I know Intuit did a similar thing when they developed QuickBooks

Simple Start, living in the field with customers and using the proto-type products themselves [an example from class]. They used the data from their field research to create a blockbuster product." Notice that she didn't criticize the project; instead, she subtly suggested a way to quickly run experiments about the key uncertainties. She could let the data from the field reshape or destroy the project.

There was a silence in the room after Anne spoke. She began to get nervous. After what seemed a long pause, a senior manager spoke up, praising Anne's great idea to save time and money on the new project. Several others chimed in, and a colleague came up to her afterward and mentioned how impressed he was with her. Over time, people started to look at Anne with new respect, and some requested her help on new ideas they were considering.

Anne's experience illustrates how you can still apply the principles of the innovator's method even when they're not widely understood or explicitly supported by your organization. Others may not always accept your proposals, but over time, if you suggest experiments to test key assumptions in a positive spirit, you will gain a reputation as a care-ful thinker.

Moreover, you can apply these same ideas to your own life, think-ing through how you might design experiments to test key assump-tions about actions you should take. For example, rather than quitting your job to jump into a new career, find a way to be involved in the new occupation for a few hours a month over the course of a year to explore how much you like it. We both did this in making our career decisions as we voluntarily participated in multiple research projects before jumping from consulting to academia. If you feel you want to change the nature of your relationship with a particular family mem-ber or friend, write down your assumptions regarding the key rela-tionship problems, and design an experiment to test an approach for improving the relationship. Whenever you face a problem in life char-acterized by uncertainty, try deeply investigating the problem, and then consider various experiments to test a solution.

Applying the Innovator's Method in a Team

In 1983, while traveling in the United States with a Toshiba R&D team, Tetsuya Mizoguchi had the idea for the first laptop. Having observed that Japanese workers often lived and worked in small spaces that discouraged the use of large desktop computers, Mizoguchi came to believe that a smaller laptop could become a huge success by allowing computer use at work and at home.

But Toshiba had already tried to enter the mainframe market and failed to beat out IBM. Its personal computer entry also failed, largely because it was not compatible with the IBM and NEC standards that eventually emerged. So when Mizoguchi presented the idea for a laptop to the executive team, he was quickly denied. The executives told him that they were considering exiting the computer business altogether and so did not want to commit funds to new projects. When Mizoguchi continued to push, arguing he could find the funds, the executives claimed that an engineering shortage meant they couldn't divert any engineers to high-risk projects. Despite these denials, sensing the eminent opportunity, Mizoguchi secretly assigned ten engineers to the laptop project at the Ome factory, twenty-five miles from headquarters.

Mizoguchi didn't have the innovator's method framework, but he applied many of the principles to manage the large risks inherent in pioneering a new product category. For example, he designed a five-stage development process that started much as we would have prescribed, first trying to understand the problem by observing computer users as well as dealers and then trying to nail the solution using a series of prototypes. Furthermore, Mizoguchi pushed for rapid iterations toward an awesome product. For example, after several rounds of rapid iteration during which the engineers felt they had reached the limit of what they could fit into a small laptop case, Mizoguchi ripped the cover off the prototype, poured a glass of water into the case, and then held the ruined prototype upside-down. As a few drops of water fell to the table, Mizoguchi shouted, "See, there is some space left!"[1]

When Mizoguchi's team finished a prototype that he felt was ready to share with the executive team, they denied him the chance to sell it in Japan. Fortunately, Atsutoshi Nishida, a senior vice president of Toshiba Europe, offered to sell the laptop in his territory—quickly selling thousands of units. With this new evidence, central administration swiftly changed their minds, and the Toshiba laptop was launched worldwide, achieving 38 percent market share in Europe and 46 percent market share in Japan by 1988. Mizoguchi's story shows that it's possible to apply rapid experimentation methods on new ideas in your team, even if you don't have top-level support. But you have to do so with small wins and with supporting data.

Sometimes the bottom-up approach of applying the innovator's method must be kept secret, particularly for large or controversial projects, as was the case for Mizoguchi. In these circumstances, pursuing a project in secret requires a champion who has enough resources to shelter the project (and a willingness to take risks, such as losing her job). For the laptop project, Mizoguchi had the support of Masaichi Koga, general manager of the computer business division. Later, Mizoguchi repeated this same process, himself sheltering the development of the first notebook computer, a project also rejected by corporate headquarters. Furthermore, these projects must be fast and frugal, being revealed only when there is adequate proof of the concept to convince the rest of the company. In the Toshiba case, the team revealed the project after there was a solid prototype, but perhaps this was too early: the executive team accepted the project only after it had demonstrated sales.

In addition, these projects are often best located away from headquarters to avoid distractions or distortions from the existing way of doing business. Like the Toshiba project, dozens of other secret projects have lived outside corporate headquarters, including IBM's successful PC experiment, which operated out of Florida, far away from IBM's New York headquarters.

But you don't need to pursue an innovation as radical as Mizoguchi's laptop in order to apply the innovator's method to the problems your team faces. The key is to educate your team regarding the process and then generate potential innovation insights, picking one or two to test (see "Taking a Page from Agile"). Consider it an experiment to see what you learn. If you're in the middle of a problem-solving or product development process, ask yourself whether you've nailed the problem and you're using fast and frugal experiments to test various solutions with customers. Try to keep whatever you do simple, inexpensive, and focused on learning and action.

Taking a Page from Agile

Some of the best thinking about how to apply the innovator's method as a team comes from the world of software. Because software development teams often face high uncertainty, a number of practitioners (Jeff Sutherland, Ken Schwaber, and Ken Rubin, to name a few) developed the concept of a *scrum* as a better way to organize a team for innovation and development. A scrum, a concept that comes from rugby, is the formation that allows the team to restart after stopping. Several useful ideas from the scrum may help you lead your team.

In software development, every agile scrum team has three components: a product owner, a scrum master, and a development team. The product owner sets the product vision and requirements, the scrum master coaches the team, and the team self-organizes to accomplish the tasks. Beyond software, consider the importance of a scrum master to helping a team apply the innovator's method. The scrum master has several important roles, each one essential: coach, helping the team members learn the method; process leader, helping the team apply the method; change management counselor, helping team members adapt to a new process; and champion, protecting team members from outside demands and removing barriers. Similarly, as a team member you need to realize your role in self-organizing and applying the process to your work.

Second, every scrum team follows an internal process of defining a *product backlog,* executing a *sprint,* and reviewing the sprint. The product backlog is a list of pending activities prioritized by those most critical to success. The sprint involves planning how the work (experiment) occurs within a short time-frame (between one week and one month), and the sprint review focuses on reviewing the product (completed work in the form of shippable products) and process (how well the sprint worked).

The scrum process has several valuable lessons. For starters, think of your team's backlog as the prioritized list of the most important assumptions you face. The concept of a sprint suggests the importance of identifying the tasks to test those critical questions, time boxing (scheduling) these tasks to go fast, and then adapting quickly as you discover the facts. And scrum teams engage in a daily fifteen-minute review, when they synchronize and adapt their activities to produce a finished outcome at the end of the sprint. After the sprint, the team members assess what worked and what they could have done better.

You could apply the daily process of the scrum to any stage of the innovator's method. As the scrum master, you could coach your team through the definition of a series of sprints to tackle your backlog quickly and effectively, all while learning how to improve the process. For more detail, we recommend Ken Rubin's *Essential Scrum: A Practical Guide to the Most Popular Agile Process* (New York: Addison-Wesley, 2012).

Igniting Innovation from Within Using the Innovator's Method

What if your organization is focused on execution but would like to ignite innovation from within? We recommend applying the innovator's method itself to the problem of building innovation capabilities. Now that you understand the need to develop innovation capabilities, follow the process we have described: assemble a small team, reach out to early adopters inside your company to understand their problems, use prototypes to test your solutions as quickly and inexpensively as possible, and then find the right business model for innovation inside your organization.

Consider how Kate O'Keeffe applied the method to build innovation capabilities at Cisco Services, a major business unit within Cisco employing more than thirteen thousand people and delivering almost one-quarter of Cisco's revenue. Although Cisco Services had made efforts to encourage innovation, for the most part they were ad hoc efforts across a large, diverse, and fragmented organization. So when Joe Pinto, a senior vice president in Cisco's Technical Services group, encouraged O'Keeffe to develop Cisco's innovation capabilities, the project was daunting by every measure. Moreover, she would have to do it without much budget, credibility, or infrastructure. Faced with this challenge, O'Keeffe said, "I needed to start small, demonstrate proof points, and earn organizational support organically."[2]

O'Keeffe began by assembling a small team composed of T-shaped people (people with breadth across many disciplines and depth in some disciplines) who were passionate about innovation and willing to voluntarily help her test their assumptions about igniting innovation. Included were an experienced facilitator, a serial entrepreneur, an expert in organizational behavior, and an expert in six sigma and product management. The team called itself the Services Innovation Center to create early legitimacy and connect to influential parts of the organization, for example, engaging executives such as Carlos Pignataro, a Cisco Distinguished Engineer who brought the members of that community with him.

Then, much as we have described, the team set about understanding the job-to-be-done. To do so, the team reached out to early adopters (people inside the company who wanted more innovation) to understand the problems they were trying to solve. O'Keeffe described this process: "We have a really different model. It's a client (customer) model, meaning we define what we do around what our customers (managers and executives) need to innovate."[3] As part of the process, the Services

Innovation team discovered that different customers wanted different things. Some wanted help generating new insights, others wanted help assessing and developing their innovation capabilities, and still others needed experimentation tools and instructions for how to innovate.

With a clearer picture of the job-to-be-done, O'Keeffe and her team could start to prototype solutions for a focused set of customers. Rather than wasting resources building full-featured solutions to every problem at once, O'Keeffe and her team prototyped solutions one at a time. For example, in one early effort the Services Innovation team developed a rapid prototype of an idea day and an idea tea time that spread virally throughout the company.

In a later example, several senior leaders expressed a desire to explore new business models and markets for existing technologies (the functional job) while also inspiring employees to innovate (emotional job). With these "jobs" in mind, the Services Innovation team prototyped a potential solution: a "LaunchPad" event that they pitched to Parvesh Seth, the senior vice president of Advanced Services, who agreed to conduct a pilot program. With this validation from an internal customer (similar to a payment test with an external customer), the Center assembled teams of six people from across the Cisco Services businesses, grouped around nine global regions. Each team worked to generate insights, explore the job-to-be-done with customers, and then rapidly prototype potential solutions. Then the teams converged in front of a combined live and virtual audience of senior executives to describe the problem and their most promising prototype. Although a rapid experiment, the LaunchPad proved a success, creating a $9 million impact and inspiring the excitement executives were searching for. In the words of Rosette Nguyen, one participant, "This was an incredible experience— what we learned from the process, the networks we built, and the exposure we received was incredible. I have everything I need to drive greater innovation in the future." [4] But just as important, it also led to innovation: the winning team developed a services dashboard for health care that one customer literally begged to buy or invest in.

By rapidly iterating on solutions for internal customer problems, the Services Innovation team generated the proof that they could solve key innovation problems inside the company. Over time, they have iterated from rapid prototypes to more feature-rich solutions, such as an innovation capabilities assessment and tools to capture and develop ideas. In another example, the team started without an idea capture tool, then adopted a version developed by Brightidea, then rapidly iterated to develop a tool that allows crowd-sourcing ideas across the entire services division. They have leveraged the platform, called Smartzone, to capture, select, nurture, and develop ideas.

For example, O'Keeffe recalls a team of service engineers who were discussing the daily challenge of trying to get customers' technical issues solved faster. The core issue was access to pieces of code, called scripts, which enable a customer issue to be resolved. Trying to find these scripts could be time-consuming and often delayed resolution of the customer issue. The engineers came up with an idea that would be like an app store for service engineers. This solution, a social networking platform that quickly connected service engineers to the required scripts, had the potential to change the way service engineers performed their work. The team, led by Sam Grimée, a senior manager in Technical Services, immediately submitted it to Smartzone, which attracted the feedback, interest, resources, and sponsorship needed to move through the steps of the innovator's method and bring the innovation to the service engineers. Grimée recalls, "Smartzone was a great medium to test whether potential customers found our idea useful, and it helped us identify and build a network of stakeholders to engage with and later partner with. The exposure and feedback we received were instrumental to define our plans and guide our solution development." They generated enough enthusiasm and funding to make a viable demo, a prototype, and to secure the people needed to help them succeed internally. The result is more than six thousand scripts being made available on a social media platform inside Cisco Services, each one saving precious minutes or hours of engineering time.

Finally, as the Services Innovation team prototyped and deployed solutions, they also experimented to validate the business model. For example, as with the launch of any other innovation, O'Keeffe's team had to find a way to deliver a value proposition, acquire customers, and manage costs. Recall that customer acquisition requires understanding what motivates your customers (the job-to-be-done), how they make decisions (the consumption chain), and how to communicate through channels that influence them (the influence pyramid). The team started by understanding the unique job-to-be-done for different customers; for example, junior engineers are looking for time and recognition, whereas senior executives are looking for big ideas that will create value through engaged employees. The team also looked at the consumption chain—the points at which innovation messages can influence their customers, such as company communications, annual evaluations, high-profile events, compensation, and so on. Finally, the team tackled the influence pyramid for their customers. For example, even though newsletters and e-mails have some effect, the team discovered that a range of events, such as an Innovation Summit (for advocates) and an Innovation Leadership Forum (a speaker series), along with rewards (a $1,500 Innovation Catalyst Award), had an even greater effect. Similarly, when it comes to costs, the team thought carefully about leveraging the resources already in Cisco, using partners inside and outside Cisco to develop and deliver solutions.

By applying the innovator's method, O'Keeffe and her team have been successful in igniting innovation within Cisco Services. In the last quarter alone, they've generated dozens of insights and more than $12 million of business impact, including lifting employee innovation engagement scores by more than 8 percent in the teams they engaged.[5] Moreover, people feel energized and inspired, saying things like, "I have never felt so much like a part of Cisco" and "People who were originally skeptics are now genuinely excited."[6] Having nailed the problem, solution, and business model, the team now faces many of the challenges described in chapter 8: developing the whole-product solution, standardizing the solution, and finding ways to deliver it at scale.

Adjusting for Disruptive versus Incremental Innovation

Imagine you work at Google and you're asked to work on bringing a new solution to market. You've been given two projects to choose from: Google Offers, an idea for a service offering discounts and coupons that is integrated with both Google Wallet (for payment) and Google Maps (to identify the location of the offering company), or Google Glass, an idea for a wearable computer with an optical head-mounted display (OHMD) that responds to voice commands and displays information in a smart phone-like hands-free format.[7] Both projects involve trying to bring something new to market, but clearly the Google Glass project involves a more radical innovation with higher uncertainties and higher risk. How might applying the innovator's method be different for an incremental versus a more radical, disruptive innovation (see "What Is a Disruptive Innovation?")?

What Is a Disruptive Innovation?

Innovations fall into two general categories: incremental and disruptive (radical). An *incremental* innovation builds on a firm's established knowledge base and either improves a product or offers product line extensions—for example, a Gillette razor with five blades instead of four; a Samsung TV with 3-D instead of 2-D imaging; and improvements to internal operations to accomplish a task faster, better, or with fewer resources.

In contrast, a *disruptive* innovation draws on a different knowledge base, technologies, or methods to deliver value in a unique way. Examples of disruptive product innovations include digital watches (versus mechanical watches), the personal computer (versus the typewriter and manual processes), cell phones (versus landline phones), and MP3 players (versus CD players).

Processes can also be changed in a disruptive way. For example, Toyota engineer Taiichi Ohno's flexible production techniques, often referred to as *lean* manufacturing, minimized inventories and waste despite being designed for rapid product changeovers. Business models, too, can be based on radical innovations. For example, Netflix used the internet, software, and warehouses to deliver video rentals through the mail and through streaming, an approach that was radically different from the brick-and-mortar stores of one-time market leader Blockbuster. Similarly, Redbox rents videos through vending machines, a method that requires different technologies—and a different distribution system—from those used by either Blockbuster or Netflix.

Strategies based on radical innovations are sometimes referred to as *disruptive* (a term popularized by Clayton Christensen) because incumbents can no longer do business as usual.[8] For example, Netflix and Redbox disrupted Blockbuster's strategy. Disruptive innovations often stem from a new technology entering at the low end—the most price-sensitive segment of the market—and then gradually moving upmarket as the disrupting company improves its technology and processes.

Although the Google Glass project may seem "cooler" because it's more disruptive, these types of innovations present significant challenges. Indeed, *The Innovator's Dilemma* argues that managers who aren't trained to deal with disruptive innovations fail when they try to apply their familiar tools for incremental management.[9] In the parlance of the innovator's method, we see the difference between incremental and disruptive innovations in terms of degrees of uncertainty. Disruptive innovations involve much greater uncertainty—sometimes orders of magnitude greater. This means that you'll need to apply the innovator's method to almost everything you do. But for disruptive innovations you must also adjust your expectations along four key dimensions: target customers, feedback expectations, timeline, and structure.

Before we describe these dimensions, we want to acknowledge that incremental innovations can also have significant benefits. By some estimates, they create as much value for companies as do disruptive innovations. For example, Hindustan Unilever discovered and implemented many small incremental innovations, generating a 40 percent revenue boost in a single year. With incremental innovations you enjoy lower uncertainty, you may already possess many of the required resources, and you can more easily integrate the change with your existing business model. However, it is also crucial to recognize that disruptive innovations create the growth markets of the future and so are a fundamental part of a firm's innovation portfolio.

Adjust Your Feedback Expectations

Most disruptive innovations are adopted first by nonusers: people who are not well served by existing solutions. Therefore, as a first rule of thumb, if you are pursuing a disruptive innovation, you should always explore your innovation with nonusers in great depth. That being said, regardless of whether you explore a disruptive innovation with users or nonusers, there are some peculiarities of the adoption process you should watch out for.

First, for disruptive innovations, customers may not fully recognize the problem, or the solution may be unfamiliar. As a result, you may receive negative feedback at first. Furthermore, for many disruptive innovations, people cannot imagine the product until they actually try it. For example, when Reebok introduced the Reebok Pump—an athletic shoe that has a button to inflate air pockets around the ankle—basketball players and coaches were skeptical until they tried the shoe. Then they loved it. *The Innovator's Dilemma* calls this the "agnostic marketing" problem, meaning that, for disruptive innovations, no one—not experts, not traditional market research, and not even customers themselves—can tell you what is wanted or whether it will succeed. Instead, customers have to try it to fully appreciate it.[10]

To complicate matters, there may be social norms or incentives that distort the feedback you receive. One entrepreneur developed a portable X-ray machine that produced such clear images that any health care provider could see bone cracks or tissue lumps, at 10 percent of the cost of existing technology. But radiologists and medical device companies were not interested. Why? The new machine conflicted with their existing financial incentives (radiologists interpret fuzzy films, and medical device companies sell expensive machines). Ultimately the company failed because it ran out of cash before it could overcome these persistent obstacles.

Similarly, if a solution doesn't seem legitimate, customers may reject it no matter how well it solves the problem. In one famous example, efforts to teach villagers to boil unclean water in the region of Los Molinos, Peru, failed because of a local tradition that hot foods were only for sick people. Because the innovation was only adopted by people lacking legitimacy (social outsiders), the practice failed to spread.[11] If your innovation faces potential legitimacy challenges, you may have to think carefully about how to create that legitimacy.

Adjust Your Timeline

In the popular lore surrounding disruptive innovation, incumbents are blindsided and respond too late, leading to their failure. For example, Swiss watchmakers dominated the mechanical watch industry for years before digital watches—most of them made by Japanese firms—entered the market. The Swiss viewed these new watches as low-quality, low-margin timepieces; jewelers did not want to sell them, and Swiss watchmakers felt certain they could maintain their advantage. But as the performance of digital watches improved, they began to move upmarket, quickly replacing Swiss watches at the market's lower end and then in the mainstream. By the time Swiss manufacturers responded, it was too late. Japanese manufacturers were making millions of units for every ten thousand units the Swiss produced. Within a decade, the Swiss watch industry had been decimated, with most manufacturers going out of business and the Swiss market share falling to less than 10 percent.[12]

On the surface, the Swiss watch example appears to be a classic case of disruption, with the incumbents being blindsided by a new technology. But let's take a closer look. In this case, as in other disruptions, the incumbents actually invested early on in digital technology, but they concluded it was too expensive and too clunky and would never succeed against the elegant Swiss watches. As a result, they simply quit investing.

The issue at stake is a matter of timing and perception. Early in the life of a disruptive innovation, it often appears "not good enough." Moreover, market adoption of disruptive innovations takes far more time than with incremental innovations. In some cases it might take decades for the disruptive product to improve to the point where customers will accept it. This means that if you're working on the Google Glass project instead of the Google Offers project, you'll need to be patient and adjust your expectations for how quickly the product will gain adoption and be seen as valuable. Moreover, you may have to patiently improve certain new technologies (or work with partners to improve them) for the disruptive product to nail the job-to-be-done. It usually takes longer to get market adoption, because customers will be unfamiliar with the solution and will need to be educated. If you've adopted a low-cost, high-experimentation approach like the one we advocate—rather than the high-profile, high-cost approach taken by many hopeful innovators—you're more likely to sustain the organizational patience needed for the idea to mature.

Adjust Your Structure

It's critical to provide the right structure—and the right mix of skills—for disruptive innovation project teams. Many organizations fail with projects, especially disruptive ones, because they fail to understand a basic organizing principle: the more radical the idea, the more autonomy the project team will require.

Let's see why that is. A company's least radical projects typically involve incremental improvements to existing products. For example, at Sony the next generation of its PS4 game console (we'll call it the PS5) will likely be developed by designers and engineers who work at Sony and are familiar with the PS4's components and architecture. Innovations are likely to come from modifying or improving existing components (graphics, storage, the convenience of online gaming) or perhaps adding a new one (perhaps the ability to digitally record TV shows as a DVR or TiVo does). The ideal team for this project is a team of engineers who specialize in each type of component, working at the component level. Alternatively, Sony might use a *lightweight* team— mainly people from the game console group but including a few engineers from other functional areas.

But imagine that Sony wants to develop a Google Glass–like device that possesses features that leapfrog Google Glass (let's call it Sony Glass) and support advanced gaming. If Sony attempts to develop the new Sony Glass device within the PS4 engineering group, the new device will likely reflect the knowledge and technology of a Sony game console. The same would be true if the device were developed by the Sony computer engineering group, or the Sony TV group. To get something more radical, Sony would be better off pulling folks from each of these areas (and perhaps elsewhere) into an autonomous project team, independent and isolated from the rest of the corporation, to protect the innovation and allow full application of these principles.

A project may differ so radically from a company's offerings that it requires a different business model (e.g., to serve different customers using different technologies). In these cases it makes sense to create a fully autonomous business unit. For example, when Amazon decided to pursue, and then launch, a cloud computing service business (Amazon Web Services), it created an autonomous business unit, because the opportunity demanded a different business model from Amazon's online retailing business.

Creating an autonomous team or business unit can be critical for several reasons. First, when the existing business model conflicts with the disruptive business model, staying with the existing business model can destroy the disruptive idea. The existing business model will starve the idea of resources, as happened in the Swiss watch case, or it will kill the innovation outright, as occurred when Polaroid shelved its market-leading digital capabilities because they conflicted with its film-based business model.

Second, large companies require growth that disruptive innovations initially cannot provide. A billion-dollar company searching for 10 percent growth ($100 million) next year will find the $50,000 revenues of an early disruptive innovation irrelevant. As a result it will either defund the effort or distort it by trying to make it generate revenue right away (usually it gets turned into a sustaining innovation that misses the market opportunity). Putting the disruptive idea into a separate group that can get excited about smaller revenues will let these folks take the steps to one day build a billion-dollar business.

Third, putting the disruptive idea into a separate unit lets the team develop the resources the innovation needs rather than those already in the firm. For example, when IBM sent a team to Florida to develop the IBM PC, the team developed new competencies and used the resources of new partners, such as Intel and Microsoft. This strategy saved the team crucial time and expense, economies that proved vital to the success of the IBM PC.

Watch Out: Are You Dependent on Someone Else?

Have you ever wondered how Nokia went from being the top phone manufacturer in the 1990s, only to be banished to the sidelines in the smart phone era? It's tempting to think the company didn't try to innovate or didn't foresee the 3G revolution, with its potential for mobile internet and a portable, digital lifestyle. But that's not it. As Ron Adner recounts in *The Wide Lens,* Nokia was an enthusiastic pioneer of the 3G era.[13] Projecting that there would be more than 300 million 3G users by 2002, Nokia pushed the development of the first 3G phone, the 6650, which was the most technically advanced mobile phone to date. Despite successfully producing the first 3G phone at an affordable price—an immense technical feat in 2002—Nokia saw less than 1 percent of the predicted market materialize.

Although Nokia delivered a solution, it overlooked a change that occurred in the transition from 2G to 3G: successful innovation shifted from being an independent effort under Nokia's control to an interdependent effort, much of it outside Nokia's control. The shift to 3G required the development of outside innovations such as video conversion software to display mobile video, changes in router technology to handle increased traffic, database tools to allow mobile operators to identify users' data access, digital rights management to ensure security for content providers, and so on. As a result, when Nokia delivered the phone, the remaining pieces of the ecosystem were still missing. Nokia failed to recognize that its success was dependent on others, and it hadn't properly addressed or managed those interdependencies.

Increasingly, innovation is shifting from independent to interdependent undertakings. Multiple partners must deploy their resources and even change their activities to ensure widespread market adoption. Some of these partners may be upstream or downstream, in areas that you might normally ignore.

To adapt the innovator's method to interdependent innovation, start by mapping the required ecosystem for your product. As you look at the uncertainties you face, look upstream at any uncertainties about the required components, downstream at the uncertainties of adoption, and laterally at the larger ecosystem of partners you need. What parties possess complementary assets or resources that will influence the successful adoption of your innovation? Once you've identified them, it's critical to bring them on board early. Otherwise you might spend significant time and resources developing an innovation that will not succeed because you did not get the support of entities that possess key complementary assets.

Adapt to Innovate

Your ability to apply the innovator's method depends on your circumstances. If you're an individual contributor, your pathway will differ from that of a team leader or an organization leader trying to achieve organization-wide impact. We've observed the successful application of elements of the method by hundreds of individuals and by dozens of companies, large and small. In most instances, managers and entrepreneurs adapted the method to fit their own circumstances. There is no one-size-fits-all prescription for success.

Despite the adaptations, there remains remarkable adherence to the basic principles: identify a problem, identify the necessary assumptions with regard to solving it, construct low-cost experiments to test your assumptions, and learn as quickly as possible. We know you can adapt the innovator's method to your unique circumstances.

In conclusion, we want to once more acknowledge that the innovation process is inherently messy and recursive. We have tried to simplify the process here to make it easier to understand, but in reality, stages overlap with one another, some steps get skipped, and often confusion or ambiguity accompanies the process. When this is the case, it helps to recognize that you aren't doing anything wrong. Rather, you are dealing with uncertainty and such messiness is part of the process. Rather than trying to stamp out uncertainty, respect and embrace it as many great things emerge from uncertainty: creativity and innovation are just one.

Conclusion

Turn Uncertainty into Opportunity

I N THE FIRST DECADES of the US biotechnology industry, most biotech companies operated according to the same rule: identify one promising candidate drug (usually following up on an insight coming from academia), and then focus virtually all your resources on bringing this drug to market. Because the cost and technical uncertainty in discovering and developing new drugs were so high, the prevailing wisdom argued that nascent biotech companies had neither the capital nor the know-how to develop a broader research base or drug pipeline. Furthermore, diluting efforts by attempting to do so was a sure recipe for failure. While many young companies raised tens to hundreds of millions of dollars to develop a single new drug, the sad truth was that the vast majority of these companies would fail, never bringing a single drug to market. The landmark sequencing of the human genome raised hopes that things would change: thousands of cures for cancer and other diseases would become instantly obvious, and the rate of drug discovery would exponentially increase. Unfortunately, things didn't change. Despite the efforts of hundreds of biotech companies, not to mention dozens of so-called multinational big pharma companies, each year only about twenty new drugs are approved in the United States, and very few are true blockbusters that change the landscape.

So when a newly formed biotech company called Regeneron, led by physician-scientists Leonard Schleifer and George Yancopoulos, held its first meeting with a board of esteemed scientific advisers, the team members were excited to share their grand vision of a better process for developing new therapeutics. Rather than focus on one solution, Yancopoulos proposed that they first invest in better understanding why treatments failed in the first place and then use better experiments to create dozens of solutions at the same time. This would require creating tools to tackle the rate-limiting factors—the accuracy and speed of experiments—in developing new therapeutics.

Much to the chagrin of Yancopoulos, formerly a professor at Columbia, the room exploded with criticism: What were Schleifer and Yancopoulos thinking? Why weren't they, like everyone else, focusing their research efforts and resources on a single high-potential therapeutic treatment? How could they possibly succeed if they scattered their resources and attention by testing multiple solutions at once?

Yancopoulos recalls being stunned and dismayed. Finally, Schleifer stepped in, asserting that Regeneron was going to try its process in spite of the advisers' rejection. Although Yancopoulos felt relieved to have Schleifer on his side, we ask you to put yourself in their shoes: some of the most preeminent thinkers in the world had told them they were going about it all wrong. Were they?

Fast-forward twenty-five years, and we find that Regeneron is one of the most innovative companies in the world. Regeneron's success in developing breakthroughs has helped it rise rapidly to the number 4 position on the *Forbes* most innovative companies list, with an innovation premium of 63 percent. Although Yancopoulos could easily look back and gloat, he says he now recognizes how fortunate the founders were. Most companies that followed the advice of their advisers failed, flaming out before they brought a single product to market. As it turned out, many of Regeneron's early guesses, although seemingly founded on strong science, also turned out to be dead ends. Had Regeneron focused too narrowly, it too might have become a forgotten failure.

At the core, a single insight differentiated Regeneron from its contemporaries: in a highly uncertain environment, you need to do fast and frugal experiments to solve problems. Whereas many of Regeneron's contemporaries unwittingly borrowed traditional management tactics from established pharmaceutical firms (which faced comparatively greater certainty), Regeneron started with the assumption that it faced unprecedented uncertainty. Yancopoulos says that even though many of Regeneron's contemporaries have a healthy respect for peer-reviewed science, he started with a healthy disrespect. "In my view 60 to 90 percent of discoveries in biology are either wrong or irrelevant," he says. "Just take a look at the *New York Times* science section: Of a hundred breakthroughs, how many have materialized? I remember seeing the cover of the *New York Times* in 1998 that cancer would be cured in two years . . . the point is, most of what we believe to be facts are not."[1]

Because they recognized such fundamental uncertainty, the Regeneron team designed a different process to deal with such uncertainty. As Yancopoulos recalls, "Our core belief was that if you don't know for sure about things, you are going to make a lot of wrong turns, wasting a lot of resources. Our belief was that we could actually use genetics as the most powerful way to rigorously test an idea. We are doing something fundamentally different than the way a lot of companies innovate."[2]

Although the two men describe this process in more scientific terms, in essence, the Regeneron team discovered and applied the innovator's method (see figure C-1).

FIGURE C-1

The innovator's method

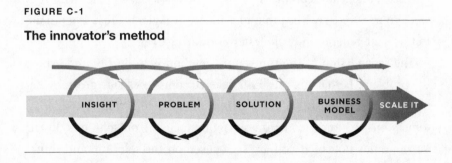

Here's how. In the first step—insight—we recommend searching broadly rather than focusing on a narrow set of ideas. Regeneron searches much more broadly for insights than most biotechnology companies before settling on the problems it wants to tackle. Whereas many biotech companies are based on a single insight from a scientist's lab, the Regeneron team members go beyond the lab, scouring the broader academic literature, searching for potential associations or even hints of associations between genes and a disease. Then, when they find a reported association, the team does experiments in genetically modified mice, created using its VelociGene platform technology, to test it. In this way, the Regeneron team can generate and validate insights, using real data, much more quickly than many competitors. Yancopoulos argues, "Using this approach we could re-create reported associations and quickly jump on them. Instead of following the literature, we can sample a thousand associations and jump on the most promising ten to fifty."[3]

For example, in the mid 2000s, Regeneron teams became aware that researchers at the University of Texas had found a specific genetic mutation in people who have "bad" (LDL) cholesterol levels that are 20 percent as high as those of the rest of the population (and who have correspondingly lower rates of heart disease). Putting VelociGene to work, Regeneron scientists quickly created this mutation in their mice and watched the effect, quickly observing and validating an insight—an association between a specific gene, a biochemical marker (low "bad" cholesterol), and heart disease. Today, Regeneron and its big pharma partner, Sanofi, are completing phase three trials with the drug they went on to develop, while other pharmaceutical giants are in hot pursuit in this next generation of cholesterol-lowering drugs.

The second step of the innovator's method is to deeply understand the problem. Perhaps because life science companies face greater technical uncertainty (will it work?) than demand uncertainty (will customers buy it?), most companies start by focusing on solutions. But as Yancopoulos notes, "If you are so focused on the solution, and things aren't working, and you are trying to get things to work, you don't understand the reasons you are failing . . . Rather than slapping solutions on top, we were trying to deeply understand the problem, which is the first step."[4]

Regeneron doesn't interview customers, because most customers care about problems like curing their cancer or lowering their blood pressure (the demand uncertainty). But Regeneron still invests in understanding the physiological and biological problem before working on the solution. For example, before developing solutions to block the way disease-related genes instruct the body to bind proteins with one another, the Regeneron researchers experimented to understand how the relevant proteins bind with each other in the first place so that they could better create solutions to block the binding process. Because Regeneron focused on the problem first, says Yancopolous, "we were able to come up with a therapeutic solution better than anyone else's solution . . . in fact, whereas most companies would develop only one drug for a particular target, by understanding that first step really well, we ultimately came up with three drugs and five disease applications."[5]

The third step of the innovator's method is to iteratively match a solution to the problem using a series of prototypes to avoid wasting resources on unwanted solutions. Of course, all life science companies test their solutions to make sure they work. But they often use a long, expensive testing process that starts with testing in animals and then progresses through three rounds of clinical trials in humans, ultimately costing hundreds of millions of dollars and resulting in failure rates as great as 97 percent.[6] Many companies have tried to overcome this liability by pushing as many solutions as possible through the clinical trial pipeline in hopes of increasing their hit rate, resulting in a sharp increase in the cost to develop new treatments.

Clearly some of the prototypes we have recommended, such as virtual prototypes drawn in PowerPoint, would not work here. But consider how Regeneron has applied the principle. Rather than push solutions into clinical trials, Regeneron executives adopted the idea of early, rapid experimentation, developing a technology that would allow them to rapidly generate and test many solutions more accurately in that first step of animal trials. Most companies test one or a few solutions in mice. Mice are inexpensive but are imperfect models for human disease. Rather than accept the status quo and rely on an imperfect experiment with a small number of solutions, Regeneron redesigned the experimentation process, creating a technology to generate a larger number of higher-quality solutions by replacing mouse immune genes with human counterparts, but at a scale millions of times larger than any gene replacement attempted previously. These "humanized" mice were then used to develop what was effectively a multitude of "prototyped" solutions that were also more specific to human disease: human antibodies, rather than mice antibodies, to treat a disease. A different humanized mouse would then be used to quickly test which of the prototyped solutions actually worked to treat the disease, in what was essentially a prototype of a human model. Whereas their closest competitors could test one or two mouse antibodies (which are imperfect models of human antibodies), the Regeneron approach lets the company prototype and then test hundreds of human, rather than mouse, antibody solutions. Not only did Regeneron experiment during the earliest stage to find the best solutions, but it also invented a technology that allowed it to experiment better and faster—a hundred times faster.

As we look back, part of what makes Regeneron successful is that it has applied the principles of the innovator's method to test unknowns more quickly and more effectively than most competitors. It has made mistakes, but applying rapid experimentation has allowed it to quickly test multiple solutions, thereby enabling it to rapidly resolve some of the huge uncertainties during treatment development. This approach has helped Regeneron successfully develop for approval three treatments in the past few years, a remarkable achievement for all but the largest pharmaceutical firms.

EYLEA, the most successful so far, treats a form of adult vision loss known as wet age-related macular degeneration. The product achieved nearly $1 billion in sales during its first full year, a rare feat in a field that rarely sees blockbuster treatments. What's more, Regeneron produces these breakthroughs at a cost dramatically lower than the industry average: according to a recent analysis, most companies that have produced three or more approved treatments spend an average of $4.3 billion in R&D per treatment. Some of the larger companies have spent as much as $10 billion. By contrast, Regeneron has spent an average of $736 million per treatment, a number that includes both the cost of development and the extra investment in experimentation tools.[7]

Innovate on the Method Itself

Beyond its remarkable application of the innovator's method in an industry characterized by complex science and high technical uncertainty, Regeneron's experience teaches us a deeper lesson. The company has been so successful because it innovated on the process itself. It identified the rate-limiting elements of its ability to nail the problem and solution and then developed innovations that dramatically increased the speed at which the company could follow the steps. As Yancopoulos describes it, "We went broad, beyond the technology, to come up with tools that would allow us to make better choices in the first place."[8]

These tools include data sets to test insights, the technology to replace genes (VelociGene), the tool to create human antibodies in mice (VelocImmune), and a number of other approaches. These process improvements allow Regeneron to test problems and solutions more quickly, inexpensively, and accurately than competitors. "History is proving that our approach was better," says Yancopoulos. "We've been able to come up with faster, better ways to make those crucial decisions: How do you pick the right problem and how do you know if your solution will really work."[9]

Gain a Competitive Advantage

As uncertainty increases, companies will have to reorganize for innovation, adopting new ways to effectively create new products, services, and solutions. But rather than view such a change as a threat, leaders should view it as an opportunity to create an advantage by designing better experimentation tools to speed innovation.

At the beginning of this book we argue that you should ignore strategic issues such as competitive advantage or first-mover advantage until you determine that you've found a problem worth solving and a solution that nails the job-to-be-done. As professors of strategy and innovation, we're being fairly heretical in advising you to ignore strategy during the first stages of the method (of course, strategy matters as you begin to nail the solution). But ask yourself, in an era of uncertainty, what competitive advantages truly persist? As we show in chapter 1, competitive advantages are more fleeting than ever. We argue that in high uncertainty, the only durable advantage is the ability to manage uncertainty: to capture opportunities more quickly and to learn more effectively than competitors, and to bring those innovations to market. Although it takes time to develop and practice this capability, once developed, it's hard to imitate. That makes it durable.

By applying the innovator's method to the problems of increasing the speed and effectiveness of experimentation, Regeneron has created a competitive advantage. Although the company has been criticized for working in diseases crowded with competitors, Yancopoulos and Schleifer make these seemingly counterintuitive choices because they believe they can learn—and develop effective solutions—more quickly than others. Using its rapid experimentation processes, Regeneron can test assumptions so quickly that often it simultaneously tests its competitor's solutions as well as its own as it looks for opportunities to leapfrog a competitor. Whether it can continue to develop these capabilities and stay a step ahead remains to be seen. But its remarkably high hit rate and low development costs suggest that it has developed a durable advantage through its innovation capabilities.

Professional and Personal

We start this book by asserting that as we move from the industrial age to the information age, we face a surge in uncertainty that calls for a new way of management. Established companies will no longer be able to rely on traditional management alone if they hope to innovate or survive. Instead, managers and entrepreneurs alike will have to apply the new management science of innovation—what we labeled the i-school— to the uncertainty of creating new growth from innovation.

Each major discipline, upon encountering uncertainty, has developed its own answer to the challenge of how to manage uncertainty. Each perspective offers valuable insight into solving high-uncertainty problems. Each perspective has generated thoughtful contributions. But rarely do the holders of these perspectives talk to each other or consider how their overlapping approaches could be combined to effectively address the need for innovation.

In this book, we've tried to synthesize these perspectives into a single method, an end-to-end process that you, your team, or your company can use to generate disruptive insights and bring them to market. In a sample of companies we studied, we found a significant correlation between implementing elements of the innovator's method and an increase in innovation premium and market value. Indeed, the average boost in innovation premium is more than 50 percent, an increase that translates into billions of dollars in market capitalization. Similarly, companies that have instituted these ideas, even after trying to innovate using other approaches, have claimed significant increases in revenues from new products: for example, both Intuit and Cisco Services earned more than $100 million in new revenues, and Hindustan Unilever enjoyed a 40 percent increase in revenues.

But more important than shorter-term revenues and market value, these companies discover new opportunities and bring them to market at lower cost and at higher success rates than their competitors. Regeneron is not alone in saying, "We've been able to come up with faster, better ways to make those crucial decisions";[10] Jeff Bezos cites a reduction of the costs of experimenting and a resulting boost in the number of experiments the company is able to conduct.[11] For Intuit founder Scott Cook, the approaches described here have "totally transformed" the way the company operates. Our firsthand research showed that every Intuit leader, manager, designer, and engineering lead used the process of developing a hypothesis, framing an experiment, and then using the data to make decisions.

This approach has allowed companies working in a wide range of industries, from software to cement, from pharmaceuticals to food products, to discover the tools to innovate repeatedly. Those that apply the method are finding the returns speak for themselves. "Our innovation program sharpens the focus of our employees and our ecosystem on the direction we're going," says John Donovan of AT&T technology and network operations. "But it also is providing elite venture capital returns, so there's real value in it."[12]

Whether you're a leader, a manager, an entrepreneur, or an individual contributor, we know you can apply this method to resolve uncertainty, wherever you face it, whether in internal processes or external innovations, at lower cost and with greater success than ever before. The innovator's method will help you creatively solve problems that you face in both your professional and your personal life. Most of all, you can use these tools to learn more quickly than others—and in this era of uncertainty, speed of learning is the new competitive advantage. We look forward to seeing you use these tools to cross each new finish line first, wherever that may be.

Appendix

An Overview of the Innovator's Method

I N THE FOLLOWING figure A-1, we summarize all the steps and tools of the innovator's method. This graphic features the key activities for each step of the innovator's method, the tools, and the tests to know whether you have resolved the key uncertainties of each element sufficiently to have confidence in your innovation. Additional insights on how to apply these, and other tools and tests, are available at www .theinnovatorsmethod.com.

FIGURE A-1

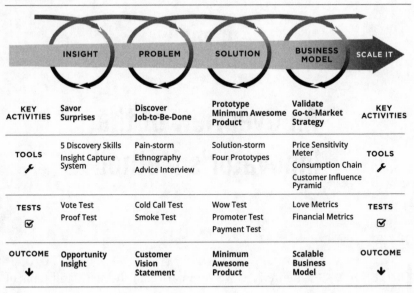

KEY ACTIVITIES	Savor Surprises	Discover Job-to-Be-Done	Prototype Minimum Awesome Product	Validate Go-to-Market Strategy	KEY ACTIVITIES
TOOLS 🔧	5 Discovery Skills, Insight Capture System	Pain-storm, Ethnography, Advice Interview	Solution-storm, Four Prototypes	Price Sensitivity Meter, Consumption Chain, Customer Influence Pyramid	TOOLS 🔧
TESTS ☑	Vote Test, Proof Test	Cold Call Test, Smoke Test	Wow Test, Promoter Test, Payment Test	Love Metrics, Financial Metrics	TESTS ☑
OUTCOME ⬇	Opportunity Insight	Customer Vision Statement	Minimum Awesome Product	Scalable Business Model	OUTCOME ⬇

Notes

Introduction

1. Thomas Eisenmann and Laura Winig, "Rent the Runway," Case 812-077 (Boston: Harvard Business School, 2012).

2. Ibid.

3. Ibid.

4. Ibid.

5. Jenna Wortham, "A Netflix Model for Haute Couture," *New York Times*, November 8, 2009, http://www.nytimes.com/2009/11/09/technology/09runway.html?_r=0.

6. See http://sloanreview.mit.edu/article/rent-the-runway-organizing-around-ana lytics/.

7. Evidence suggests that writing business plans has no correlation with success under conditions of uncertainty and are largely a waste of time. See John C. Dencker, Marc Gruber, and Sonali K. Shah, "Pre-Entry Knowledge, Learning, and the Survival of New Firms," *Organization Science* 20, no. 3 (2009): 516–537; David A. Kirsch, Brent Goldfarb, and Azi Gera, "Form or Substance? The Role of Business Plans in Venture Capital Funding," *Strategic Management Journal* 30, no. 5 (2009): 487–515; Julian E. Lange et al., "Pre-Startup Formal Business Plans and Post-Startup Performance: A Study of 116 New Ventures," *Venture Capital* 9 (2007): 237–256.

8. Clayton M. Christensen, *The Innovator's Dilemma: When New Technologies Cause Great Firms to Fail* (Boston: Harvard Business Review Press, 2013); Jeff Dyer, Hal Gregersen, and Clayton Christensen, *The Innovator's DNA* (Boston: Harvard Business Review Press, 2011).

9. A company's innovation premium represents the premium that investors are willing to pay for a company's stock because they expect the company to launch innovations that will produce even bigger future income streams. It is the market value of the company minus the net present value of its existing businesses.

10. Jeff Dyer and Hal B. Gregersen, "The Secret to Unleashing Genius," *Forbes*, September 3, 2013.

Chapter 1

1. Scott Cook, personal interview, May 7, 2013.

2. The innovation premium, a metric for innovation performance that we developed and described in *The Innovator's DNA* (Jeffrey Dyer, Hal Gregersen, and Clayton Christensen, Boston: Harvard Business Review Press, 2011) represents the percentage of a firm's market value that cannot be accounted for by its existing business cash flows. We rank *Forbes* list of the world's most innovative companies using this methodology. See http://www.forbes.com/sites/innovatorsdna/2011/10/20/the-innovation-premium-our-methodology/.

3. Peter Drucker, *The Practice of Management* (New York: Harper & Row, 1954), 54.

4. For a detailed discussion of this case, see the Introduction.

5. Alternative explanations for an increase in the rate of patenting are globalization (international companies increasingly patenting in the United States), changes in patenting scope (increases in the number of patents of narrow scope), patent litigation (increasing patenting activities to create defensible intellectual property), and so on. Even in the face of these explanations, it's clear that the pace of technology invention (and adoption) has accelerated.

6. John Melloy, "iPad Adoption Rate Fastest Ever, Passing DVD Player," CNBC, October 4, 2010.

7. Robert R. Wiggins and Timothy W. Ruefli, "Schumpeter's Ghost: Is Hypercompetition Making the Best of Times Shorter?" *Strategic Management Journal* 26 (2005): 1249–1259; Rajshree Agarwal and Michael Gort, "Firm and Product Life Cycles and Firm Survival," *American Economic Review* 92 (2002): 184–190.

8. A score of 7 or 8 is deemed "passive" (see chapter 5).

9. Kaaren Hanson, personal interview, May 6, 2013.

10. Brad Smith, personal interview, May 6, 2013.

11. Hanson, 2013.

12. Ibid.

13. Roger Martin examines the role of innovation catalysts in a 2011 *Harvard Business Review* article, "The Innovation Catalyst."

14. Cook, 2013.

15. Eric Ries, in *The Lean Startup: How Today's Entrepreneurs Use Continuous Innovation to Create Radically Successful Businesses* (New York: Crown Business, 2011), uses "build-test-learn" terminology to refer to this experimentation loop. However, we prefer "hypothesis" to "build" because in many cases your experiment is testing a hypothesis without building anything.

16. Ben Blank, personal interview, May 6, 2013; Cook, 2013; and Thomas Eisenmann and Tanya Bijlani, "Intuit Inc.: Project Agranova," Case 813062 (Boston: Harvard Business School, 2012).

17. Smith, 2013.

18. Lean start-up uses the term *minimum viable product,* but Intuit says it doesn't want a minimum "viable" product; it wants a minimum feature set but one that delights customers. We discuss this more in chapter 5.

19. Hanson, 2013.

20. Cook, 2013.

21. Ibid.

22. Smith, 2013.

23. Ibid.

24. Ries, *The Lean Startup.*

Chapter 2

1. See http://www.quoteswise.com/elon-musk-quotes-2.html.

2. Frederick Winslow Taylor, *The Principles of Scientific Management* (New York: Norton, 1911).

3. Peter Drucker, *The Practice of Management* (New York: Harper & Row, 1954), 54.

4. Alfred Sloan, *My Years with General Motors* (New York: Crown Business, 1990).

5. Lawrence R. Gustin, *Billy Durant: Creator of General Motors* (Ann Arbor: University of Michigan Press, 2008).

6. Scott Cook, personal interview, May 7, 2013.

7. David Garvin, "How Google Sold Its Engineers on Management," *Harvard Business Review*, December 2013.

8. Ryan Tate, *The 20% Doctrine* (New York: HarperCollins, 2012), 26.

9. Nitin Verma, personal interview, August 26, 2013.

10. Cook, 2013.

11. Jeff Dyer, Hal B. Gregersen, and Clayton Christensen, "Innovative Companies Demand Innovative Leaders," HBR Blog Network, August 9, 2011, http://blogs.hbr .org/2011/08/innovative-companies-demand-in/.

12. Ibid.

13. Cook, 2013.

14. Paul Kirschbaum, personal interview, October 17, 2013.

15. Valve Software, "Valve Handbook for New Employees," 2012.

16. J. J. McCorvey, "AmazonFresh Is Jeff Bezos' Last Mile Quest for Total Retail Domination," 2013, http://www.fastcompany.com/3014817/amazon-jeff-bezos.

17. Ricardo dos Santos, personal interview, October 30, 2013.

18. Ricardo dos Santos, "Just Say 'Maybe,'" *Necrophone*, 2013, http://necrophone .com/2013/10/30/just-say-maybe/.

19. John Donovan, personal interview, December 20, 2013.

20. Ben Blank, personal interview, May 6, 2013.

21. Roger Martin, *The Design of Business* (Boston: Harvard Business Review Press, 2009).

22. Kaaren Hanson, personal interview, December 26, 2013.

23. "Valve Handbook," 2012.

24. Bala Iyer and Thomas H. Davenport, "Reverse Engineering Google's Innovation Machine," *Harvard Business Review,* April 2008.

25. Brian M. Carney and Isaac Getz, "Google's 20% Mistake," *Wall Street Journal*, August 27, 2013.

26. Ryan Smith, personal interview, May 10, 2013.

27. Hanson, 2013.

28. Kirschbaum, 2013.

29. "Valve Handbook," 2012.

30. Intuit Legal Department, 2013.

31. For an excellent summary of the dangers of using financial tools, see "Innovation Killers: How Financial Tools Destroy Your Capacity to Do New Things," *Harvard Business Review*, January 2008.

32. Cook, 2013.

Chapter 3

1. Stephen Remedios, "Project Bushfire: Focusing the Might of an Entire Organization on the Consumer & Customer," Management Innovation eXchange, January 1, 2013, http://www.managementexchange.com/story/project-bushfire-focussing-might-entire-organization-consumer.

2. Ibid.

3. Kala Vijayraghavan and Sagar Malviya, "Hindustan Unilever Ceo Nitin Paranjpe Targets to Work Towards Perfection in a Store," *Economic Times,* August 10, 2011.

4. Michael Dell, personal interview, June 25, 2004.

5. Scott Cook, personal interview, May 7, 2013.

6. Clayton M. Christensen, *The Innovator's Dilemma: When New Technologies Cause Great Firms to Fail* (Boston: Harvard Business Review Press, 2013).

7. Remedios, 2013.

8. Ibid.

9. Julia Kirby and Thomas A. Stewart, "The Institutional Yes: An Interview with Jeff Bezos," *Harvard Business Review,* October 2007.

10. Kirby and Stewart, 2007.

11. Larry Huston and Nabil Sakkab, "Connect and Develop," *Harvard Business Review,* March 2006.

12. Jeff Howe, *Crowdsourcing: How the Power of the Crowd Is Driving the Future of Business* (New York: Random House, 2008).

13. Howard Leventhal, Robert Singer, and Susan Jones, "Effects of Fear and Specificity of Recommendation upon Attitudes and Behavior," *Journal of Personality and Social Psychology* 2, no. 1 (1965): 20.

14. Jeff Zias, personal interview, May 6, 2013.

15. Valve Software, "Valve Handbook for New Employees," 2012.

16. Paul Kirschbaum, personal interview, October 17, 2013.

17. Teresa Amabile, "Motivating Creativity in Organizations," *California Management Review* 40, no. 1 (1997): 39–58.

18. "Valve Handbook," 2012.

19. Ryan Tate, *The 20% Doctrine* (New York: HarperCollins, 2012), 26.

20. Ibid, 28.

21. Matthew Herpen, "The Miracle Workers," *Forbes,* September 2, 2013, 94.

Chapter 4

1. Mike Maples, personal interview, May 13, 2009.

2. As recounted by Maples, 2009, and in Jeffrey Rayport, Marco Iansiti, and Myra Hart, "Motive Communications," Case 699-157 (Boston: Harvard Business School, 2001).

3. Quoted in Clayton Christensen, Scott Cook, and Taddy Hall, "Marketing Malpractice: The Cause and the Cure," *Harvard Business Review,* December 2005.

4. Anthony Ulwick, "Turning Customer Input into Innovation," *Harvard Business Review,* January 2002.

5. Gianfranco Zaccai, "Why Focus Groups Kill Innovation, from the Designer Behind Swiffer," 2012, http://www.fastcodesign.com/1671033/why-focus-groups-kill-innovation-from-the-designer-behind-swiffer.

6. See Jeffrey Dyer, Hal Gregersen, and Clayton Christensen, *The Innovator's DNA* (Boston: Harvard Business Review Press, 2011).

7. Juan Carlos, "DaviPlata: 'Self-Service' Financial Inclusion," Management Innovation eXchange, 2013, http://www.managementexchange.com/story/daviplata-financial-inclusion-all-using-self-service-transactional-product-going-kyc-kyc-know-.

8. Ibid.

9. Mark Sandhill, personal interview, January 5, 2009.

10. Alistair Barr, "Amazon Lending: Company Offering Loans to Its Online Sellers," *Reuters*, September 28, 2012; Sarah Needleman, "What to Know Before Borrowing from Amazon," *Wall Street Journal*, October 4, 2012.

11. Ibid.

12. Ibid.

Chapter 5

1. Isak Bukhman, *TRIZ Technology for Innovation* (Taiwan: Cubic Creativity Company, 2012); Genrich Altshuller, *And Suddenly the Innovator Appeared: TRIZ, the Theory of Inventive Problem Solving* (Worcester, MA: Technical Innovation Center, Inc., 1996).

2. Juan Carlos, "DaviPlata: 'Self-Service' Financial Inclusion," Management Innovation eXchange, 2013, http://www.managementexchange.com/story/daviplata-financial-inclusion-all-using-self-service-transactional-product-going-kyc-kyc-know-.

3. Andrew Hargadon, *How Breakthroughs Happen: The Surprising Truth about How Companies Innovate* (Boston: Harvard Business School Press, 2003).

4. Wendy Castleman, personal interview, January 13, 2014.

5. Brad Stone, "Inside Google's Secret Lab," *Bloomberg Businessweek*, May 22, 2013, http://www.businessweek.com/articles/2013-05-22/inside-googles-secret-lab.

6. Austin Carr, "Google's Project Glass: Inside the Problem Solving and Prototyping," *Fast Company*, June 5, 2012, http://www.fastcodesign.com/1669937/googles-project-glass-inside-the-problem-solving-and-prototyping.

7. Jessica Livingston, *Founders at Work* (New York: Apress, 2008).

8. Doug Berger, "Interview on Extreme Innovation: With Alberto Savoia (Google) and Jeremy Clark (Fxx)," The Innovators, 2011, http://www.innovate1st.com/newsletter/january2011/eXtreme_Innovation.pdf.

9. Jeanne Liedtka and Tim Ogilvie, *Designing for Growth* (New York: Columbia University Press, 2011).

10. Mark Goldenson, "Ten Lessons from a Failed Startup," VentureBeat, 2009, http://venturebeat.com/2009/04/29/10-lessons-from-a-failed-startup/.

11. Marc Pincus and Bing Gordon, "A Serious Take on Internet Game Play," video, Stanford Technology Ventures Program, October 28, 2009.

12. The term *minimum viable product* was first used by Frank Robinson and later popularized by Eric Ries.

13. Nathan Furr and Paul Ahlstrom, *Nail It then Scale It* (Lehi, UT: NISI Publishing, 2011).

14. Jared Allgood, personal interview, December 10, 2009.

15. Geoffrey A. Moore, *Crossing the Chasm* (New York: Harper Paperbacks, 2002).

16. Anonymous, personal interview, February 20, 2012.

17. Scott Cook, personal interview, May 7, 2013.

18. Amir Eftekhari, personal interview, January 7, 2014.

19. Gary Rhoads, Michael Swenson, and David Whitlark, *Boomstart* (Dubuque, IA: Kendall-Hunt, 2009).

20. Ryan Tate, *The 20% Doctrine* (New York: HarperCollins) pg. 22.

21. Ben Blank, personal interview, May 6, 2013.

22. Massolution, *The Crowdfunding Industry Report* (Massolution, 2013).

Chapter 6

1. "ChotuKool: An Innosight Impact Story," video, Innosight, 2013. An abbreviated version is available online at: http://www.innosight.com/impact-stories/chotokool-case-study.cfm.

2. Ibid.

3. Ibid.

4. Ibid.

5. Additional sources for this story include G. Sunderraman, personal interview, February 14, 2013; and Eric Bellman, "Indian Firms Shift Focus to Poor," *Wall Street Journal*, October 21, 2009.

6. Alexander Osterwalder and Yves Pigneur, *Business Model Generation: A Handbook for Visionaries, Game Changers, and Challengers* (New York: Wiley, 2010).

7. Jeffrey Dyer, Hal Gregersen, and Clayton Christensen, *The Innovator's DNA* (Boston: Harvard Business Review Press, 2011).

8. *Upsells* refers to companies like Zynga or Skype offering a free product and then trying to get customers to purchase a premium version. Among free business models this is often referred to as "freemium."

9. Suzanne E. Taylor, *Inside Intuit: How the Makers of Quicken Beat Microsoft and Revolutionized an Entire Industry* (Boston: Harvard Business Press, 2003).

10. Ibid.

11. Ian C. MacMillan and Rita McGrath, "Discovering New Points of Differentiation," *Harvard Business Review*, July 1997.

12. Ibid.

Chapter 7

1. Jessica Livingston, *Founders at Work* (New York: Apress, 2008).

2. Peter Thiel, personal interview, March 16, 2004.

3. Livingston, 2008.

4. Ibid.

5. Phanish Puranam, Benjamin C. Powell, and Harbir Singh, "Due Diligence Failure as a Signal Detection Problem," *Strategic Organization* 4, no. 4 (2006): 319–348.

6. For more detail on different kinds of pivots, see Eric Ries, *The Lean Startup: How Today's Entrepreneurs Use Continuous Innovation to Create Radically Successful Businesses* (New York: Crown Business, 2011).

7. The research project consisted of two parts: first, a formally structured, multicase inductive study following ten innovators for a year, observing how innovators managed the change process, and second, a convenience sample of established corporations pivoting during innovation.

8. For more detail about Aardvark's evolution, see Thomas Eisenmann et al., "Aardvark," Case 811064 (Boston: Harvard Business School, 2001).

Chapter 8

1. For example, see Noam Wasserman, "Founder-CEO Succession and the Paradox of Entrepreneurial Success," *Organization Science* 14, no. 2 (2003): 149–172; Warren Boeker and Rushi Karichalil, "Entrepreneurial Transitions: Factors Influencing Founder Departure," *Academy of Management Journal* 45 (2002): 818–826.

2. Ryan Smith, personal interview, May 9, 2013.

3. Nathan Furr and Paul Ahlstrom, *Nail It then Scale It* (Salt Lake City, UT: NISI Institute, 2011).

4. Everett Rogers, *Diffusion of Innovations,* 5th ed. (New York: Free Press, 2003).

5. Geoffrey Moore, *Crossing the Chasm: Marketing and Selling Disruptive Products to Mainstream Customers,* revised ed. (New York: HarperBusiness, 2006).

6. Ibid.; and Geoffrey Moore, *Inside the Tornado: Strategies for Developing, Leveraging, and Surviving Hypergrowth Markets* (New York: HarperBusiness, 2004).

7. Filipe M. Santos and Kathleen Eisenhardt, "Constructing Markets and Shaping Boundaries: Entrepreneurial Power and Agency in Nascent Fields," *Academy of Management Journal* 52, no. 4 (2009): 643–671.

8. Ryan Smith, personal interview, May 9, 2013.

9. Corey Wride, personal interview, October 13, 2013.

10. Meg Whitman, personal interview, November 5, 2004.

11. T. R. Weiss, "Q&A: Craig Newmark," *Computer World*, February, 2007, http://www.computerworld.com/s/article/print/9053838/Q_A_Craig_Newmark_of_Craigslist_fame_looks_back_and_ahead.

12. Ibid.

13. Marc Benioff, "How to Create Alignment within Your Company in Order to Succeed," Salesforce Blog, April 9, 2013, http://blogs.salesforce.com/company/2013/04/how-to-create-alignment-within-your-company.html; also discussed in Marc Benioff, *Behind the Cloud: The Untold Story of How Salesforce.com Went from Idea to Billion-Dollar Company and Revolutionized an Industry* (New York: Jossey-Bass, 2009).

14. Ibid.

15. Ibid.

16. Jim Cavalieri, personal interview, September 24, 2013.

Chapter 9

1. Everett Rogers, *Diffusion of Innovations,* 5th ed. (New York: Free Press, 2003).

2. Kate O'Keeffe, John Marsland, Carlos Pignataro, and Lisa Voss, "Unleashing Inclusive Innovation at Cisco," Management Innovation eXchange, January 7, 2013, http://www.managementexchange.com/story/unleashing-inclusive-innovation.

3. Kate O'Keeffe, personal interview, October 24, 2013.

4. Kate O'Keeffe, personal interview, March 11, 2014.

5. Ibid.

6. Ibid.

7. See http://en.wikipedia.org/wiki/Google_Glass; Jared Newman, "Google's 'Project Glass' Teases Augmented Reality Glasses," *PC World*, April 4, 2012; Nick Bilton, "Behind the Google Goggles, Virtual Reality," *New York Times*, February 23, 2012.

8. Clayton M. Christensen, *The Innovator's Dilemma: When New Technologies Cause Great Firms to Fail* (Boston: Harvard Business Review Press, 2013).

9. Ibid.

10. Ibid.

11. Rogers, 2003.

12. History of the Swiss watch industry adapted from Amy Glasmeier, "Technological Discontinuities and Flexible Production Networks: The Case of Switzerland and the World Watch Industry," *Research Policy* 20, no. 5 (1991): 469–485.

13. Ron Adner, *The Wide Lens: What Successful Innovators See That Others Miss* (New York: Penguin/Portfolio, 2012).

Conclusion

1. George Yancopoulos, personal interview, December 10, 2013.

2. Ibid.

3. Ibid.

4. Ibid.

5. Ibid.

6. William Bains, "Failure Rates in Drug Discovery and Development: Will We Ever Get Any Better?" *Drug Discovery World*, Fall 2004, http://www.ddw-online.com/business/p148365-failure-rates-in-drug-discovery-and-development:-will-we-ever-get-any-better-fall-04.html.

7. Matthew Herper, "How Two Guys from Queens Are Changing Drug Discovery," *Forbes*, September 2, 2013, http://www.forbes.com/sites/matthewherper/2013/08/14/how-two-guys-from-queens-are-changing-drug-discovery/.

8. Yancopoulos, 2013.

9. Ibid.

10. Ibid.

11. Jeff Bezos, personal interview, July 30, 2007.

12. John Donovan, personal interview, December 20, 2013.

Index

Acknowledgments

Nathan Furr

For almost a decade, I've had a deep suspicion that we might not really understand how to manage the uncertainty of innovation. While everything I learned at business school was highly relevant to the relative certainty of capturing value, I began to wonder if traditional management might not work so well given the relative uncertainty of creating value. My suspicion grew during my time at Stanford, as I watched the design school being formed at the same time as the Lean Startup movement gathered near-religious fervor among entrepreneurs who were also angry about the failure of the methods they had learned in business school. I found it stunning that in most academic entrepreneurship texts, there was plenty of information about the antecedents of entrepreneurship and its outcomes (e.g., IPOs, acquisitions), but the sections on the process—how to create value under uncertainty—were basically blank. I concluded that perhaps we hadn't truly understood the process of creating new value in the first place and wrote a book to explain it called *Nail It Then Scale It* to help new entrepreneurs avoid the mistake of scaling an unproven innovation too early: a mix of motivation and "how to" that came out simultaneously with my colleague Eric Ries's book, *The Lean Startup*.

However, as I reflected on the first book and researched the history of management, I concluded that, as a field, management faces a much deeper and graver challenge. If we look at the history of management (and most other fields, with the possible exception of the humanities), it was founded in response to a particular problem: how to manage and optimize the large firms created by the Industrial Revolution. In other words, management was designed to make trains run on time. The topics of innovation and entrepreneurship were scarcely studied at all until the last few decades, and even when they did finally appear in business schools, we carried over many of our existing management theories—designed for conditions of relative certainty—into the context of innovation. Only now are we awakening to the fact that because these theories were founded on the assumption of relative certainty and for a different purpose (capturing value), they work poorly for uncertainty and creating value. It is an awakening that has occurred in other fields that have encountered uncertainty: design thinking in engineering, lean startup in entrepreneurship, agile software in computer science, and active learning in physics are the individual responses of each field to managing radical uncertainty.

Although I became convinced that we need a new set of theories and tactics to manage under conditions of radical uncertainty, I confess I lacked the courage to swim upstream against the prevailing current. When I began discussing my ideas with Jeff Dyer, he believed I might be onto something and gave me the courage to move forward on this book and on my broader research agenda. I don't mean to say that others have not made great strides in the right direction on innovation (I'm particularly appreciative of the academic work of Clay Christensen, Kathy Eisenhardt, Vijay Govindarajan, Ian MacMillan, Roger Martin, Rita McGrath, Tina Seelig, and Bob Sutton). However, it takes courage to suggest that the field might have gotten a foundational assumption wrong and, as a result, although all that we have discovered has immense value in many contexts, we need a different, or at least dramatically modified, set of theories for the context of radical uncertainty.

I would like to thank Jeff Dyer for helping me find the courage to share this message and for being such a supportive friend, robust thinker, and wonderful coauthor. He is one of the finest human beings I will ever meet. I would also like to thank my Stanford mentors, colleagues, and friends who started me on this journey, particularly Kathy Eisenhardt, my adviser, and Steve Barley, Tom Byers, Tina Seelig, and Bob Sutton. I would also like to thank Steve Blank for his interest and mentorship, Eric Ries, with whom I forged an early research partnership, Tom Eisenmann, who provided his rigorous thinking, and Alex Osterwalder, who has been a friend and thought partner. In addition, my friends at BYU have been particularly instrumental, especially Professor Nile Hatch, Tom Peterson, and Gary Cornia who, as dean of the Marriott School of Management, helped me create time to work on this book. Thanks also to Gary Crocker, who provided significant insight and support, Paul Ahlstrom, who encouraged me to write the first book, and the team at the Center for Entrepreneurship and Technology, led by Scott Peterson and Steve Liddle, who provided enthusiasm and financial assistance. I would also like to thank my academic colleagues Chris Bingham, Ben Hallen, Rahul Kapoor, Rory McDonald, Jackson Nickerson, Rob Wuebker, and the faculty at INSEAD, who encouraged me and helped me refine the ideas presented in this book. Furthermore, I owe a particular debt of gratitude to my team of research assistants, led by Salvael Ortega and complemented by some particularly fine researchers: Aaron Boswell, Sean Brown, Spencer Calvert, Kenton Nicholls, James Oakes, Jane Thomas, Mason Wooley, and Pavel Yurevich. I also want to thank the many executives who gave their precious time for the research and who are mentioned in this book, as well as those who are not mentioned. Your participation was crucial to making this research happen, and you have made the world a better place for it.

Last but not least, I'd like to express the depth of my gratitude to my wife Susannah for her endless support and belief in me and in my work. I am also deeply grateful to my parents and my four children, who have suffered through the research and writing of this book. Any thanks I could express here would be insufficient by countless orders of magnitude.

Moving forward, I hope to further develop the management science of uncertainty—what I have come to call the "Innovation School" in contrast to the more familiar business school. Many of my colleagues have already made excellent progress in this direction, and I hope that by setting the boundaries of our basic assumptions we can work together to create a new and richer perspective on how to manage uncertainty and innovation.

Jeff Dyer

When Nathan Furr and I started discussing this project almost three years ago, I didn't fully grasp the potential of what we would learn as we did the research for this book. *The Innovator's Method* research has opened my eyes to the fact that we need a contingent view of management: managing under conditions of high uncertainty is really different than managing under conditions of low uncertainty. It also helped me see that "The Innovator's DNA" is typically just the starting point for innovation—and that we can all get better at testing and validating our ideas to make sure they will work before we invest in launching them into the market. I would first like to acknowledge and thank Nathan for being such a terrific coauthor. I've really enjoyed the collaborative process as we tried to make sense of what we'd learned from our research together. Moreover, Nathan gets things done. It's a delight to work with someone so capable.

The data collection effort for this book has been significant, and I have many research assistants to thank who worked countless hours on the manuscript. I would especially like to thank Mason Wooley, Chad Howland, Samuel Stapp, Kyle Nelson, Tyler Cornaby, and Zach Rogers. In addition, I'd like to thank Curtis Lefrandt, principal and VP of training and product development at Innovator's DNA, for his helpful comments on the manuscript and for his role in working with Ben Terres to develop the visual graphic of the Innovator's Method.

Ben Terres deserves special mention for his excellent design work on the main graphic, and Mason Wooley similarly deserves special mention for his capable assistance on the majority of the graphics that appear in the book. I would also like to extend my thanks to Michael McConnell, an adviser of HOLT (a division of Credit Suisse), who conducted the Innovation Premium analysis for the companies we analyze in the book. The transcriptions of all of the interviews carried out by me and/or Nathan were done by Nina Whitehead and her staff, who always seemed to meet my ASAP deadlines. Indeed, all of the staff members that support me at Brigham Young University are terrific and deserve my thanks, especially my assistants Holly Jenkins, Stephanie Graham, Stephen Powell Gustin, Marissa Tenney, and Preston Alder. I also must extend my heartfelt thanks to former BYU dean Gary Cornia and Entrepreneurship Center directors Steve Liddle and Scott Peterson, who have provided research funding over the last three years to support this project.

I would also like to thank a number of folks who provided extremely useful insights during the research phase of the book. Many of them come from Intuit; most notably Scott Cook, Brad Smith, and Kaaren Hanson, but also Josh Walker, Amir Eftekhari, Ben Blank, Alan Tifford, Jeff Zias, Wendy Castleman, Joe Hernandez, and Rachel Evans. I'd also like to thank Jodi Maroney (PR Access), who helped facilitate our visits and interviews with Intuit executives. Thanks also to Marc Benioff and Jim Cavalieri of Salesforce.com, John Donovan and Rob Lister of AT&T, Jeff Bezos of Amazon.com, and Paul Kirschbaum of Valve Software for the valuable insights they provided during numerous interviews. Finally, I would like to thank my friend Clayton Christensen for writing the foreword to the book and also our endorsers, Marc Benioff, John Donovan, Brad Smith, Bob Sutton, and Steve Blank for kindly reviewing the manuscript and sharing their thoughts about it.

I wish I could write a book without it taking over my life for a least a short period of time. As always, I owe a deep debt of gratitude to my wife Ronalee, who has always supported me in my work and patiently listens to me drone on about this and that related to whatever project I am working on. Ronalee especially deserves recognition for taking such great care of our family and catching the balls I invariably drop when I am focused on completing a book.

About the Authors

Nathan Furr earned his PhD from the Stanford Technology Ventures Program at Stanford University and is currently a professor of innovation and entrepreneurship at Brigham Young University (ranked among the top five in entrepreneurship education) and a visiting scholar at INSEAD and ESSEC. Furr is a recognized expert on innovation, entrepreneurship, and change, coauthoring *The Innovator's Method* and *Nail It Then Scale It: The Entrepreneur's Guide to Creating and Managing Breakthrough Innovation.*

Furr's research focuses on innovation and technology strategy, particularly on how new and established firms manage the uncertainty of technological change and innovation. His research has been published in leading journals such as *Strategic Management Journal, Organization Science,* and *Strategic Entrepreneurship Journal,* as well as being featured in *Forbes, Sloan Management Review,* and similar outlets. His research has received multiple national and international awards from the Academy of Management, the Kauffman Foundation, the Sloan Foundation, and other highly recognized academic institutions. Based on this research, Professor Furr has created or taught interdisciplinary innovation programs at BYU, Stanford, ESSEC, and other schools. He also cofounded the International Business Model, a competition that reinforces the methodologies he teaches and that attracted over 2,500 teams from more than 250 universities around the world in its most recent year.

Professionally, Professor Furr has acted as the founder or adviser to corporations and start-ups in the health care, clean technology, professional services, internet, retail, and financial services industries. He also sits on the investment board of the Kickstart Seed Fund, an innovative early-stage venture fund. Furr was a management consultant at Monitor Group, a premier international strategy consulting firm, working with senior executives on a range of strategic and market discovery initiatives. Clients have included AT&T, Sony, Tec de Monterrey, USTAR, and other leading companies and organizations.

Jeff Dyer (PhD, UCLA) is the Horace Beesley Professor of Strategy at Brigham Young University as well as a professor of strategy at the Wharton School. Before becoming a professor, Dyer spent five years as a consultant and manager at Bain & Company. His book, *The Innovator's DNA*, coauthored with Clayton Christensen and Hal Gregersen, is a business bestseller, has been published in more than thirteen languages, and won the 2011 Innovation Book of the Year Award from Chartered Management Institute. The December 2009 article of the same name was runner-up for the prestigious McKinsey Award for best *Harvard Business Review* article of the year.

Professor Dyer is the only strategy scholar in the world to have published at least five times in both *Harvard Business Review* and *Strategic Management Journal*, the top academic journal in strategy. In 2012 he was ranked the world's #1 "most influential" management scholar among scholars who completed their PhDs after 1990 by the peer-reviewed journal, *Academy of Management Perspectives*. This ranking was based on more than thirteen thousand academic citations and almost five hundred thousand Google searches on his name. Dyer's book, *Collaborative Advantage*, won the Shingo Prize Research Award, and his *Team Building* book (with Gibb Dyer and William Dyer) is in its fifth edition.

Professor Dyer's research has been covered by *Forbes*, the *Economist*, *Fortune*, *Businessweek*, the *Wall Street Journal*, CNN, and many other publications. He delivers speeches and workshops on innovation to clients such as Adobe, AT&T, Cisco, General Electric, General Mills, Gilead Sciences, Harley-Davidson, Hewlett-Packard, Intel, Life Technologies, Medtronic, and Sony.